WALTER LYNWOOD FLEMING LECTURES
IN SOUTHERN HISTORY

DIXIE BOHEMIA

A French Quarter Circle in the 1920s

JOHN SHELTON REED

LOUISIANA STATE UNIVERSITY PRESS
BATON ROUGE

Published by Louisiana State University Press
Copyright © 2012 by Louisiana State University Press
All rights reserved
Manufactured in the United States of America
First printing

Designer: Laura Roubique Gleason
Typefaces: Chaparral Pro, text; Gill Sans, display
Printer: McNaughton & Gunn, Inc.
Binder: Acme Bookbinding

Library of Congress Cataloging-in-Publication Data

Reed, John Shelton.
  Dixie Bohemia : a French Quarter circle in the 1920s / John Shelton Reed.
    p. cm.
  Includes bibliographical references and index.
  ISBN 978-0-8071-4764-1 (cloth : alk. paper) — ISBN 978-0-8071-4765-8 (pdf) —
ISBN 978-0-8071-4766-5 (epub) — ISBN 978-0-8071-4767-2 (mobi)
  1. Vieux Carré (New Orleans, La.)—Intellectual life—20th century. 2. Vieux Carré (New
Orleans, La.)—Social life and customs—20th century. 3. Vieux Carré (New Orleans, La.)—Bi-
ography. 4. New Orleans (La.)—Intellectual life—20th century. 5. New Orleans (La.)—Social
life and customs—20th century. 6. New Orleans (La.)—Biography. 7. Spratling, William,
1900–1967. Sherwood Anderson and other famous creoles. I. Title.
  F379.N56V5357 2012
  976.3'35—dc23

                                                                2012006535

CONTENTS

PREFACE

HIS BOOK BEGAN ITS LIFE as the Fleming Lectures at Louisiana State University in April 2011. I was both delighted and intimidated to be invited to give those lectures—delighted because of the distinguished company of Fleming lecturers I would be joining, but intimidated . . . for the same reason. No doubt many other lecturers have felt that way, but in my case there was the added complication that the full title of the lectures is "the Walter Lynwood Fleming Lectures in Southern History," and (although historians have always been very gracious about it) I am not an historian. I was in fact the first sociologist ever to give the lectures, so I feared that a poor performance would embarrass not just me, but my discipline.

Anyone who studies the South will know a great many of the books resulting from earlier Fleming Lectures, but to get a more systematic idea of what was expected I consulted Burl Noggle's historiographical essay on the series. There I found that since Charles W. Ramsdell gave the first lectures in 1937 different speakers have gone about their task in many different ways. Some have used the occasion to look back and to summarize their previous work, but I started doing that some time ago and really ought to give it a rest. Others have taken the opportunity to plow new furrows in the fields they had been working, but my old field suffers from soil exhaustion—or maybe it's just me who is exhausted. Anyway, if it is to be restored to production, someone else will have to come manure it (and this metaphor is getting out of hand).

The point is that I didn't want to write on a subject where I had nothing new to say, so I started casting about for topics that (1) would make suitable

Fleming Lectures and (2) wouldn't bore me, but (3) I had a reasonable chance of addressing satisfactorily. There are fewer of those than I like to admit. I kicked around three or four that fell short on one count or another, until one day my sometime coauthor and longtime wife, Dale, suggested that I write about the French Quarter in the 1920s. Neither of us can remember why she suggested it, but it surely has something to do with the fact that she and I have collected Mexican silver for years. William Spratling designed some of the best of it, and we were interested in him even before we knew that William Faulkner shared his apartment in the Quarter. I haven't had many "Eureka" moments in my life, but when Dale made that suggestion, the figurative light bulb lit immediately: I got to work the next day, and have not once regretted the choice. I hope readers will come to see why I found that topic such fun to work on. (Of course it didn't hurt that it required me to spend a couple of months in New Orleans doing research at the Historic New Orleans Collection, Tulane, and Galatoire's.)

DIXIE BOHEMIA

INTRODUCTION

Two Bills and a Book

I N OCTOBER 1926 TWO YOUNG men named Bill, an artist and a writer who shared an apartment in the French Quarter of New Orleans, decided to publish a little book. It was to be "a sort of private joke," the artist said later, just his sketches of some of their friends and themselves, with captions and the writer's introduction. They'd get it out in time for Christmas, amuse their friends, and maybe make a little money. Sure enough, by mid-December they had the manuscript in hand and paid a local printer to run off 250 copies. The artist signed and hand-tinted fifty or so, mostly for the friends who were included. The rest of the copies sold within a week at $2 apiece, so after Christmas the printer ran off another 150 copies and they sold, too.

Ordinarily, that would have been the end of it. The book was a strictly amateur production, it was full of allusions that were unintelligible to anyone not in the circle, some of the sketches were decidedly amateurish, and the authors even misspelled a half-dozen of their friends' names. But two facts turned this little jeu d'esprit into what *The Booklover's Guide to New Orleans* calls "one of the great literary curiosities in the city's history." One of the Bills was named Faulkner. And the friend featured most prominently was the novelist Sherwood Anderson.

Let's go back and start over.

When William Faulkner arrived in New Orleans in 1925, he moved in with William Spratling, an artist who taught at Tulane's architecture school. In the fall of 1926, they were living in a fourth-floor garret on St. Peter Street. The year before, Miguel Covarrubias, a New York-based Mexican artist, had published *The Prince of Wales and Other Famous Americans,* a compilation of his caricatures of celebrities; Spratling, who admired Covarrubias, persuaded Faulkner that it might be fun to do a New Orleans version of the same thing. Soon their friend Natalie Scott (who was also their landlady) was writing breathlessly in her social column for the *States* newspaper that "Bill Spratling is working on a series of caricatures to be called *Sherwood Anderson and Other Eminent Creoles*" and "everybody is wondering who is going to be who in this new New Orleans *Who's Who*." The fact that Scott got the title almost right suggests that Spratling, who had a gift for self-promotion, wasn't exactly keeping the project a secret.

Ready in December

THE PELICAN BOOKSHOP PRESS ANNOUNCES ITS FIRST PUBLICATION
"SHERWOOD ANDERSON AND OTHER FAMOUS CREOLES"
A GALLERY OF CONTEMPORARY NEW ORLEANS

DRAWN BY WM. SPRATLING AND
ARRANGED BY WM. FAULKNER

Among the Forty or More Included are Drawings of

Grace King	Mr. Whitesell	Lyle Saxon
Sherwood Anderson	Mark and Lucile Anthony	Caroline Wogan Durieux
Ellsworth Woodward	Marion Draper	Flo Field
Franz Blom	Daniel Whitney	Albert Bledsoe Dinwiddie
Meigs Frost	Helen Pitkin Schertz	Samuel Louis Gilmore
Richard Kirk	Keith Temple	Emmett Kennedy
Genevieve Pitot	Ronald Hargrave	Alberta Kinsey

A LIMITED EDITION OF 250 NUMBERED COPIES, BOUND IN BOARDS AND DONE ON IMPORTED PAPER, THE FIRST FIFTY DECORATED BY HAND WITH WATER COLOR AND AUTOGRAPHED, AT $5.00, THE OTHERS AT $2.00.

THE PELICAN BOOKSHOP, 407 ROYAL STREET, NEW ORLEANS.

Publication announcement for *Sherwood Anderson and Other Famous Creoles*

The Pelican Bookshop on Royal Street was a favorite hangout of the French Quarter's literary crowd, and the "Pelican Bookshop Press" seems to have been conjured into being for the sole purpose of publishing *Sherwood Anderson and Other Famous Creoles: A Gallery of Contemporary New Orleans*. The book was printed by the Robt. H. True Company, practically around the corner on Bienville Street, and it was for sale by December 19, when Natalie Scott wrote in her column that it was "really a delight" (without mentioning that she was in it). Bound in green boards, it opened "With Respectful Deference to Miguel Covarrubias," followed by a dedication "To All the Artful and Crafty Ones of the French Quarter" and the dog Latin epigraph, "Ave et Cave / per Ars ad Artis." A classicist friend shudders at the grammar, but suspects this may be a lame attempt to say something like, "Look out—we're using art to portray the artist." He suggests that it might make more sense after a few drinks, which is probably how it was written.

Sherwood Anderson took pride of place in the title not only because he was far and away the most Famous of those included, but also because he and his wife, Elizabeth, were at the center of the French Quarter's social life, their apartment on Jackson Square abuzz with the comings and goings of writers and artists, practicing and would-be. Anderson's is the first portrait in the book and Faulkner's introduction is an unmistakable parody of the older man's sometimes pompous style. ("When this young man, Spratling, came to see me, I did not remember him. Perhaps I had passed him in the street. Perhaps he had been one of the painters at whose easel I had paused to examine. Perhaps he knew me. Perhaps he had recognized me when I paused, perhaps he had been aware of the fellowship between us. . . .")

Faulkner and Spratling seem to have meant their book to be a sort of teasing tribute to Anderson, but that's not exactly how it worked out. Spratling recalled that when he and Faulkner proudly gave Anderson a copy of the book the evening it came off the press, he looked it over, scowled, and said, "I don't think it's very funny." Spratling joked that Anderson was taking himself very seriously at the time because someone had recently called him the "Dean of American Literature," but Faulkner, a writer himself, was more sympathetic; he came to believe that he had truly hurt Anderson by making fun of his style at a time when the older man was beginning to recognize that he had passed his prime and had nothing left *but* style. Faulkner regretted what he called "the unhappy caricature affair" for the rest of his life—although in fact Anderson may not have been all that hurt: he apparently gave his copy away and asked Spratling for another.

Anyway, these days *Famous Creoles,* as I'll call it for short, is a curiosity and a collector's item, of interest primarily to literary scholars and bibliophiles as one of Faulkner's earliest works (original copies fetch upwards of $2,000). But is it anything more than that? Spratling himself thought so: "Though certainly not literature," he wrote in the 1960s, "it may now be considered a sort of mirror of our scene in New Orleans," and I intend to use it that way—as an introduction to a Bohemian crowd of artists, writers, journalists, musicians, poseurs, and hangers-on found in the French Quarter in the mid-1920s. I am going to provide a sort of annotated edition of *Famous Creoles,* but first I want to say something about that scene, the people and institutions it included, and why it happened where and when it did.

❦

The title of *Famous Creoles* is, of course, part of the joke. Of the forty-three Famous Creoles (as I'll call *them* for short), only pianist Genevieve Pitot and artist Caroline Durieux were actually Creoles, as Creoles understand that word—that is, descended from French or Spanish colonists. Sherwood Anderson certainly wasn't. Not only that, but many weren't famous by any standard, and such fame as others had was fleeting, or the kind that one of them, Meigs Frost, had in mind when he wryly remarked that "so many of us here are internationally famous locally." To be sure, a handful have received a great deal of attention. Faulkner scholarship now provides employment for

The book's title page

hundreds around the world, and there's a respectable, if much smaller, body of work on Sherwood Anderson. Lesser literary lights like Grace King, Hamilton Basso, and Lyle Saxon have at least had their biographers, and Ellsworth Woodward gets some respect as a painter from students of Southern art. A surprising amount has been written about Spratling, although this owes less to what he was doing in the 1920s than to his later fame as a jewelry designer. (Neither of the major museums of Southern art holds any of his work, and he is not, to my knowledge, mentioned in any survey.) But most of the Famous Creoles appear only in supporting roles, if at all, in the stories of these few. I will have more to say about their individual and collective merit later; here I'll just observe that in a few cases this neglect is completely undeserved. Durieux, Pitot, journalist Frederick Oechsner, and even writer Roark Bradford deserve at least entries in *Wikipedia,* yet when I started this project in 2009 none had one. The obscurity in which others languish is fitting, if we are to judge by literary or artistic achievement alone, but even these least famous can be interesting in their own ways, often in their own right (like, say, Marian Draper, cheerleader and architecture student), but especially when viewed collectively.

It's important to note that the Famous Creoles were not a tightly knit group. In fact, they weren't a group at all, in the sociological sense. They were divided by generation—in 1926 the oldest was seventy-six, the youngest twenty—and by social class: some had been born to wealth or social distinction; others had worked their way up, to varying degrees, from humble origins. Some were Yankees, some Southerners, and among the Southerners the native New Orleanians held themselves somewhat apart. A few were establishment figures, a few a bit raffish. Not all were friends, or even acquaintances. It seems unlikely that Marian Draper and Grace King ever met, or that photographer Cicero Odiorne and President Dinwiddie of Tulane were ever in the same room. But if the Famous Creoles weren't a *group,* they did make up a *social circle,* a loose network of relationships linked by friends in common (if nothing else, they all knew Bill Spratling), by association with the same institutions, and by common interests.

By their nature, social circles have no formal leaders, but they may have their notables, and this one had Sherwood Anderson, "our Royal Personage," according to Hamilton Basso, and "the Grand Old Man of the literati in New Orleans at the time" in Spratling's judgment. But Anderson was more than an honored elder. A social circle usually has a core, and the core of this one comprised those who were regularly part of the Quarter's busy social life, a nucleus that would certainly have included Anderson and his wife, as well as Lyle Saxon and Spratling himself. If some Famous Creoles were at the core, it follows that others were peripheral, and some were so much so that it may be a puzzle why they were included at all (although I'll suggest some reasons when I discuss them individually). Finally, the Famous Creoles in the book were not the only members of this circle. I'll have a bit to say about a few New Orleanians who could easily have been included, but weren't.

A social circle almost always exists in symbiosis with one or more institutions, and this one was no exception. Institutions bring people with common interests together in the first place, and the circle they form may create other institutions, which then operate to keep the circle going. The Newcomb College Art School, Tulane University, and the daily newspapers (especially the *Times-Picayune*) brought the Famous Creoles' circle into being; its members and future members then created the *Double Dealer* magazine, the Arts and Crafts Club, Le Petit Theatre du Vieux Carré, and other, less important institutions. Nearly all of the Famous Creoles were associated with more than one of these enterprises, and the criss-crossing patterns of interaction—in effect, overlapping circles within the larger circle—held the larger circle together. The interests that created these institutions also tied the circle together and provided topics for conversation (other than the gossip about individuals that seems always to have been a feature of New Orleans life). Those interests included art, literature, drama, and historic preservation. I don't believe that any one member of the circle was seriously interested in all of these areas, but, with the possible exception of President Dinwiddie, each was deeply engaged with at least one and almost always more than one.

Finally, although I'll be examining the Bohemian world that the Famous Creoles shaped and populated, for the most part I am not going to talk about "Bohemia" in general. Rattling on about the concept would be mere theoretical ruffles and flourishes unless there were some question about whether the French Quarter was an instance of it or the Quarter's example illuminated poorly understood aspects of it. Since there isn't a question and the Quarter doesn't, I will merely refer readers to the extensive literature on Bohemia and usually let it go at that, except (1) when the French Quarter case is unusual and (2) in the case of the Quarter's evolution from slum to Bohemia to tourist trap, which was so thoroughly typical that I have used it to illustrate a few generalizations.

Dramatis Personae

I N WHAT FOLLOWS, I have usually referred to the players by name. Most were colorful and memorable characters who deserve better than the anonymity of "one member of the circle," or "a young artist." But it may be hard to keep this cast of dozens straight, so let me briefly introduce them before I turn to the set and the drama. (You may want to dog-ear this page for reference.)

Here is an alphabetical list of all the Famous Creoles, followed by some other members of their circle who will make frequent appearances. I have provided approximate ages in 1926 and shorthand descriptions. The Famous Creoles' names are followed by page references in brackets to the fuller biographical sketches beginning on page 99.

FAMOUS CREOLES

Conrad Albrizio, twenty-seven [178]
New York-born, serious artist, Spratling's neighbor, Arts and Crafts Club stalwart.
Sherwood Anderson, fifty [108]
"Lion of the Latin Quarter," éminence grise, generous to respectful younger writers.
Marc Antony and **Lucille Godchaux Antony**, both twenty-eight [168]
Love-match between heiress and lower-middle-class boy, both local artists.
Hamilton "Ham" Basso, twenty-two [198]
Star-struck recent Tulane grad, aspiring writer, good dancer.
Charles "Uncle Charlie" Bein, thirty-five [165]
Director of Arts and Crafts Club's art school; lived with mother, sister, and aunt.
Frans Blom, thirty-three [116]
Danish archeologist of Maya, Tulane professor, colorful resident of Quarter.
Roark Bradford, thirty [158]
Newspaperman, jokester, hit pay dirt with Negro dialect stories.
Nathaniel Cortlandt Curtis, forty-five [113]
Tulane architecture professor, preservationist, recorded old buildings.
Albert Bledsoe Dinwiddie, fifty-five [223]
President of Tulane, Presbyterian.
Marian Draper, twenty [175]
Ziegfeld Follies alum, Tulane cheerleader, prize-winning architecture student.
Caroline "Carrie" Wogan Durieux, thirty [216]
Genuine Creole, talented artist living in Cuba and Mexico, painted by Rivera.
William "Bill" Faulkner, twenty-nine [241]
Needs no introduction, but wrote the one to *Famous Creoles*.
Flo Field, fifty [104]
French Quarter guide, ex-journalist, sometime playwright, single mother.
Louis Andrews Fischer, twenty-five [201]
Gender-bending Mardi Gras designer, named for her father.
Meigs O. Frost, forty-four [123]
Reporter's reporter who lived in Quarter; covered crime, revolutions, and arts.
Samuel Louis "Sam" Gilmore, twenty-seven [225]
Greenery-yallery poet and playwright, from prominent family.
Moise Goldstein, forty-four [142]
Versatile and successful architect, preservationist, active in Arts and Crafts Club.
Weeks Hall, thirty-two [231]
Master of and slave to Shadows-on-the-Teche plantation, painter, deeply strange.
Ronald Hargrave, forty-four [194]
Painter from Illinois formerly active in Quarter art scene, relocated to Majorca.
R. Emmet Kennedy, forty-nine [192]
Working-class Irish boy, collected and performed Negro songs and stories.

Grace King, seventy-four [228]
Grande dame of local color literature and no-fault history, *salonnière*.

Alberta Kinsey, fifty-one [204]
Quaker spinster, Quarter pioneer, indefatigable painter of courtyards.

Richard R. Kirk, forty-nine [140]
Tulane English professor and poet, loyal Michigan Wolverine alumnus.

Oliver La Farge, twenty-five [130]
New England Brahmin, Tulane anthropologist, and fiction-writer; liked a party.

Harold Levy, thirty-two [213]
Musician who ran family's box factory, knew everybody, turned up everywhere.

Lillian Friend Marcus, thirty-five [180]
Young widow from wealthy family, angel and manager of *Double Dealer*.

John "Jack" McClure, thirty-three [162]
Poet, newspaper columnist and reviewer, *Double Dealer* editor, bookshop owner.

Virginia Parker Nagle, twenty-nine [145]
Promising artist, governor's niece, Arts and Crafts Club teacher.

Louise Jonas "Mother" Nixon, seventy [137]
A founder of Le Petit Theatre and its president-for-life, well-connected widow.

William C. "Cicero" Odiorne, forty-five [134]
Louche photographer, Famous Creoles' Paris contact.

Frederick "Freddie" Oechsner, twenty-four [148]
Recent Tulane graduate, ambitious cub reporter, amateur actor.

Genevieve "Jenny" Pitot, twenty-five [219]
Old-family Creole, classical pianist living in New York, party girl.

Lyle Saxon, thirty-five [208]
Journalist, raconteur, bon vivant, host, preservationist, bachelor.

Helen Pitkin Schertz, fifty-six [185]
Clubwoman and civic activist, French Quarter guide, writer, harpist.

Natalie Scott, thirty-six [125]
Journalist, equestrian, real-estate investor, Junior Leaguer, social organizer.

William "Bill" Spratling, twenty-five [236]
Famous Creoles illustrator, Tulane teacher, lynchpin of Quarter social life.

Keith Temple, twenty-seven [189]
Australian editorial cartoonist, artist, sometimes pretended to be a bishop.

Fanny Craig Ventadour, twenty-nine [155]
Painter, Arts and Crafts Club regular, lately married and living in France.

Elizebeth Werlein, thirty-nine [172]
Suffragette with colorful past, crusading preservationist, businessman's widow.

Joseph Woodson "Pops" Whitesell, fifty [151]
Photographic jack-of-all-trades, French Quarter eccentric, inventor.

Daniel "Dan" Whitney, thirty-two [183]
Arts and Crafts Club teacher, married two students, beauty pageant judge.

Ellsworth Woodward, sixty-five [119]
Artistic elder statesman, old-fashioned founder of Newcomb art department.

SOME OTHER MEMBERS OF THE CIRCLE

Elizabeth Prall Anderson, forty-two [see page 246]
Sherwood's third wife, hostess, den mother, should have been in the book.

Dorothy Dix (Elizabeth Meriwether Gilmer), sixty-five
Popular syndicated advice columnist, local society leader.

Esther DuPuy, twenty
Debutante, avid dancer, frequent date for Spratling.

James Feibleman, twenty-two
Local kid from mercantile family, hanger-on, aspiring poet, keen observer.

Julius Weis Friend, thirty-two
Lillian Marcus's brother, cofounder (with Albert Goldstein) of *Double Dealer*.

William Ratcliffe Irby, deceased (1860–1926)
Tobacco millionaire, philanthropist, preservationist, lay in coffin and shot himself.

Adaline Katz, twenty-six
Banker's daughter, M.A. from Columbia, free spirit, Anderson's walking companion.

Richard Koch, thirty-seven
Ubiquitous preservation architect with many projects in Quarter and elsewhere.

Olive Leonhardt, thirty-one
Beardsley-esque illustrator for *Double-Dealer* and Junior League.

Gideon Stanton, forty-one
Stockbroker, amateur painter, grandson of Lincoln's secretary of war.

Will Henry Stevens, forty-five
Newcomb College art teacher and painter, Taoist, directed Cane River art colony.

Basil Thompson, deceased (1892–1924)
High-spirited editor of *Double Dealer*, poet, drank himself to death.

William Woodward, sixty-seven
Ellsworth's brother, helped found Tulane architecture school, retired in Biloxi.

The World of the Famous Creoles

Life in the Quarter

Hamilton Basso wrote that "if I never much hankered after Paris during the expatriate years, it was because, in the New Orleans of that era, I had Paris in my own back yard." The Vieux Carré of his youth, he said, was "a sort of Creole version of the Left Bank," and in six blocks or so, clustered around the cathedral of St. Louis, *les bons temps* did roll in a Bohemian sort of way. Many who were part of that scene knew the Left Bank firsthand, or Greenwich Village, and did their best to follow those models, as we shall see.

But the life of the Quarter also reflected some demographic characteristics of its habitués. At the core of the Famous Creoles' circle were the twenty-three Famous Creoles who actually lived in the Vieux Carré in 1926. That figure included the notable hosts (Sherwood and Elizabeth Anderson, Spratling, Lyle Saxon) and their most frequent guests and companions, as well as the most important of the journalists who covered the New Orleans cultural scene (Saxon, Natalie Scott, John McClure, Freddie Oechsner). Seventeen of the twenty-three were men, and only three of those were over thirty-five. Eliminate those three and throw in Basso (who

Young Men in the French Quarter, 1926
SINGLE
Ham Basso, 22
Freddie Oechsner, 24
Oliver La Farge, 25
Bill Spratling, 25
Keith Temple, 27
Dan Whitney, 28
Bill Faulkner, 29
Harold Levy, 32
Conrad Albrizio, 32
Frans Blom, 33
Lyle Saxon, 35
Sam Gilmore, 35
MARRIED
Marc Antony, 28
Roark "Brad" Bradford, 30
Jack McClure, 33

spent so much time in the Quarter that he might as well have lived there) and you have most of the members of a group of newspapermen, freelance writers, artists, and Tulane faculty members who called themselves, for reasons now lost, the Shasta Daisies Society. You also have a concentration of young men, nearly all unmarried—the makings of what Basso's biographer calls a "boyish and boisterous atmosphere" that often lent a sort of fraternity house flavor to the goings-on.

The Atmosphere

The last drawing in *Famous Creoles* repays close study. Faulkner and Spratling are shown in their garret. Spratling— art teacher, author of *Pencil Drawing*— is holding his pencil at arm's length in the classic technique for determining proportions. The joke is that the proportions of the drawing are totally haywire. Faulkner holds a glass and under his chair are several liquor jugs. Next to the "Viva Art" motto on the wall hangs a pump-action BB gun, which (Spratling recalled) was used "on a rainy day, or when there were distinguished visitors to be entertained," to shoot out the windows of an empty house across the street. "From the street below no shot could be heard—only the slight tinkle

Spratling and Faulkner, from *Famous Creoles*

of glass as it hit the pavement." (The gun is a Daisy. Could this be where the Shasta Daisies got their name?)

The boys also shot passing pedestrians, and they had a scoring system posted on the wall: "If you managed to pink a Negro nun, that rated ten points (for rarity value) and that was the highest you could go," although bearded men were almost as valuable. When Sherwood Anderson's teenaged son Bob visited New Orleans he became particularly fond of this sport, and made a nuisance of himself by coming around when Faulkner was writing. Bob didn't take hints, so one day Spratling and Faulkner "grabbed him, took

Spratling standing in garret apartment with Hamilton Basso (?) seated.

Spratling drawing of rooftops

his pants off, painted his peter green and pushed him out on the street, locking the door." After that, Spratling recalled, he "didn't bother us much."

The walls of the apartment's bathroom featured nude figures Spratling had painted, with shower faucets and parts of other fixtures incorporated as anatomical features. Another attraction was what their friend Flo Field remembered years later as a "death-defying platform" built over the roof.

Another rooftop view by Spratling

Reached through a window, it offered an escape from the stifling heat of a New Orleans attic, and at one party Faulkner unsuccessfully tried to persuade Mrs. Field to crawl outside—four floors above the street—with him. The platform also offered access to adjoining roofs, across which, Ham Basso recalled, some daring partygoers once had "a fine game of tag." (One of them was Faulkner: one slip would have profoundly altered American literary history.) Anthropologist Oliver La Farge, who shared a cook and dining expenses with Spratling and Faulkner, was very much a part of his messmates' larky scene. His tabletop mock-Indian "Eagle Dance" and his systematic destruction of some expensive glassware (see page 132) became part of the circle's lore.

Wine, Women, and Song

For young Americans in the 1920s the French Quarter was an exotic and exciting place. La Farge described it in his memoirs as "a decaying monument and a slum as rich as jambalaya or gumbo":

> There were sailors of all kinds, antique dealers, second-hand dealers, speakeasies galore, simple workmen, a fair variety of criminals, both white and coloured nuns, the survivors of a few aristocratic Créole families clinging to their ancestral homes, merchants of all sorts, and whole blocks of prostitutes. Except for part of Royal Street and a section around the Cathedral which had been brushed up and enjoyed the tourist trade, this was the real thing in slums. Most of these assorted inhabitants were united by love of playing the ponies, by the pleasures of eating good red-beans-and-rice and gumbo and of connoisseurship of coffee, by liking their Quarter just as it was, and by pride in its peculiarities. . . . Anything could happen there, in the

blocks of houses too beautiful to be true, under balconies and in the shadows of the arches, and where the jangling, jerry-built shacks have fought their way in among the ancient bricks. The hot nights stirred you until you had a cat's longing to prowl, down streets turned utterly silent, past speakeasies, by doors that gave out snatches of music, and the blocks where the whispers and eyes of the whores behind the shutters made a false promise of romance. Anything could happen in a town where the signs on the trolleys along Canal Street showed that one line ran to Desire and one to Elysian Fields.

The Vieux Carré's version of Bohemia was tamer than the classic nineteenth-century Parisian version, which floated on the surface of an underworld of opiates and prostitution. Some Bohemians patronized the relatively wide-open bordellos, but they didn't socialize with the working girls, and for the most part the drug of choice was bootleg alcohol. Still, things were pretty spicy for 1920s America. The vice to be found in the Quarter and nearby was a sort of tourist attraction, even for tourists who weren't themselves in the market. When New York writer Carl Carmer and his wife, Betty, came to town, Carl was taken to see Louise's, "a whorehouse of great distinction in the Quarter," while Keith Temple took Betty to meet Aunt Rose Arnold, a wealthy retired madam with a fondness for artists and writers. Sherwood Anderson enjoyed Aunt Rose's company, introduced Faulkner to her, and wrote the three of them into a short story. John McClure took the visiting H. L. Mencken to Tom Anderson's tavern on Rampart Street, which had a brothel upstairs. (The Cadillac Bar next door was even dicier, allegedly with rooms for smoking opium.) Anderson's was a favorite eating and drinking place for McClure, Faulkner, and Roark Bradford, while other members of the circle patronized Celeste's, which Carmer described as "the lowest joint in New Orleans—filled with lesbians, homosexuals, and the rest of us." It was across from the police station.

Flo Field stumbled on a link between the art scene and the *demimonde* of male prostitution when she met a young artist at an Arts and Crafts Club exhibition. When she went back to his apartment to see his drawings, she found that he and his two roommates were "all starving." The good-hearted Flo took them under her wing, bought them milk, and gave them money. But she was dismayed when one of them, "a boy like a beautiful 16 year old girl, but no front teeth" who worked as an artist's model, made his "girlish confessions" to her. He had posed for an uptown artist and teacher, he said, and the man had "assaulted" him, but he "wasn't going to let anything stand between him and making two dollars posing!"—and was going to pose for the man again. He also told Field that his artist roommate was "selling his body every night." (When Flo wrote to her son, Sydney, that she regretted having been "a fairy godmother" to the three boys, the double entendre was probably unintended.)

A more respectable component of the Famous Creoles' circle was what Basso remembered as "a fairly dazzling collection of pretty girls [whose] part in this here twentieth century American literary renaissance will never be fully appreciated." Half a dozen Famous Creoles met this description. Thirty years later William Odiorne particularly remembered cute Lucille Godchaux Antony, who often wore a painter's smock, and the elegant and vivacious pianist Genevieve Pitot. Odiorne also recalled Odette Goldstein, a Brazilian reputed to be the most beautiful woman in New Orleans, and an Arkansas girl known as "Musetta," so chic she could have been a Parisienne, whom Spratling gallantly escorted to and from Tulane to pose au naturel for his art classes. But many of the pretty girls remain nameless, like the "New Orleans debutantes" Elizabeth Anderson remembered (not with pleasure), who "visited us regularly," one of whom "dropped her purse, knocked over her chair, and ran away in fright" when Sherwood rushed at her with his shirt completely open, to grab her for a dance.

These girls and their boyfriends puzzled Sherwood. He wrote a friend about the local boys who ran the *Double Dealer* and socialized with "society women": "one goes evening after evening among these women—at least these fellows do—and . . . one never goes to bed with one of them and gets clear. As far as that is concerned they will go further without going anywhere than any people I ever saw." Anderson's young friend Adaline Katz agreed. Although everyone probably believed in "free love," she recalled—certainly they talked about it a lot—there was less than one might have expected: the men, she told an interviewer (perhaps a bit scornfully), "drank a lot and talked a lot and then drank a lot."

She was certainly right about that. Bootleg liquor was as much a part of the scene and emblematic of it as marijuana would be for a later generation of Bohemians. "The big thing that bound all those artistic people together was alcohol," cartoonist Keith Temple claimed, and his neighbor and fellow Famous Creole Louis Andrews Fischer recalled that "*everybody* was a heavy drinker then." Genevieve Pitot remembered "well lubricated" parties, where women might wear shawls in the summer heat to conceal bottles. Liquor was a social necessity, Pitot said, and Spratling agreed. "We could do our friends proud," he said. "We always had plenty of liquor for all comers."

Opinions differed about why alcohol was so important. Temple told an interviewer later that, paradoxically, Prohibition was the reason: "We did not know whether or not we would be able to get a drink tomorrow or ever again, so we drank whatever came to hand," and Pitot said something similar: "It was that horrible thing of 'You can't do this.' We drank because they told us we couldn't." Elizabeth Anderson added, "We all seemed to feel that Prohibition was a personal affront and that we had a moral duty to undermine it."

That wasn't difficult. James Feibleman acknowledged that Prohibition was in force, "but New Orleans did not seem to have heard of it." When Marc and Lucille Antony had parties, they invited the neighborhood cops up for drinks. Floods of liquor came from Cuba and the Bahamas through any of several bayou routes to the Mississippi or Lake Pontchartrain. (Faulkner spun fantastic yarns all his life about his involvement in this romantic business, complete with circumstantial details about hidden sand spits where Cuban schooners stashed barrels of alcohol.) In the city, the thirsty could easily get a drink at one of the seventy-four French Quarter bars that Elizebeth Werlein once counted in a nine-block radius, or served more discreetly in teacups at restaurants like Arnaud's. "Speakeasies flourished openly," Elizabeth Anderson recalled, "and far into the night their music blared out and mingled on the still busy streets." The bars also added a "winy-beery smell" to the Quarter's "rich, spicy aroma" of roasting coffee and seafood. Those who wanted a bottle could get one at an Italian grocery store like Joe Cascio's at

Spratling's Christmas card shows Joe Cascio's grocery store.

St. Peter and Royal, or Manuel and Teresa's across the street,—although the "bourbon," "Scotch," and "gin" were most likely Cuban grain alcohol flavored with iodine, creosote, and juniper-berry essence respectively. (Faulkner's rum-running fantasy incorporated a little Italian lady who did the flavoring.) Alternatively, one could easily find a bootlegger. Faulkner got his liquor from a priest at the cathedral (later defrocked, it was said, for "impairing the morals of young girls"), while Spratling bought ten large jugs from a woman whose bootlegger husband had died. And do-it-yourselfers could easily make their own. Musician Harold Levy was a well-connected local, so he got his alcohol and "essential oils" from a druggist friend, but anyone could go "fishing" by paying a fisherman to rent a skiff and picking up a five-gallon can of alcohol stashed in the marshes. With alcohol in hand, you could make the popular "needle beer" by injecting (legal) near-beer with it or your own mock-gin with juniper essence from Solari's grocery at Royal and Iberville. (Spratling rolled the cans across the floor for aeration; otherwise, he said, the taste was rather flat.)

The favorite drink of all was what was called "absinthe"—possibly just licorice-flavored Cuban alcohol, but whatever it was, as "the green fairy" it

THE LOCALE, WHICH INCLUDES MRS. FLO FIELD

Faulkner's bootlegger, "the bad priest," urinating against a wall (detail from the frontispiece to *Famous Creoles*).

had a decadent Continental allure. A Swiss man living in the Quarter made it himself, and at six dollars a bottle (about $72 in today's money) it wasn't cheap, but Spratling recalled making up "great pitchers for all our parties." When it was poured over crushed ice with just a touch of water to make an "absinthe frappé," Mrs. Anderson attested, it had very little taste of alcohol, so "it was consumed in quantities." "Was it good?" Temple asked of all this homemade hooch. "Indeed it was! It was cheap and tasted fine, and we certainly drank a very great deal of it."

Oddly, given what was going on practically next door, most of the Famous Creoles' crowd seem to have been indifferent to jazz. This was, after all, the Jazz Age, and Bohemians elsewhere took the music to heart. Hamilton Basso, an avid dancer, must have appreciated jazz; pianist Genevieve Pitot played it for her own and her friends' amusement; Roark Bradford and John McClure and sometimes Faulkner went to a club to hear clarinetist George "Georgia Boy" Boyd; but in general there seems to have been far less interest in jazz than in other forms of black music. It may be that work songs and spirituals were seen as less commercial and more "authentic" than jazz. Emmet Kennedy collected and performed black "mellows" (melodies), Sherwood Anderson liked to listen to dockworkers singing at their labor, and Pitot would later arrange spirituals for a modern dance troupe in New York. Excursions to hear the music and sermons at black churches seem to have been a popular form of entertainment. Bradford frequented the church of a black Baptist evangelist in Algiers, while Natalie Scott and her friends liked hearing "all the colored people sing, with a big orchestra" and the "very funny sermons" of Mother Catherine, "an old colored woman, fat and good-natured, who has started what she calls a church."

Socializing

Above all, Mrs. Anderson recalled, this was "a social and congenial time." Even Faulkner was only occasionally antisocial, although by local standards he was an exceptional loner. On Sundays he and Spratling often went for breakfast with Baron Hanno von Schucking, a Quarter character said to have a wealthy lady friend; drinks after breakfast extended into lunch, followed by more drinking, and the abandonment of whatever plans had been made for the day. Most days the *Double Dealer* crowd gathered at the Pelican Bookshop on Royal Street after business hours for "tea"—wine, salami sandwiches, and talk—just "a happy hour," Ham Basso recalled, not "an intellectual hour." And there were parties most nights: Oliver La Farge recalled that "a bottle or so of absinthe, some sandwiches, some Saratoga chips were all we needed for a gathering which would last from nine o'clock to three the next morning."

Spratling wrote that he and his French Quarter friends "saw each other every day, almost every evening. If it wasn't at Lyle Saxon's house, it was at Sherwood and Elizabeth's or my own." People just dropped in. According to Mrs. Anderson, "No one was ever invited, for that would make it seem as though they had to be invited before they would be welcome." Almost every Saturday night the Andersons had a dinner party for a rotating group of friends and visitors to New Orleans. Spratling remembered that the guests might include "John Dos Passos, or perhaps Carl Sandburg or Carl Van Doren or a great publisher from New York, Horace Liveright or Ben Huebsch, all people we were proud to know." If the Andersons weren't entertaining at home, they met friends for supper at one of the Quarter's inexpensive restaurants like Tujague's or Tortorici's, a Sicilian place on Royal Street that people called "the Bucket of Blood." After supper, the gang might move on to a newspapermen's hangout called Max in the Alley, where Elizabeth Anderson recalled "a large ceiling fan that languorously revolved, stirring flies into brief action [and] all the men dressed in rumpled, messy seersucker suits, patched with perspiration."

Once, some Famous Creoles took their socializing afloat when, on the eve of the Ides of March, 1925, they set sail for Mandeville, twenty-three miles across Lake Pontchartrain from New Orleans. Sherwood Anderson had organized the trip as a treat for a visiting writer; when she begged off, citing a deadline, the party went ahead without her. That much seems to be undisputed, but not much else is. It's not even clear who was there. Almost everyone agrees that the party included the Andersons, Faulkner, Spratling, Marc and Lucille Antony, Lillian Marcus and her brother Julius Friend, young Ham Basso, Sam Gilmore, and Virginia Parker. Elizabeth Anderson included in her tally, disapprovingly, "a giddy young girl" with Basso and "several young girls Sherwood had casually asked along." Sam Gilmore remembered Colonel Charles Glenn Collins, a bizarre Scottish confidence man with a knack for marrying heiresses. The Antonys remembered Collins, too, as well as Lucille's sister (who may have been one of the "young girls"), Natalie Scott, and maybe Harold Levy. Marc Antony thought Lyle Saxon was there, while Faulkner's biographer Joseph Blotner adds Frans Blom and Richard Kirk, and Spratling's notoriously unreliable autobiography reports that "Ben

Hecht, Carl Van Doren, and—perhaps—Carl Sandburg" were present—but he must have been conflating this excursion with another, since surely someone else would have remembered them.

It's not clear who paid, either. Elizabeth Anderson said that Sherwood hired the boat, but Sam Gilmore and Marc Antony told Blotner that everyone in the party kicked in. Anyway, *someone* engaged the *Josephine* and her captain ("a professional sailor who seemed greatly amused by his motley load of passengers," Mrs. Anderson recalled) and the group set out on its adventure. Blotner tells what happened next:

> The day darkened and a drizzle began to fall. Then, as a storm rumbled in the distance, the engine started to smoke and miss, steadily losing power. Although they were now virtually stranded, the shore was close enough for the mosquitoes to find them. The passengers took refuge in the main cabin, but the smoke from the engine hung in the air and soon they were coughing as they scratched their bites.

Blotner says the party spent a day on the water (Elizabeth Anderson remembered it as two days, but maybe it just seemed like it) and nothing much happened. The boat did reach Mandeville, but only Faulkner and Virginia Parker braved the mosquitoes ashore to check out the amusements. As for the others, Mrs. Anderson recalled, "we might as well have remained at home, for we all sat around the galley talking, just as we did every night on our patio. The only real difference was the food, which was bad." Blotner concludes his account: "It was dark when they got back to New Orleans. Some had mosquito bites. Others, doubtless, would have hangovers. Faulkner had literary material."

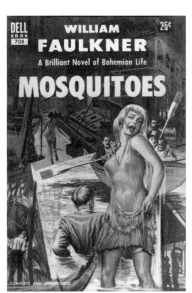

And that's why the voyage of the *Josephine* has received so much attention. A thinly fictionalized account of it appeared two years later as *Mosquitoes,* Faulkner's "Brilliant Novel of Bohemian Life" (according to the lurid cover of the 1953 paperback) and his "one truly negligible book," in Hamilton Basso's opinion. Some critics have disagreed, but Faulkner himself soon came to think it was "trashily smart" and eventually simply called it a "bad book." Even so, it was a source of innocent merriment for Faulkner's companions as they tried to figure out which characters were based on whom, and it still provides hours of harmless diversion for literary critics and historians as they do the same. We should remember that *Mosquitoes* is not a documentary, but it's hard for anyone familiar with the Famous Creoles' circle to resist this parlor game. No points for identifying Dawson Fairchild as Sherwood Anderson, and Major Ayers was obviously drawn from Colonel Collins. But how much Talliaferro is based on Lyle Saxon and how much on Faulkner himself, or whether Spratling was the model for Mark Frost, as Elizabeth Anderson believed, or for Gordon (with Sam Gilmore as Mark Frost), as Blotner has it—although many think *Faulkner* was Gordon. . . .

One disputed identification is amusing. Elizabeth Anderson, who disliked Lillian Marcus, believed that Marcus was the original for what *Time*'s reviewer called "unctuous Mrs. Maurier, queen mosquito," an arrogant, affected, and wealthy widow, but Marcus's brother thought the character was based on Mrs. Anderson. Blotner thinks they're both mistaken and that the imperious Elizebeth Werlein was the prototype, with Marcus rendered as the "sharp and perceptive" Eva Wiseman. Cicero Odiorne agreed: Wiseman, he said, had "the right amount of acid." Whoever she thought she was, Marcus always fumed about Faulkner's portrayal of her, although she also claimed that she had never read the book.

Balls

The high point of the French Quarter's social calendar in the 1920s was a more or less annual "Bohemian" costume ball, modeled on the Bal des Quat'z Arts, held in Montmartre each spring by students of the Ecole Nationale des Beaux-Arts. "The first time an imitation of this ball had been conceived of in New Orleans," according to the *States* newspaper, was in December 1922, as a fund-raiser for the *Double Dealer*. Albert Goldstein, one of the editors, recalled that the "Folies du Vieux Carré" were helpfully promoted by "our friends in the newspapers." Ticket prices were steep—$10 for a single, $15 for a couple—but tickets did entitle their holders to unlimited drink (illegal, of course, but the two hired policemen guarding the proceeds looked the other way), and more liquor had to be procured midway through the evening. There was also a band to pay and the organizers rented a parrot "which sort of lent color to the proceedings," so in the end the fund-raiser netted only about $200. But the *States* called the party "one of the most sensational and interesting that has ever taken place in the social history of New Orleans"—which is saying something.

At midnight on the night before New Year's Eve a costumed crowd including Conrad Albrizio in a bear suit, someone in a police uniform that almost got him in trouble, and many others in what the newspaper described as "futuristic and original" garb arrived at the Quartier Club in the lower (i.e., down-river) Pontalba building, facing Jackson Square, to be greeted by "raucous ribald ragtime, jangling jazz, the moaning of saxophones, the blare of cornets, and the high, shrill notes of the clarinet." The evening's entertainment began with a torchlight procession as "stalwart slaves" carried a "Moorish bride" on a palanquin from Ronald Hargrave's studio in the upper Pontalba building across Jackson Square to the club. (A photograph of the wedding party appeared in the next day's newspaper: Hargrave had designed all of the costumes, as well as "highly futuristic" murals to decorate the ballroom.) The nuptials that followed were the first of "several skits and stunts that added life and interest to the party"; others included "an up-to-date jazz dance by Miss Kingsley Black" and a "doll-dance" by a couple in costume. The highlight of the evening, however, was "the dance of Salome," which Genevieve Pitot performed in attire "that made the seven veils look like an arctic explorer's costume." The *States* reporter found "words . . . entirely inadequate to describe this dance and costume," but tried anyway with "unique, bizarre, queer, original and startling." The dance, "greeted with much enthusiasm," was "one of the most Bohemian features of the evening's entertainment." (Pitot danced barefoot all evening and couldn't wear her shoes the next day.)

Lyle Saxon's *Times-Picayune* account of the evening led with subheadlines including "Dowagers Dance Till 5 A.M.," "Riot of Color and Gaiety as Society Touches Fingers With Art," and "Old-Fashioned Girl in Low-Neck Nightie." A monumental figure of the "Great God Silenus" near the entrance "watched the whole rout with its pagan smile," as "bare-legged girls [in] fur-trimmed costumes of white . . . shrieked with delight"; "Turkish ladies reclined languidly on cushions upon the floor, smoke rising in long spirals from their cigarettes"; "pretty little talcum-powdered debutantes of this year's crop" were "'tasting life' with a vengeance, deliberately devilish"; and "more sophisticated girls of last year's vintage" wore "daring costumes of brilliant reds and greens." (Saxon himself was no doubt at least as interested in some dashing

French naval officers from the ship *Jeanne D'Arc,* in their gold-braided uniforms.)

A couple of years later, some students at the Arts and Crafts Club held the first of what became a series of Bals des Artistes. The announcement stated that the event would be "a costume and mask affair and even those coming in evening clothes will be refused admission" and promised that "stunts under the personal direction of Miss Louise [Louis] Andrews" (later Fischer) would include many "features which are unmentionable—remember, it is the Bal des Artistes." Spratling came in costume "as a dashing Arab, bearded and turbaned and short-coated," and "won much applause." His girlfriend Esther DuPuy was one of the featured dancers; another hoofer had "studied under the personal direction of Ned Weyburn of the Ziegfeld Follies." (Faulkner was there, too—in what costume is not reported—but didn't enjoy it.) It's not clear which features were unmentionable—surely not the Russian puppet show. Nevertheless, the *Times-Picayune* announced triumphantly afterward: "The Paris of America has its Montmartre."

The announcement had said that the ball was to be, "my dear, just another night of fun and frolic for members of the club," open to students and their guests at a dollar a head (a bit more for Club members and their guests), but it also attracted a sizable contingent of slumming debutantes and their beaus, and even a few dowagers. By 1927, newspaper society pages were listing the names of socially prominent partygoers, who by then outnumbered the more Bohemian element. Admission charges had crept up, couples had become the basic unit, there were no longer cheap tickets for students, and proceeds went to upkeep of the Club's Royal Street quarters. The ball was moved to a larger hall and opened to the public. The *Times-Picayune* announced that what had formerly been "a gorgeous hidden panorama for the artists themselves, a brilliant revel that most persons could only hope to read about in gay but ambiguous descriptions in the morning papers," could now be enjoyed by anyone with the price of a ticket. The writer boasted that this was "a spectacle that no other city in America can offer," and promised that it would "make ordinary folk drop their jaws."

The Club's friends at the newspapers could always be counted on for a steady flow of publicity like this. Typical headlines teased that "Secrecy Shrouds Preparations for Arts, Crafts Ball," or promised a "Gay Soiree," a ball to "Rival Any This Side of Paris." Quoting Famous Creoles or members of their circle like illustrator Olive Leonhardt, reporters told readers to expect "lavish and daring schemes of color" and "weirdly costumed revelers," as

At the Arts and Crafts Ball

"This drawing by T. Kemp is one of the many which are being made to illustrate the spirit of the Arts and Crafts Club ball" (*Item-Tribune*, 1927).

well as "models and others" performing "spicy sketches, tableaux and other events." Some stories were accompanied by mildly suggestive drawings by members of the Club. In 1927, all four dailies promised "professional entertainment in the modernistic mode," "a spirit of mysticism and beauty," the presence of many an "out-of-town celebrity," and the return of a "zippy" Junior League chorus line that had enlivened an earlier ball. There was much heavily facetious joshing about the promised appearance of three Lady Godivas at the ball, thereby topping a recent Chicago Arts Ball, which had only promised one, and produced a wax dummy at that. *States* reporter Meigs Frost wrote a long and not especially funny story about try-outs for the roles and the need for bearded ladies since all the good-looking girls had bobbed their hair. (In the event, the five hundred or so partygoers encountered only a painting of the three bearded Godivas, but the chorus line performed in person.)

In short, every attempt was made to portray the ball as "like the Beaux Arts ball of the Parisian artists' quarter," a spectacle "rivaled by nothing but the Montmartre balls themselves" (the words of the *Times-Picayune*), and to "herd" into it "all who like pseudo Bachannalian [*sic*] revels" (the words of the *New York Times*, which took notice). Some New Orleanians who had been to Paris would have known about the French original by hearsay or might even have experienced firsthand the public nudity and debauchery for which it was famous (Sherwood Anderson hinted at its nature in his novel *Dark Laughter*). By those standards—or even by the standards of 1920s

London, where Evelyn Waugh was writing of "almost naked parties in St John's Wood" and "any really successful party included somebody stripped to the waist or beyond"—the New Orleans balls were rather tame. Still, by American standards some of the entertainment was a little racy, and Julius Friend's wife, Elise, recalled that many costumes were "very scanty." At one ball, the *States* reported enough "abbreviated costumes" to "strain the optics," adding that many partygoers "seemed to find interest in less congested localities [and] wandered off to commune with the wonders, consisting of various types of Nature," and that the party was still "going strong as Dawn streaked the dove-colored sky with a lipstick-reddened finger."

The scanty costumes doomed an experiment with a December date in 1927 (the balls were usually held just after Easter). The night turned out to be wet and bitterly cold, and a newspaper report the next day said that "the red-hot jazz band and the red-hot stove were easily the most popular parts of the ball [and those] who wore leopard skins were wishing for coonskin coats." Although the reporter said that everyone agreed that it had been "the best, dampest, and most colorful party that New Orleans has seen in more than many a moon," the experiment was not repeated.

Scanty or not, costumes were certainly varied. At one ball, a crew of pirates "whooped it up with damsels representing every country, including Iceland and the West Indies," while a tribe of Indians, a host of devils, and a "horde of Russian gentlemen," bearded and booted, cavorted with ballerinas, scrubwomen, Indian princesses, Gypsy girls, "demure young things, vampires, snake charmers, Egyptian dancing girls, hula dancers, queens and celery stalks." Newspaper accounts of another mentioned Peter Pan, a "Chinee girl and boy," Pierrot and Pierrette, a chef, several peasants, "Rose of Washington Square," Trappist monks, a chimneysweep, a Fascist blackshirt, a pirate, ballet dancers, clowns, toreadors, policemen, sailors, and doctors. Famous Creoles at that one included Spratling, who came as a beachcomber (with Esther DuPuy as "a Nautch bride"), Charles Bein as a baby, Oliver La Farge as a Mayan prince, and Weeks Hall in some outlandish costume that baffled interpreters.

Decorations tended to excess. Dan Whitney of the New Orleans Art School faculty and his students set the tone with their murals for the first ball, including one of Father Time "reclining on a cross-word puzzly crazy-quilt flung over the clouds, . . . flanked by a spectacled female artist seated on a garbage can and doing a landscape," and another of "charming little cherubs in quaint postures." A later ball offered murals of a large and colorful octopus with "a comely maid and handsome youth" in its tentacles, "something or someone who might have been Bacchus," and "a pale, long, aesthetic man" surrounded by "mischievous little red devils." For another, the *Times-Picayune* reported, two clubrooms were transformed into "a haven of angels and devils" and "a dream room of romance" with "statuary, fiery red paintings, and ornamental draperies." (A philistine from the *States* wrote that the place was "profusely decorated with splashes of color meant to represent futuristic painting.")

Entertainment ran to skits and dances. The planning committee for April 1927—including Spratling and his fellow Famous Creoles Dan Whitney, Charles Bein, and Alberta Kinsey—laid on a parody by Spratling and Kinsey of Flo Field's play *A La Creole*, staged just the month before at Le Petit Theatre, as well as the popular Junior League chorus line in "black costumes with full tarlatan skirts and big ruffs around the neck." The ball "rose to a fever pitch about 3 o'clock," according to one account, and "a stranger dropping in might have thought himself in the Latin Quarter of Paris, so alike was the scene." All in all, said another observer, carried away, the ball "surpassed any other ever given in cleverness and gaiety."

Arts and Crafts Club balls were still being held as late as 1930 and 1931—although they had moved back to the warmer post-Lenten season—but they seem to have run out of steam about that time. The Depression put a damper on all sorts of frivolity, of course; moreover, as we shall see, changes in the French Quarter may also have reduced the market for what James Feibleman later recalled as "imitation Greenwich Village parties."

Making a Scene

F UTURE FAMOUS CREOLES and others like them began to gather in New Orleans in the years during and just after World War I. Writers and artists and architects and anthropologists came to work at Tulane University or for the city's newspapers, and they encountered like-minded natives, some just back from military service or from living somewhere else. They began to form a community, based on common interests and friendships. As the circle took shape the newspapers and the university helped to maintain it by providing publicity and more recruits. The phrase "critical mass" is not just a cliché in this case: Eventually enough people were involved that they could create and sustain new institutions, which in turn maintained the circle and attracted new members.

The Tulane Connection

Although Tulane University and Newcomb, its associated women's college, were located nearly five miles uptown, their importance for the emergence and maintenance of the French Quarter scene cannot be overstated. Fully half of the Famous Creoles had some sort of Tulane connection. Seven taught there, at least a dozen were alumni or alumnae, one received an honorary doctorate, and another was the university's president. A major conduit to the Famous Creoles' circle ran from Newcomb, especially from its School of Art, where Ellsworth Woodward had been director since the school's founding and Louis Andrews Fischer, Caroline Durieux, and Fanny Craig Ventadour had been among his students. (Alberta Kinsey came to New Orleans intending to enroll at Newcomb, although it's not clear whether she ac-

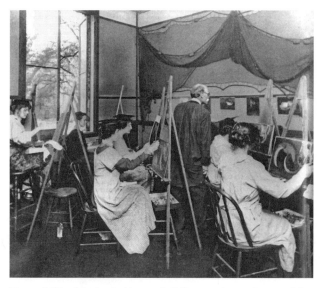

Ellsworth Woodward and a Newcomb College art class at the turn of the century.

tually did.) Other Famous Creoles with a Newcomb connection included Flo Field, who went to a secondary school attached to the college; Natalie Scott and Lillian Friend Marcus, who played together on the college's pioneering women's basketball team; and Helen Pitkin Schertz, a student some years earlier.

While Newcomb art students drew the French Quarter's picturesque architecture to use on postcards and calendars, students and faculty from Tulane's architecture school went to the Quarter to measure and sketch its historic buildings, and many became early and active members of the preservation movement. The school had been cofounded by Ellsworth Woodward's brother William, and in 1926 Famous Creoles Spratling and N. C. Curtis were teaching there, while Moise Goldstein and Charles Bein (both also alumni) had done so in the past. Tulane cheerleader Marian Draper was an architecture student—and apparently a good one. She and Tulane undergrads Ham Basso and Freddie Oechsner were all important figures on campus, put by the yearbook in its Hall of Fame.

Tulane's English department was home to Famous Creole Richard Kirk, a poet and regular contributor to the *Double Dealer* (about which, more later), while the university's Department of Middle American Research pur-

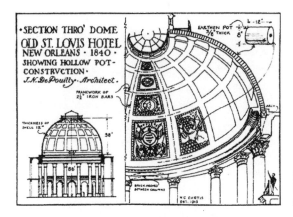

Measured drawing of St. Louis Hotel dome, by N. C. Curtis (1915).

sued "advanced research into the history (both Indian and colonial), archaeology, tropical botany (both economic and medical), the natural resources and products, of the countries facing New Orleans across the waters to the south." That department's chairman, Frans Blom, lived in the Quarter and commuted to the university, as did his younger colleague Oliver La Farge. Together, the two Famous Creoles did important archeological work in Mexico and Central America, and Blom was assiduous in passing on his findings

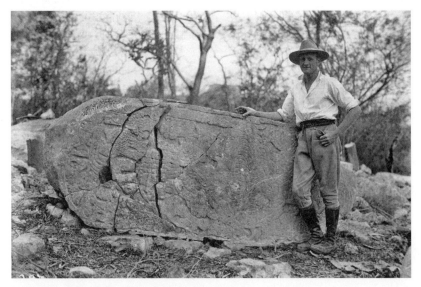

Frans Blom of the Department of Middle American Research in the Yucatán

to an interested public, with an eye to securing funds for future expeditions. At one lecture on Mexico in 1925, his audience included Spratling, Natalie Scott, and Caroline Durieux, who would all eventually live there, as well as Virginia Parker Nagle and Charles Bein, who would paint in Orizaba with "a number of the New Orleans boys and girls" in 1930. Blom also showed his movies, photographs, and reproductions of architectural details at the Arts and Crafts Club, and his enthusiasm spread (probably through his friend and fellow commuter, Spratling) to the architecture school where, one student from the 1920s recalled, it was a "standing joke" that "no matter what the problem was—whether it was a bank, office building, or a school; if you did it in Mayan architecture, you got a good grade."

The Newspapers

As important as Tulane and Newcomb in shaping the Famous Creoles' social circle were the daily newspapers of New Orleans. There were three in the early 1920s, four after 1924, and no single paper was comfortably dominant. The morning *Times-Picayune* always led in sales, but the combined circulation of the afternoon papers, the *Item* and the *States,* was greater, and when the *Item* brought out a morning edition called the *Morning Tribune* in 1924, soon *those* two papers together outsold the *Times-Picayune. Time* magazine described New Orleans as "one of the hottest competitive newspaper towns in the country." The resulting scramble for readers led to extensive coverage of local news, like the goings-on in the French Quarter, and created jobs for reporters to cover it. At one time or another, nearly a quarter of the Famous Creoles were working journalists. Flo Field and Helen Pitkin Schertz had

THE PRESS
THE TIMES-PICAYUNE, NEW ORLEANS

ROARK BRADFORD   JOHN McCLURE
Story-Teller   *Ballad-Maker*

"The Press," from *Famous Creoles.*

been pioneering newspaperwomen in the 1890s, although both had given it up by the 1920s. When *Famous Creoles* was published in 1926, Lyle Saxon and Roark Bradford had just left the *Times-Picayune* to try to write fiction, Hamilton Basso would soon do the same, and Natalie Scott would leave the *States* to move to Mexico. Frederick Oechsner left the *Item* and *Morning Tribune* in the late 1920s for a distinguished journalistic career elsewhere. But Meigs Frost stayed on at the *States,* and John McClure and editorial cartoonist Keith Temple remained at the *Times-Picayune* for their entire careers.

Many others in the circle relied on their friends at the newspapers for extra income. As editor of the *Picayune*'s Sunday features section, Roark Bradford had $15 a week to parcel out among his friends. Natalie Scott lined up an architecture column for Spratling and used his pencil portraits with her stories, while the *Morning Tribune* used a sketch by Louis Andrews Fischer with a story by Oechsner, Dan Whitney illustrated at least one feature by Saxon, and McClure persuaded the *Times-Picayune* to print sixteen of Faulkner's stories and sketches.

The newspapers also publicized the circle's activities (and defined its boundaries by choosing whose activities to cover). All the working journalists among the Famous Creoles wrote at least occasionally about what other members of the circle were up to. McClure's *Times-Picayune* column, "Literature and Less," could be counted on to review local authors, almost always gently, while Natalie Scott's social column in the *States* was filled with the doings of her friends, many of them Famous Creoles. Saxon used his "What's Doing" column to promote both historic preservation and the activities of his crowd; in what must have been a record, a single column in 1925 mentioned fourteen other Famous Creoles. Even Keith Temple occasionally devoted an editorial-page cartoon to French Quarter happenings. An Oechsner story in the *Morning Tribune* headlined "Summer's End Brings Artists Home to Plan Many Exhibitions" was typical. It read like an ordinary society-page story, except that it was about the comings and goings of local artists, including a half-dozen or so Famous Creoles. ("William Spratling is in New York and will return shortly to continue his professorship in Architecture at Tulane University.") And these stories didn't always confine themselves to simple reporting. When Meigs Frost covered a 1924 Arts and Crafts Club exhibit, he closed by exhorting his readers, "If New Orleans has any pride in the fact that painters of genuine and splendid artistry live in this city, then [this exhibit] should be crowded from opening until closing hours."

Incidentally, "full disclosure" was not yet the norm for journalists. Just as Scott had plugged *Sherwood Anderson and Other Famous Creoles* without revealing that she was one of the Famous Creoles, she also plugged each of the *Double Dealer*'s forty-two issues in her column without disclosing that she was an investor in the magazine (eventually one of its four largest stockholders). Similarly, Oechsner wrote an article promoting Flo Field's play *A La Creole* that neglected to mention that he was playing the lead.

Le Petit Theatre du Vieux Carré

A La Creole was staged at Le Petit Theatre, one of the earliest and most important of the institutions founded by members of the Famous Creoles' circle. In 1916 a group of friends who called themselves the Drawing Room Players had begun performing for their own amusement in the Garden District house of Rhea Loeb Goldberg, wife of a New Orleans lawyer, and by 1919 there was so much interest in their activities—450 dues-paying members at $5 each—that they listened when Lyle Saxon suggested in the *Item*, "What about a Little Theater in one of the Pontalba buildings?" Saxon envisioned "a place where drawing-room plays could be acted, and which would seat approximately 200 spectators." In November of that year the Players

The Drawing Room Players on the lower Pontalba building's gallery (Mrs. Schertz, Mrs. Nixon, and Mrs. Goldberg seated, left to right).

rented a shabby upstairs space in a former flophouse in the lower Pontalba building for $17.50 a month and changed their name to Le Petit Theatre du Vieux Carré. Mrs. Goldberg, Helen Pitkin Schertz, and Mrs. James Oscar Nixon, the group's first president, were later honored as the Theatre's "fairy godmothers." The Players had been very much an uptown group, in every sense, but that move began an association with the Quarter that persists to this day. (In 1921 Mrs. Nixon received the *Times-Picayune* Loving Cup for the "revival of public interest in the French Quarter," and Spratling and Faulkner probably put her and Mrs. Schertz in *Famous Creoles* for the same reason.)

Three years later, the Theatre had doubled its dues and more than doubled its membership (to a thousand), so when its Board became concerned about matters like crowding and the absence of fire escapes, they confidently bought property at the corner of St. Peter and Chartres streets and engaged architect and preservationist Richard Koch to design a new building for the Theatre's use. *Lady Windermere's Fan* was the last of twenty-one productions in the lower Pontalba building; the new theater opened its 1922–1923 subscription season with a bill of three one-acters: a couple of stylish English numbers and a more somber pseudo-Slavic item ("There is an atmosphere of silence, solitude and Russian monotony. The clock ticks.").

Bird's-eye view by William Spratling of Le Petit Theatre's new playhouse

The Theatre's success was never in doubt. A subscription season of seven or so productions from October until June offered works by morose Scandinavians or Russians offset by drawing-room comedies, and most seasons included an evening of one-act plays and something by Oscar Wilde or George Bernard Shaw. Many of the plays were by authors now largely forgotten, though well known at the time (like the Anglo-Irish playwright Lord Dunsany who had helped to open the Pontalba building theater), but modern audiences might recognize names like Edna St. Vincent Millay, Booth Tarkington, John Galsworthy, James M. Barrie, A. A. Milne, Arnold Bennett, and William Alexander Percy, not to mention Strindberg, O'Neill, and Tolstoy. (Oddly, Shakespeare wasn't attempted until the 1927–1928 season, and then only the first three acts of *Hamlet*.) In addition to the subscription season, "workshop" performances featured more experimental plays or untried actors, playwrights, and directors.

A scene from Alphonse Daudet's *L'Arlésienne* at "Le Petit," ca. 1921

Famous Creoles were well represented on the Theatre's programs. Marc Antony designed the sets for a half-dozen productions, for example, and the Theatre staged plays written by Sam Gilmore and Natalie Scott. Gilmore also appeared onstage, while his sister, Martha, was in *The Devil's Disciple* with Scott, and directed at least two of the Theatre's plays. Helen Pitkin Schertz also acted and directed (her nephew Waldo acted, too), and her fellow fairy

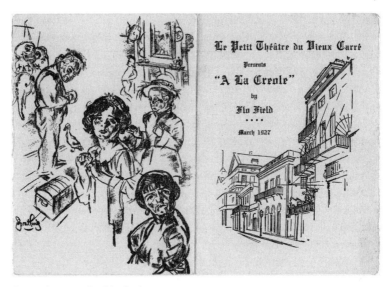

Cover of program for *A La Creole*

godmothers, Rhea Goldberg and Louise Nixon, each appeared in at least one production—Mrs. Nixon as the lead in a French-language one-acter. The *New York Times* remarked that Le Petit Theatre was "the only Little Theatre in this country which can present French plays in French" (although, in fact, that may have been the only one presented).

Undoubtedly the high point of Famous Creole involvement with Le Petit came in March 1927 when that play by Flo Field, *A La Creole,* had its world premiere. The opening had good advance publicity in the local papers, including leading man Oechsner's article, "Le Petit Theatre Eager for Flo Field's Play." Spratling illustrated the program and shared credit for scenery, which included "a real bit of the architecture about which visiting scribes, notables, tourists, and others like to rave." Spratling's lady friend Esther DuPuy had a bit part and Harold Levy's Orchestre du Petit Theatre du Vieux Carré made its debut between the acts. The play itself was a bit of local color fluff, set in Madame Toup's French Quarter carnival costume shop. The author played Mamzelle Tintine, "a little Creole spinster doing job work" in the shop ("It was a religion my Pappa had for opera, yas. Me, I can show you that box at the opera where I am almost born! It was *Les Huguenots* and when the chorus sing—'La-Lal-la'—Mommon say to Pappa, 'Felix, me, I cannot wait for that ballet, NON!'"). Oechsner's poor but handsome character was revealed at the end to be the heir to an earldom. Field's friend Hermann Deutsch (whose own one-acter had been staged by the Theatre's workshop) meant it as a compliment when he wrote in the next morning's *Item* that this "whimsy in three acts" was as if the offspring of Peter Pan and Pollyanna had been reared "on a diet of bubbles and rainbows." The *Times-Picayune*'s reviewer, especially touched by "Mrs. Field's tear-spattered curtain speech," hailed the play as a "triumph."

By 1928 Le Petit Theatre had thirty-five hundred members, and another story in the *New York Times* concluded that it had become "undoubtedly the greatest single cultural force in the community." Calling it "a fine manifestation of the guild spirit," the *North American Review* observed that "it has been artistically successful and has consistently made money, furnishing a theatre-loving city with the kind of entertainment it might otherwise have had to go without during the movie-ridden period." But the Theatre's importance went beyond the drama that it brought to New Orleans. The *Times* remarked that going to its performances had become "the thing to do," bringing its mostly uptown subscribers into the Quarter, where they patronized the shops and restaurants, and were introduced to the more Bohemian element to be found among the Theatre's actors and crew. An after-theater party at the nearby Quartier Club described in one of Natalie Scott's newspaper columns mixed society with "musicians, artists, actors, authors." Mrs. Schertz played her harp and another lady the violin, an actress recited humorous poetry, and the Creole proprietress of the fashionable Patio Royal gave a tabletop "imitation of a French Opera ballet girl." Other entertainment included recitations in Scottish and cockney dialect by a visiting English actor, and a sing-along with Harry Loeb at the piano concluded with the "Marseillaise," which everyone sang, "as though to prove we have a right to the French Quarter."

The *Double Dealer*

Another important institution founded in the early years of the Quarter's Bohemian scene was the *Double Dealer* magazine. It drew on the Famous Creoles' circle, to be sure, but (like the other new institutions) also on other, older social circles in New Orleans. Both of its founders, Julius Friend and Albert Goldstein, came from prominent Jewish families in New Orleans and had been friends since childhood. After serving together in the army medical corps in World War I they found themselves back home with time on their hands. "We were disillusioned, we were at loose ends and we belonged to what some people in those days called the 'Lost Generation,'" Goldstein recalled a half-century later. "One day Julius said to me or I said to him, 'Let's publish a magazine. You and I publish a magazine here in New Orleans.'" They enlisted Paul Godchaux Jr., scion of another established Jewish family, who helped them raise the money to get started, much of which came from their own pockets and from their families. (Sherwood Anderson wrote a friend later that the *Double Dealer* was "run by the sons of several rich men.") Friend and Goldstein also recruited John McClure, an experienced journalist who put them in touch with a youthful but published poet named Basil Thompson. Friend's uncle, Sam Weis, let the boys use the vacant third floor of a building he owned just across Canal Street from the French Quarter. The filthy place came with some overstuffed furniture, a set of dueling pistols, and two human skulls. The only heat was provided by a fireplace that burned coal hauled up the stairs by a "little old colored man." Over the fireplace was a mural of a recumbent Sam Gilmore, painted by an artist who had previously occupied the place. (Gilmore would become a benefactor, a major contributor, and eventually a Famous Creole.) Friend's sister, Lillian Marcus, lent them a typewriter, they engaged the services of a printer whose specialty was feed catalogs for farmers, and in December 1920 the *New Orleans Illustrated News* announced that the *Double Dealer* would appear the next month, with its title from a Congreve play where the hero deceives all parties by speaking the truth and its motto to be "a plague on both your houses."

In the event the motto was "honesty is our policy" instead, but the little magazine did ride forth (as Friend put it) "like a literary Don Quixote to slay the monsters of American letters and succor the good and the beautiful." "We mean to deal double," the editors wrote, "to show the other side, to throw open the back windows stuck in their sills from disuse, smuttered over long since against even a dim beam's penetration. To myopics we desire to indicate the hills, to visionaries the unwashed dishes." They asked their readers to defy Prohibition and to "drain a beaker of the forbidden juice to— THE DOUBLE DEALER."

Although the magazine seemed terribly modern at the time, Friend later acknowledged that in fact it was a period piece, like the flapper and the speakeasy, part of a "wider cultural movement—a revolt from current American restrictions and stereotypes in favor of more freedom of expression." It was "infected with the first wave of Freudianism innocently understood as the doctrine that anything less than complete sexual freedom was

First issue, February 1921

Olive Leonhardt cover

The magazine's serious new look, 1922.

devastating." Friend called particular attention to the early covers drawn by Olive Leonhardt, featuring "nymphs and satyrs aplenty done in the Beardsley manner, suggesting I know not what amounts of naughtiness and challenge to Mrs. Grundy." The editors shared H. L. Mencken's scorn for "puritanism" and the "booboisie" and Sinclair Lewis's disdain for Babbitry and the values of Main Street. "As to Southern writing, we were bored with colonial mansions and antebellum nostalgia. With 'Old New Orleans' steeped in fabled sinfulness and Creole culture (a gold mine still unexhausted) we had no truck."

In its early days the magazine's editorials and many of its reviews were written by the editors under various pseudonyms jokingly identified in the "Notes on Contributors" (e.g., "Narcisse Smathers . . . resides on the banks of the Atchafalaya [with] the largest collection of Poland Chinas in Louisiana"). The tone was usually arch or world-weary, often both. Friend remarked that the magazine suffered from "a youthful facetiousness wherein we wished to exhibit ourselves as properly and mellowly scornful of all popular ideals and pretentions—terrible fellows indeed." The editors' judgments were confident, if fallible. (They predicted that "several decades hence, such writers as James Joyce, Wyndham Lewis, Ezra Pound, T. S. Eliot . . . will have been either entirely forgotten or recalled only as eccentric clowns," and dismissed "the flapper philosopher" Scott Fitzgerald as "a modern young man lately come up from Rutgers or some such institution.")

When the magazine was founded, the editors' idols were Mencken and the Richmond writer James Branch Cabell, whose fey novel *Jurgen* had been the subject of a celebrated obscenity trial in 1919. Cabell sent an encouraging letter that was printed in the magazine's first issue, but he wasn't heard from after that, and in any case the editors didn't much like his books after *Jurgen*. Mencken, on the other hand, oversaw, criticized, and encouraged the young publication throughout its life. Albert Goldstein said later that the *Double Dealer* had been founded in part to show Mencken "that he didn't know what he was talking about" when he dismissed the South as a cultural desert, "the Sahara of Bozart [Beaux Arts]," and after reading each of the first year's issues "diligently" Mencken declared that the magazine "has the right air" and "doesn't give a damn for the old gods."

It's not surprising that Mencken liked the magazine—his influence was evident on almost every page—but an even more important influence was Sherwood Anderson, who showed up at the magazine's office in January 1922, pleased with a review of his work by Hart Crane, and stayed around to become not just a mentor and an elder statesman but actually one of those who met each month to put the issue together. If they didn't have enough material, they wrote some. Anderson wrote for four of the next five issues and generously used his considerable influence on the magazine's behalf.

Many contributors were local literati like Gilmore and a half-dozen other Famous Creoles, or members of the magazine's unofficial and unpaid "staff" like the teenaged Jimmy Feibleman, stockbroker and amateur artist Gideon Stanton, and Adaline Katz, a banker's daughter who was one of Anderson's early handmaidens. Eventually, however, this "National Magazine from the South" attracted an impressive roster of out-of-town contributors, ranging from the Harlem Renaissance writer Jean Toomer to planter-littérateur William Alexander Percy, from the English writer and roué Frank Harris to at least five of the Nashville "Fugitive" poets. Some, like Ezra Pound and Amy Lowell, were famous even at the time, but others were up-and-comers like Djuna Barnes, Thornton Wilder, Edmund Wilson, Malcolm Cowley, and Hart

Crane, or even unknowns like William Faulkner and "a young American living in Paris" named "Ernest M. Hemingway" (the magazine was the first to publish both).

To be sure, the material was not always top-drawer. As Hemingway later remarked, the *Double Dealer* published a lot of "2nd rate stuff by 1st rate writers" (including—he could have added—his poems). Sensitive to the charge that the editors were too hospitable to big names, Friend wrote later: "Let it be recorded that we once rejected a story by Theodore Dreiser and a poem by Gabriele D'Annunzio." But for the story I'm telling, the *Double Dealer* was less important for what it published than for what it *was*—a rallying point and gathering place for the writers and writer-impersonators of New Orleans's emerging Bohemia. Young Jimmy Feibleman first climbed the stairs in 1921, and became a regular after the magazine accepted one of his poems. Nearly fifty years later, he described the scene:

> Itinerant literary men, restless painters, and all manner of odd fish drifted in and out, submitting manuscripts, borrowing money, and talking interminably about art. Here among second-rate men the aesthetics of the day was aired a thousand times, revealing itself behind and within the most casual as well as the most profound observations. . . . In this mephitic air I felt at home at first but later became very uncomfortable. . . . One Saturday afternoon . . . a number of would-be writers were sitting around smoking, drinking whiskey and talking. Being only eighteen, I sat quietly and listened. All of them, I gathered from the conversation, were destined to be famous men of letters. Now it just happened that while I said nothing I had planned to be one, too. Could it come about that all of us would make the grade? On a sheer statistical basis, I did not see how.

Feibleman wasn't exaggerating about the "odd fish." The magazine seemed to attract them, especially after its office became a sort of flophouse for migratory poets. Among the "welcome and unwelcome habitués" was one penniless young man who had bicycled from New York. Another visitor left with as many review copies of books as he could carry and some blank checkbooks, but was arrested in Illinois for another theft before he could drain the magazine's (virtually empty) account. Those who actually wrote for the *Double Dealer* could be at least as odd. Frances Jean Bowen's history of the magazine records an Anglo-Irish nobleman who wrote with a quill pen, a Chicago lawyer who successfully posed as an African poet, a writer said to have cornered the Mexican bean market, and another who became press agent for heavyweight boxing champion Gene Tunney. One contributor moved to a leper colony in the Philippines; another had "a romantic yen for actresses," married two of them, and ended by jumping from a window. The FBI came around to check on one who was involved with the German-Alsatian separatist movement, another was charged as a Japanese agent after Pearl Harbor, and still another contributor wound up in wartime Chungking, spying for the United States.

The *Double Dealer* always lived hand-to-mouth. For a time, a managing editor served as "typist, file clerk, office manager and advertising solicitor" for "a miserly weekly wage," but after 1924 Lillian Marcus did all that for nothing. The other editors and the volunteer staff were never paid, and after the first year neither were contributors. Although circulation reached about three thousand and advertising came in from local businesses like Jimmy Feibleman's family's department store, income from those sources never sufficed to pay the bills. Eventually Marcus enlisted local "guarantors," who pledged at least $10 a month; Famous Creoles on an early list of fifty-two included Marcus herself, editor John McClure (all the other editors were there as well, plus a good many of their relatives), Lucille Godchaux Antony (Paul Godchaux's cousin), musician Harold Levy, architect Moise Goldstein, and writers Lyle Saxon, Sam Gilmore, and Natalie Scott. Other familiar names were those of Adaline Katz, Gideon Stanton, Arts and Crafts Club patron Hunt Henderson, and philanthropist W. R. Irby. On the bright side, the magazine's constant financial woes provided the excuse for the Folies du Vieux Carré (see page 24) and a series of other ostensibly fund-raising parties. Julius Friend confessed in later years that the guests were mostly "friends and acquaintances whose interests were frankly less literary than convivial."

Nevertheless, the magazine was successful enough that after 1922 or so it began to take itself seriously. The jokey "Notes on Contributors" and baroque editorials were discontinued, Olive Leonhardt's racy covers gave way to a sober image of a Roman coin showing the two-faced Janus, and the magazine's tone became "almost sedate." Some of the fun had gone out of the enterprise, and much of the rest went in 1924 when thirty-year-old Basil Thompson—described by one observer as "charming, lovable, witty, dramatic in his own way, the spark of the joint-undertaking"—died of pneumonia after one of his many drinking bouts. The *Double Dealer* scene had "fizzed and effervesced under [Thompson's] influence," and things were just not the same without him. The magazine appeared less frequently, issues were postponed or skipped altogether, and eventually the surviving editors just seem to have lost interest. Goldstein said later that the magazine "bowed out mainly because its work was done"; it had done its part "to kick over the traces of a decayed literary tradition." Friend echoed that view: the "crusade for liberty of expression, against puritanism and complacency had quickly succeeded," he said, adding, "Perhaps the citadel had never been so formidable as it appeared." The forty-second issue of the *Double Dealer* appeared in May 1926, and when *Famous Creoles* appeared that winter it wasn't clear whether there would be another. There was not.

The Arts and Crafts Club

Of all the institutions founded by the Famous Creoles' circle, the single most important one for setting the tone of the French Quarter scene was unquestionably the Arts and Crafts Club (and not just for its Bals des Artistes). The Club's beginnings can be traced to 1919, when a small group of artists met in Alberta Kinsey's Toulouse Street studio—possibly at Lyle Saxon's instigation and certainly with his encouragement—and engaged one of their number as a teacher. (Conrad Albrizio, later another Famous Creole, was one of the first three students.) The "Artists' Guild," as the group came to call itself, bounced around among several French Quarter locations, including some exhibition and sales space provided rent-free by the city in the old Bank of Louisiana building on Royal Street. Along the way they attracted the attention and patronage of some wealthy members of New Orleans society, one of whom, Martha Gasquet Westfeldt, gave them temporary quarters in the Green Shutter Tea Room, which she owned.

With the support of these socially elevated backers, the Artists' Guild was reconstituted as the Arts and Crafts Club in 1921 and chartered in 1922. Its charter was signed by Mrs. Westfeldt, her husband, George, who ran his family's coffee importing business, and five others with impeccable social credentials, including Sarah Henderson, a sugar refinery heiress whose fortune was substantial enough for her to have spent several Belle Époque winters in Cannes. (During World War I she returned to France to do relief work with "Secours de la Louisiane a la France.") Miss Henderson could easily afford the contributions that kept the Club afloat for many years: in 1922 she was fifty-two years old and living in a Garden District mansion alone, except for a housekeeper, two maids, a butler, and a chauffeur. A few months after the Club was chartered, preservationist W. R. Irby gave it a new clubhouse,

Courtyard 520 Royal St. New Orleans
Old Brulatour Mansion remodelled
now The Arts & Crafts Club

Drawing by Louis Andrews [Fischer]

the huge slave quarters in the rear of the historic Seignouret-Brulatour house, which he had converted for its use. The building had space for a long exhibition room on the ground floor, as well as classrooms, studios, and a salesroom, and its picturesque courtyard became probably the most often painted scene in New Orleans.

From its early days the Club brought together artists from the faculties of Newcomb College and the Tulane architecture school, freelancers like Kinsey and Ronald Hargrave, and serious amateurs like Gideon Stanton, who would become one of the Club's most faithful advocates and supporters. Unlike the Artists' Guild, which was only open to working artists, the Club was open to everyone, including mere art lovers like those who signed its charter. The professionals were always a minority, and nearly all of the Club's officers were "lay members"—Sarah Henderson was the Club's president for its first several years, and the Westfeldts and other signers of the charter passed lesser offices around. The social tone of the operation was evident in exhibition announcements that included notes like, "Tea will be poured Sunday by Miss Amelie Roman and Miss Eloise Walker Duffy from 3 to 5 p.m."

The Famous Creoles had been very much in evidence ever since the meeting in Alberta Kinsey's apartment. Architecture professor N. C. Curtis was an "indefatigable worker" in getting the Club organized, and in its first year in the new clubhouse, Spratling, Marc Antony, and Louis Andrews (Fischer) were among those who taught classes. Coeducational instruction made the Club the only institution in New Orleans offering serious art training for

"GREAT STUFF!"

Times-Picayune cartoon by Keith Temple

men (women could study art at Newcomb College). Kinsey and Albrizio were on the exhibition committee, and the Club showed work by Kinsey, Antony, Fanny Craig (Ventadour), and Lucille Godchaux (Antony), and etchings, block prints, and oriental rugs from William Odiorne's collection. The next year saw exhibitions of watercolors by Charles Bein and cartoons by Keith Temple, and by 1924 nine Famous Creoles were teaching at the Club or on its executive committee, and another eight were members.

When the Club formally established its New Orleans Art School, the same division of labor between artists and patrons applied. In 1926 George Westfeldt was the school's president and Sarah Henderson its first vice president; avocational artists Gideon Stanton and Moise Goldstein were on the executive board, and the part-time teaching staff included working artists Spratling, Dan Whitney, and Charles Bein, who would soon be named the school's first director. There were 144 students, up from sixty-one the year before, many of them on scholarships provided by "sustaining" members of the Club, who paid dues of $25 a year ("contributing" members paid $10 and ordinary "active" members $5). The Club's secretary described the scene at 520 Royal Street: "On any day one may pass through the lovely old courtyard of the club and see serious and

In The Arts And Crafts Life Class

The image (Olive Leonhardt drawing for newspaper).

The reality

ambitious students at work . . . and in the evening an incongruous lot—foreigners intent upon modeling or drawing, business girls happy in 'art for recreation's sake'; professional men finding in these classes a great resource, younger men busy with the problems of drafting—persons of every type meeting on common ground." The art school, she said, had become "very like the ateliers one finds in Rome and Paris," offering day and evening classes in "drawing, painting, commercial art, metal craft, sculpture, architecture, etching, design, outdoor sketching, and so on, with classes for children on Saturday afternoons" and "educational talks provided on Sunday afternoons," open to the public. In the Club's galleries "exhibits of pictures and crafts change semi-monthly, and have provided a great attraction to tourists as well as the public." The exhibits aimed "to show the trend of Art of Today, both conservative and modernistic," and were bringing "the best of modern art and crafts" to New Orleans.

Bringing modern art to New Orleans was, in fact, one of the Club's major contributions. In both its teaching program and its exhibitions, it was more hospitable to new trends in art than the cross-town Delgado Museum, which was under the Impressionist and Regionalist influence of Newcomb College art professor Ellsworth Woodward. Sarah Henderson's brother, Hunt, a serious art collector, had been on the Delgado's board, but after he had a falling-out with Woodward over the place of modern works in the museum's collection, he turned his attention to the club that his sister had been supporting and became a major supporter himself, sponsoring a prize for work by local artists and lending works from his collection for exhibits. Modern pieces did not always meet with popular approval; a columnist in the *States* wrote of a show of expressionist paintings that "the general public . . . thinks them 'wild' and 'crazy'

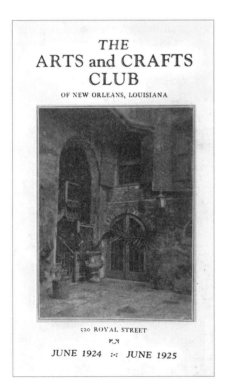

THE
ARTS and CRAFTS
CLUB
OF NEW ORLEANS, LOUISIANA

520 ROYAL STREET
≈
JUNE 1924 ∶∶ JUNE 1925

THE ART**/** and **CRAFT/ CLUB**
of **NEW ORLEANS**
520 ROYAL STREET
INVITES YOU TO ITS GALLERIES
1926-1927

works of originality and distinction by
leading local and foreign artists and
craftsmen are shown
10:00 to 5:00   visitors always welcome

and begs you to explain 'what they mean' and why the Arts and Crafts Club 'brings down such stuff.'" But the Club persevered, showing the work of "six modern local artists" in 1927 and continuing to offer instruction in the new modes.

By the 1924–1925 season the Club had nearly five hundred members and offered something for just about everybody. Exhibitions included not just paintings, drawings, and etchings, but pottery, stained-glass designs, bookbinding by Newcomb College students, South American needlework, and Central American baskets and textiles. N. C. Curtis's Lectures Committee brought in speakers on miniatures and ivories, Egyptian archeology, Russian art, and the architectural history of the Vieux Carré. The Club awarded the annual Blanche S. Benjamin Prize for Louisiana landscape painting, conducted a Pennsylvania Academy of the Fine Arts scholarship competition, and gave $25 student prizes for painting, drawing, sculpture, architectural drawing, and etching. It also raised money by subscription to buy a painting by the Russian artist Abram Arkhipov for the Delgado Museum. A notable meeting of the artistic and the literary occurred when the Club met jointly with the Poetry Society of Louisiana in 1928, pairing drawings of New Orleans with poems about Louisiana by Carl Carmer, and awarding prizes for poems by, among others, Jimmy Feibleman and Famous Creoles Flo Field, Sam Gilmore, and Richard Kirk.

The Club played a major role in introducing New Orleanians to Central America. Mexican handicrafts were sold in its salesroom, alongside art and crafts from its exhibits. Caroline Durieux, who was living in Mexico, frequently returned to the Quarter, and her work, influenced by her friend Diego Rivera, began to be shown in her hometown. After Spratling first visited Mexico in the summer of 1926 he showed his drawings at the Club and his Mexican friends began to visit. He arranged for anthropologist Zelia Nuttall and Frances Toor, the editor of *Mexican Folkways* magazine, to give talks at the Club. The next summer he went back to Mexico, and the next fall showed more of his Mexican work. He also began to arrange exhibits of work by his new artist friends, both Americans working in Mexico like George Biddle and Mexican artists like Rivera, Carlos Orozco, and Rufino Tamayo. The Club also gave archeologist Frans Blom a place to show his movies and photographs of Mayan ruins and his reproductions of Mayan cornices; later his Department of Middle American Research at Tulane held a show of Guatemalan textiles and costumes. Eventually Famous Creoles Charles Bein and Alberta Kinsey went to Mexico to paint, as did other New Orleanians, and they all showed their work at the Club.

But the Arts and Crafts Club, like the *Double Dealer,* always depended on the kindness of benefactors. Its dues, shop sales, and tuition revenues never began to meet its expenses, even when supplemented by receipts from the "Bal des Artistes." The Club needed an unknown but undoubtedly large annual subvention from Sarah Henderson and other wealthy patrons to keep going—a fact that became obvious after Miss Henderson's death in 1944. It finally closed its doors in 1951.

Outposts of the French Quarter

The Famous Creoles and their crowd also helped to establish some new institutions outside New Orleans. Those New Orleanians who painted in Mexico in the late 1920s were part of a larger exodus during the brutal heat of New Orleans summers. Others convened at Cicero Odiorne's apartment in Paris, or at Lyle Saxon's in Greenwich Village. Three of the artists summered with some other American artists in the village of El Tereno on Majorca. Closer to home, Dan Whitney set up and ran the Ocean Springs Art Colony at Mrs. Walter Anderson's house on the Mississippi Gulf Coast, which attracted more than twenty New Orleanians in 1926. It does not seem to have been repeated, but the Natchitoches Art Colony, founded by Ellsworth Woodward in 1921 (at the urging of two of his Newcomb College students, in their hometown some 250 miles northwest of New Orleans), lasted for several years, directed after the first year by Woodward's Newcomb colleague Will Henry Stevens.

Yet another colony, Melrose Plantation, just outside Natchitoches, became almost a second home for a couple of Famous Creoles. Lyle Saxon in-

Students at the Natchitoches Art Colony paint on the Cane River

troduced Carmelite Garrett Henry, widow of a wealthy planter, to Grace King, whose salon seems to have inspired her. "Aunt Cammie" decided to turn Melrose into a center for artists and writers, particularly those from Louisiana, and she ran a sort of ongoing salon until her death in the 1940s. Artists and writers were invited to stay as long as they wished, so it's not surprising that the guest list is impressive. (One writer came for six weeks and stayed for thirty-two years.) Famous Creoles who spent time at Melrose include Sherwood Anderson, Roark Bradford, John McClure, William Spratling, Ellsworth Woodward, and—especially—Saxon and Alberta Kinsey, who eventually had their own special cabins. Other members of the circle like architect Richard Koch and Will Stevens were guests at Melrose as well.

"Uptown" Institutions Downtown

These art colonies, like the community theater, the little magazine, the Arts and Crafts Club and its school—in fact, all of the new Bohemian ventures downtown—were founded and paid for by moneyed, "uptown" folk (a curious fact to which we shall return). They also established a few French Quarter institutions for themselves. One was begun sometime about 1921 by Elizebeth Werlein, the young widow of a Canal Street merchant who numbered among her many interests the protection and restoration of the French

Quarter's historic architecture, and some of her socially connected friends, including Helen Pitkin Schertz and journalist Dorothy Dix. The Quartier Club, which soon found a site in the lower Pontalba building, enrolled a group of society women who were already meeting and socializing in other settings. It was primarily a ladies' luncheon and supper club (albeit New Orleans-style—the twice-weekly supper dances began at 11:00 P.M.), but there was more to it than dining and dancing; the club had a Committee on Literature, an Arts and Distinguished Guest Committee, and a Lyceum series that offered speakers like the English novelist Hugh Walpole, who spoke in December 1922. Its founders' unstated goal may have been to bring uptown society women to Jackson Square, to introduce them to the charms of the Quarter, and to build an influential constituency for preservation. Nevertheless, the food *was* good—Werlein announced in 1923 that Arnaud Cazenave, "or 'Arnaud,' as he is more popularly known," would cater the daily lunches and dinners (75 cents and $1.25, respectively). The dining room also seems to have given members a place to have a discreet cocktail: Prohibition agents found a good deal of liquor when they raided it in 1924. (President Werlein claimed the discovery was a "revelation" to her.)

Coincidentally or not, the Quartier Club did not long survive that raid, but it was the precursor of another, longer-lived organization, Le Petit Salon, founded later that year, which met only three blocks away. That group involved many of the same women (Helen Pitkin Schertz and Dorothy Dix were officers), and its purposes were much the same—although it seems to have been a bit stuffier. Its first president was the eminent lady of letters Grace King, and the free-spirited Elizebeth Werlein is not mentioned in the organization's history. Miss King described the new organization as "a circle of distinguished ladies, animated with the desire to maintain the social prestige of the old Creole quarters and preserve its social traditions." There would be no midnight supper dances—they were replaced by a determination "to revive, promote and continue the pleasant intercourse of the SALON, which gave grace and brilliancy to the old society of this City," in order "to promote enjoyment, harmony, refinement of manners and intellectual improvements." At the early meeting which chose the group's name, Miss King gave a talk on "French Salons."

The club's charter also pledged "to keep alive the love of the old traditions of New Orleans, and wherever possible to keep and preserve old historic buildings," and it set about doing the latter almost immediately. Within a year of its founding, the Salon had outgrown its second-floor meeting place

Le Petit Salon (President Grace King seated)

on St. Peter Street, and the ladies took the confident step of buying an 1838 Greek Revival mansion next door to Le Petit Theatre. They engaged Richard Koch, who had designed the theater's new quarters, to rehabilitate theirs, and moved into their clubhouse before the organization's second birthday. The organization settled into a comfortable pattern of Monday-night receptions after performances at Le Petit Theatre and weekly meetings with guest speakers. Sherwood Anderson and Oliver La Farge were among the earliest to sign the Salon's guest book, and many others in the Famous Creoles' circle shared the club's literary, artistic, and preservationist interests, but most of Le Petit Salon's members were of a different sort altogether.

So were the principals in Le Petit Opéra Louisianais, organized "to do for music what Le Petit Théâtre has done for drama." It presented itself as successor to the French Opera House of the Quarter (its programs' covers bore a picture of the old building and its musical director had been the conductor at the old place before it burned in 1919). The Opéra offers an interesting contrast to the Theatre, its older cousin. A 1927 newspaper article observed that the public's response to the Opéra "thus far has not indicated certain success," and it never did succeed. Perhaps the problem was that theater is at least potentially more avant-garde than opera (perhaps also drama offers more scope for those of limited talent), but it also didn't help that Le Petit Opéra was more than just a musical enterprise. Like Le Petit Salon, it represented an attempt to revive a nostalgic version of the high culture of old Creole New Orleans. The Opéra was literally as well as socially more up-town than the Theatre: its performances took place at the Tulane Theater, across Canal Street from the Quarter. More Bohemian members of the Famous Creoles' circle might appreciate what they saw as the romance of old Creole days—indeed, Lyle Saxon and others celebrated it—but their con-nection to it was not bred in the bone. Most were not native New Orlea-nians (many weren't even Southerners), and natives like Hamilton Basso and Emmet Kennedy were outsiders, too, as members of recent immigrant groups. While the Opéra's "Board of Control" included the usual philan-thropic and socially prominent family names, just two members were Fa-mous Creoles: Mrs. James Oscar Nixon, perhaps unofficially representing Le Petit Theatre as well as old New Orleans, and Harold Levy, one of the circle's few serious musicians. The more distinguished and presentable Bohemians might be invited from time to time to speak at Le Petit Salon and no doubt some of the circle attended performances at the Opéra, but at base neither organization was a continuation of *their* culture. We shall examine this fault line more closely in a subsequent chapter.

The Difference Dixie Made

Bohemian New Orleanians saw themselves as creating a sort of vest-pocket facsimile of Greenwich Village and the Left Bank. As one self-published poet wrote,

> The Fact is New Orleans
> The Fable is New York,
> And the Place d'Armes challenges Washington Square.
> The Vieux Carré throws down the gauntlet to Greenwich Village.
> Rue Royal takes issue with Macdougal Alley.

But there was no real risk of confusion. Being in the Deep South rather than New York or Paris had consequences. One, justly or unjustly, was that little of the French Quarter's literature was respected and little of its art even widely known outside its region. Another, not surprisingly, was that its Bohemia was for whites only. It's true that black New Orleanians helped to make it possible and were very much a presence (both actually and in art and literature), but they were not themselves allowed to be Bohemians. Finally, the racial views of the Famous Creoles and their circle were either conventional or kept to themselves, and indeed their political opinions in general tended to be anodyne, if they had opinions at all.

Critical Disdain and Neglect

Critics have been almost universally dismissive of the literature and art produced in 1920s New Orleans. In part, there was little good work because there was little work, period: the number of writers and artists was actually quite small. Oliver La Farge once figured that the literary community of New Orleans could not possibly have numbered more than fifty and, even allowing for more aspiring painters and graphic artists than that, we are probably talking about no more than a couple of hundred people altogether. Only a small fraction actually did much creative work (as elsewhere, of course), so the serious artists and writers numbered only in the dozens. Obviously, a larger population would have stood a better chance of producing masterpieces.

But there may have been another problem as well. Both artists and writers seem to have found it hard to get beneath the colorful surface of south Louisiana's life and landscape. It was too easy to write local color instead, or to paint courtyard after courtyard, swamp after swamp. One observer, a novelist himself, believed that the reason "no really good and honest and intelligent major novel" had been written about New Orleans was that writers had been beguiled by "the superficial trappings of the city's 'atmosphere.'" Critic Lewis Simpson concurred, arguing that the "local-color damnation of New Orleans was so complete that it was virtually impossible for the imagination to transcend it." Even an attempt to produce "fierce novelistic realism," like Faulkner's in *Pylon,* turned into "a local-color image of exotic depravity." Simpson's pitiless conclusion was that the French Quarter's "bid to become a southern Greenwich Village—which for a time was backed up by a few writers of genuine talent but never by a genuine congregation—ended with Lyle Saxon and Roark Bradford." And even those "writers of genuine talent" did their best work before coming to New Orleans or after leaving it.

Landscape by Charles Bein, winner of the Arts and Crafts Club's Blanch Benjamin Prize, 1927.

Sherwood Anderson was past his prime when he lived in the city, while the younger writers were yet to reach theirs. (The exception was Oliver La Farge, who wrote his best novel, *Laughing Boy,* there.) Even most of Faulkner's early efforts were dismissed by Cleanth Brooks as "perfunctory" and "mere hackwork." The careers of Faulkner, La Farge, and Hamilton Basso illustrate the truth of English writer Arthur Ransome's observation that "Bohemia is only a stage in a man's life except in the case of fools and a very few others."

For painters and graphic artists the story was much the same. Many were of the type caricatured as "angular, retired maiden schoolteachers with a vague talent for water color and the urge for self-expression," but art historian George Jordan observes that even the professional artists are today "little known outside Louisiana except to a few knowledgeable collectors." Jordan believes that many who came from elsewhere went into decline after they arrived, but I will add that the absence of nationally significant artists in the French Quarter crowd is plainly due in part to the sociology of "national significance." As far as New York was concerned, artists who moved to Louisiana might as well have died, leaving whatever promise they had shown unfulfilled. Ronald Hargrave's last entry in *Who's Who in American Art* was in 1915, the year he last showed his work at the Pennsylvania Academy of the

Landscape by Virginia Parker [Nagle]

Fine Arts, although he painted until his death twenty years later. Alberta Kinsey produced thousands of pictures after her last entry in 1922 (which had her still teaching in Ohio). Daniel Whitney also painted all his life, but the reference work lost track of him thirty-four years before he painted his last. Weeks Hall disappeared from the book after 1924, even though he showed his work at PAFA and the Corcoran in the 1930s and 1940s. When the *New York Times* mentioned Virginia Parker as one of the "newcomers" in a show at the Morton Gallery in 1938, the former Virginia Parker Nagle was forty-one years old and had been exhibiting her work since her student days at PAFA.

But with every allowance for the metropolitan provincialism that leaves good work in other provinces to blush unseen, it is hard to argue with Laura Clark Brown's conclusion that the French Quarter of the 1920s produced "no [art]work of international significance or modernist originality." Even "the self-conscious New Orleans modernists suffered from a lack of originality, falling prey to the sentimental beauty of their surroundings or to the lure of weary, unchallenged modernist styles." Brown makes an exception for Caroline Durieux, but Durieux did her best work after leaving New Orleans. Spratling, too, would leave to make his name, although as a designer of silver jewelry and tableware, not a graphic artist. Of the artists who remained in New Orleans, Ellsworth Woodward, like his brother William, was genuinely accomplished, but in a style of painting that was already passé. Only Pops Whitesell was genuinely "world-class," but in the rarified world of salon photography.

So, neither the artistic nor literary record gives much reason to disagree with Harold Sinclair's conclusion that, "in spite of her worldliness and sophistication . . . New Orleans was no great shakes as a mother of the arts." Not all or even many of the Famous Creoles and their circle did great things. With only a very few exceptions, the interest lies less in their artistic achievement than in their larger-than-life personalities and the scene they created.

A Lily-White Bohemia

Bohemian freedom as celebrated and practiced elsewhere conspicuously— even determinedly—extended to freedom of association across racial lines. Some of the female Bright Young Things of 1920s London, for instance, were known for "their attacks on the virtue of [the] Negro artists" from West End revues. But obviously things were different in Jim Crow Louisiana. When the secretary of the Arts and Crafts Club pointed out proudly that the New Orleans Art School's classes were "open to men, women and children, with no restrictions as to age, sex, or previous training," it went without saying that race was a different matter. When a group of young black men decided in 1928 that they wanted to study art, they had to take instruction by mail. (They formed their own "Little Arts and Crafts Club," and showed their work at the Negro YMCA and the Dryades Street Library.)

All of the Famous Creoles and all of their social circle were white. Few, if any, knew that Marcus Bruce Christian was writing Whitmanesque poems just a mile or two away (while running a dry-cleaning business to make ends meet). A decade later Lyle Saxon hired Christian to head the Negro unit of the Louisiana Writers' Project, and although most of the coworkers Christian assembled—poet Octave Lilly, artist Elizabeth Catlett, and novelist Margaret Walker among them—were too young to have been part of the Famous Creoles' circle even if they had been invited, they indicate the sort of talent that white New Orleanians might have found in the black community, if they'd thought to look for it.

There were individual acts of kindness, of course. Margaret Walker recalled sixty years later that although she "dared not walk on that [Tulane] campus," English professor Richard Kirk wrote her "a nice little note" when he was shown some of her teenage poetry. Similarly, Saxon was (rightly) impressed by some clay models made by a young black man named Richmond Barthé, encouraged him to study at the Art Institute of Chicago, and remained a champion of the sculptor's work. But the color line held, sometimes even when it didn't have to: The editors of the *Double Dealer* had been delighted to publish the work of Harlem Renaissance poet Jean Toomer, and were saddened when he wrote to say that he had been in town and had wanted to come meet them, but hadn't known whether he would be received. That Zora Neale Hurston didn't look up her fellow anthropologists at Tulane to talk about the research on hoodoo she was doing in New Orleans was a lost opportunity for all concerned.

Of course, the absence of African Americans from the Famous Creoles' social circle does not mean that they were invisible. All interaction between black and white was ritualized, rigidly structured by law and custom to keep blacks and whites from interacting as equals, and even when whites saw blacks from a distance—working on the docks, for instance, or worshiping in their churches—what was seen was largely structured by whites' own preconceptions. But there was a great deal of contact between the races, and

Lyle Saxon attended by Henry Tyler.

black people were always nearby, sometimes *very* nearby. Oliver La Farge recalled that he and his friends had lots of parties, even though for a long time "we didn't even have a phonograph." What he and the others usually did have, though, was a Negro servant or two. Even impecunious young men could afford some "help." La Farge shared with Spratling and Faulkner the services of "a slatternly washerwoman named Leonore" who washed, cleaned, and cooked "food fit for a king." Their neighbor Joyce Stagg's cook, Cecile, fed not just her but Famous Creoles Cicero Odiorne and Conrad Albrizio as well. Elizabeth Anderson acknowledged that her "accomplished cook," Josephine, "created "a marvelous cuisine." (Once, when Sherwood was away, Josephine was arrested for stabbing a rival for her boyfriend's attentions. Elizabeth didn't know what to do until Ham Basso told his Yankee friend that she was expected to go to night court and pay the $10 fine.) Harold Levy borrowed his mother's cook, Victoria, for a while to cook for a "dinner club" he'd formed with Jenny Pitot and Ronald Hargrave. When Natalie Scott's brother died, Lyle Saxon's condolence letter invited her to breakfast with him and Spratling—"Just the three of us, in my apartment, with Nubian Louis making an omelet or something." Saxon always had a manservant around; Weeks Hall had two or three, and a cook as well. Presumably most of the other Famous Creoles had servants, too, whose presence in the kitchens (if not in the historical record) did much to make the incessant entertaining possible.

Far from "Invisible"

Black people were as ubiquitous in the circle's art and literature as they were in real life. Much of the artists' work has been lost—as far as I know, for example, none of Lucille Antony's "notable negro studies" survives—but what remains suggests that they did not disgrace themselves. Many of their pictures of black people are essentially documentary. When Ellsworth Woodward showed a black pedestrian in the foreground of a painting of Lafitte's Blacksmith Shop, for instance, his portrayal of the woman was strictly representational and her presence almost incidental; she might well have walked past while Woodward was painting. Similarly, when Alberta Kinsey painted former slave cabins in Pointe Coupee or Spratling drew a New Orleans dockyard scene, the black figures were simply those of folks going about their

William Spratling, untitled dockyard scene

lives. To have painted black people *out* of these scenes is what would have been objectionable. Even when treating black subjects more directly, the artists in the circle did well. Spratling's sketches of Afro-Creoles living near Melrose Plantation (the same group Lyle Saxon wrote about in his novel *Children of Strangers*) are among the best portraits he ever did. Caroline Durieux did some biting caricatures of black subjects, but she treated them as individuals, not as types, and her sketches of white Creoles were equally acid. Just so, Conrad Albrizio's Regionalist portrayals of African American life—a painting of a river baptism shown at the Whitney Museum, for example—are very much of a piece with his representations of white Southern subjects.

Caroline Durieux, *Andre*

William Spratling, portrait of Madame Aubert-Rocque, from "Cane River Portraits," in *Scribner's Magazine* (1928).

Some may find it easier than I do to object to even-handedness, arguing, for example, that Albrizio's *Jordan* could reinforce stereotypes of the primitiveness and emotionality of black religion, but to my mind artists should not be judged on what prejudiced observers see in their work. It wasn't Kinsey's fault that one critic saw her slave cabins as "quaintly picturesque monuments to a fast-fading era," and particularly praised an "especially lovely

Conrad Albrizio, *Jordan*

cabin" with "a negro mammy stepping out the gate" and others with "pick-aninnies playing 'round the door." When Charles Bein showed some of his pastels in Chicago, it is not to his discredit that the *Daily News* saw them as images of "nature's own setting for the simple and emotional Negro."

But the work of the writers in the Famous Creoles' circle can be more troublesome than that of the artists. This is not the place to discuss Faulkner's black characters or his views on race. (In 2007 an entire symposium at the University of Mississippi made a start.) Sherwood Anderson's anguished, contradictory, admiring, condescending, self-deceiving views of black life and culture are also too complicated to treat in passing. (He liked to watch black stevedores at work because he saw them as primitive—and thought that was a good thing to be. "They laugh, rub shoulders with each other, love like healthy animals, are no neurotics.") But other writers' views were less complex. Grace King's portrayals of white paternalism and black loyalty were utterly conventional for a genteel white writer of her generation. One critic's typology of white writers' racial stereotypes puts Emmet Kennedy's "Gritney" (Gretna) people in the same "contented slave" category, along with Lyle Saxon's Negro characters (although Saxon's personal views were evidently more nuanced than the "affectionate paternalism" that usually goes with that stereotype). Others in the circle worked more or less the same vein. Flo Field wrote a number of magazine stories based on a "famous old darkey" [*sic*] she had known as a child, while Natalie Scott's cookbook, *Mirations and Miracles of Mandy,* was laced with dialect quotations supposedly from "Mandy," a composite character based on black New Orleans cooks she had known. Helen Pitkin Schertz peopled her 1904 novel, *An Angel by Brevet,* with Afro-Creoles fairly described by a recent critic as "childlike, irresponsible, hopeless creatures who were meant to serve others," while her friend and fellow journalist Dorothy Dix wrote stories about a mammy named "Mirandy" that were published as far afield as the *London Daily Mail.* (Dix "suffered from the delusion that the Mirandy stuff was her best work.") Even the most hackneyed of these characters, however, were not as crude as those of Roark Bradford, who wrote that "there is nothing really funnier than a funny 'nigger'" and presented figures straight out of the blackface minstrel tradition. After all this, it comes as something of a relief to encounter young Hamilton Basso's 1929 short story "I Can't Dance," which portrays a black prostitute as a sympathetic and three-dimensional character.

It should be pointed out that most of these writers made their livings from their craft, so much of this "darky" material was produced for the market—which, incidentally, was mostly not in the South. As Sherwood Anderson observed, "The trick is to write nigger stories. The North likes them. They are so amusing." Kennedy and Bradford, the two most successful purveyors of such stories, both tried to sell something else and had it made clear to them that the reading public wanted them to stick to their genre. Kennedy, whose interest in black life and culture was genuine, if condescending, thought he was going to New York to pursue a career as a concert pianist, but wound up telling dialect stories in blackface at Town Hall. Bradford actually went so far as to write two serious novels about black folk, but neither reviewers nor customers liked them half as well as books like *Ol' Man Adam and His Chillun. Time* magazine called *This Side of Jordan* "an unpleasantly realistic, unpleasantly tragic novel of Negro life," and the public seemed to want what one editor called "a good Roark Bradford Southern-Negro story" in comic dialect—so Bradford obliged with dozens of them.

Racial Orthodoxy and Innocuous Politics

Still, it is obvious that most of the Famous Creoles and their circle—like nearly all white New Orleanians at the time—had serious vision problems when it came to seeing the African American life that surrounded them, and their racial ideologies seem to have been as monochromatic as their complexions. All either shared the conventional white Southern views or kept their mouths shut. One dissenter who admitted that he kept his own counsel was Oliver La Farge. As an anthropologist, he observed that for his New Orleans acquaintances, "born in the South and not specially trained, to think other than as they did would be remarkable." Of course, for a New Englander and a social scientist to agree with them would be equally remarkable, but he wrote in his autobiography that it seemed to him that "it would be gratuitously ugly for me to flaunt my opinions or my anthropological theories in the faces of my new friends," so when the subject came up, as it inevitably did, he said frankly that he was a Yankee, grandson of a Union soldier, and "reared in the Abolitionist tradition," but that "for the present, I wanted to learn." He said this "was generously and understandingly received," and his Southern friends tried to help him understand their point of view.

In later years the Famous Creoles went their different ways, ideologically. Some became more conservative. By 1972 Cicero Odiorne had come back from Paris and was living in Los Angeles; that year he and his old friend Sam Gilmore were planning to vote for George Wallace. After Gilmore's death the next year, Odiorne wrote Gilmore's sister, "Our old world seems to be going to pieces. Los Angles now has a negro Mayor! It is a step closer to the end. New Orleans will surely never suffer that indignity . . . I visualize a night of burning super-markets." On the other hand, after La Farge moved back to New York he served with James Weldon Johnson and W.E.B. Du Bois on the nominating committee for the NAACP's Du Bois Literary Award (endowed by his mother-in-law). Hamilton Basso also moved to New York and became the conventional suburban liberal that you'd expect a New York magazine writer to be, while Fanny Craig Ventadour and Caroline Durieux moved in seriously left-wing circles in France and Mexico, respectively, and presumably adopted appropriate racial views. In the early 1960s Ventadour, by then living in Florida, even turned up on a Mississippi State Sovereignty Commission blacklist of suspected integrationists.

But at the time a stifling orthodoxy on racial matters prevailed, which may go a long way toward explaining what seems to have been a striking absence of political expression altogether. Elsewhere, Bohemians have often been attracted to extremist politics of the Left or, less often, of the Right, but most of the French Quarter's seem to have been apolitical aesthetes. (Suffragist Elizabeth Werlein was a conspicuous exception.) When an emissary from Greenwich Village—Michael Gold, editor of the *New Masses*—

tried to talk politics with Lyle Saxon at the Andersons' one day, Saxon said that he "had no quarrel with the capitalists or the workingman either" and really "wasn't very much interested in this capital and labor business." (Gold "glared" at him, Saxon reported.) Julius Friend said later that he and his colleagues at the *Double Dealer* "were nearly ignorant of politics and entirely scornful of it," and that seems to have been true of most of the New Orleans Bohemians. This fact made the emerging Bohemia more acceptable "uptown," and had important implications for the future of the Vieux Carré.

Three Populations

RTISTS FOUND MATERIAL APLENTY in the Quarter's picturesque architecture and the nearby waterfronts and cypress swamps, while writers were taken with Louisiana's fascinating cultural gumbo, but the presence of subject matter is not sufficient to explain why a Bohemian community was created in New Orleans, or why one was not created elsewhere in the South. That story is much more complicated. In part, it has to do with the presence and numbers in New Orleans of three groups that were smaller and more marginalized in every other Southern city. Gay men and Jews were disproportionately likely to be sympathetic observers and supporters of Bohemia, if not actually Bohemians themselves, and the Quarter's Italian community—although it contributed few if any members of the social circle—created an easygoing environment that nurtured the Bohemian life.

Gay Men

Gay men are usually overrepresented in literary and artistic circles, and they clearly were in this one. Most had come from elsewhere, attracted to a city where "the milieu enabled them to indulge their sexual oddities," as Oliver La Farge put it, obliquely. University of New Orleans professor Kenneth Holditch reports "an old saying" that his fellow New Orleanians "don't care what you do. They want to know about it, but they don't care."

In 1927 *New Orleans Life* magazine had a two-part feature on "Popular Bachelors of New Orleans." Seven were Famous Creoles, and three or four of those—Spratling, Weeks Hall, Sam Gilmore, and probably one other—

were homosexual, or at least not exclusively heterosexual. The same could be said of Lyle Saxon, Cicero Odiorne, and Pops Whitesell—at least a half-dozen Famous Creoles altogether. It's true that some—Spratling and Saxon, for instance—were very discreet. (Weeks Hall and Sam Gilmore were another matter.) When Spratling's frequent date Esther DuPuy was told later of his proclivities, she said that she'd never been given cause to believe it, and Harold Levy found it hard to credit, exclaiming "Anyone who sleeps with as many women as he does!" But Spratling's "artful and crafty" sketches of Saxon and Gilmore in *Famous Creoles* suggest a familiarity and comfort with the gay scene that would be more typical of someone in the closet than someone in denial. The same sort of sly innuendo seems to have been one of Saxon's specialties. Surely he knew exactly what he was saying when he wrote that preservationist William Ratcliffe Irby had been "the good-fairy of Frenchtown," or when he referred in a review to the "peculiar virility" of Weeks Hall's paintings. (In 1941, when Saxon received a jocular letter from Hall complaining that "miasmas" were causing "yaws among our new Negroes," he replied, "As for the miasmas rising from the Teche, I cannot bring myself to think that the effluvia does aught save stir indiscreet thoughts, and, alas, perhaps indiscreet actions as well. I remember in my own case, on certain summer evenings . . . but why speak of our gaudy youth, dear Coz, as we approach Life's Sunset?")

Anyway, if you take these six or seven and throw in a couple of the "confirmed bachelors," roughly a third of the male artists, writers, and musicians among the Famous Creoles seem to have been homosexual or bisexual, even if we assume that everyone else was not, which is of course a shaky, even improbable, assumption. When an artistic and socially well-connected young man is described in a document as the "intimate friend" of another, for instance, are they just *close* friends? Both were husbands and fathers, but was this code for what some New Orleanians call an "uptown marriage"? (Holditch describes that "not-uncommon union" as one in which "a gay man, born into New Orleans society, marries an appropriate debutante from his own class and fathers children by her but keeps an apartment in the Quarter for liaisons with male companions.") Obviously, there's often simply no way to know the inclination of an individual or the nature of a particular relationship, but fortunately any single instance is immaterial to the general point that Huey Long was trying to make when he observed a few years later, "I tell you that this town is aswarm and alive and criss-crossed with perverts."

That applied *a fortiori*, of course, to the artistic and literary scene, where

W. R. Irby, pioneer preservationist

gay men made at least two contributions, apart from their literary and artistic work. In the first place, as we shall see (pages 78–82), the effort to protect and restore the French Quarter was initiated and led by gay men like Lyle Saxon, philanthropist W. R. Irby, and architect Richard Koch. The reasons for gay men's disproportionate involvement in historic preservation have been ably explored elsewhere; here, just let it be noted that, in alliance with elite women, they were a vital part of the movement that transformed the French Quarter from a slum to an artists' colony to whatever it is today.

Their other major contribution was social—in the Perle Mesta, "hostess with the mostest" sense. Two in particular made this contribution. Bill Spratling and Lyle Saxon each had the ability and the sort of social-director inclinations needed to keep a constant round of parties, suppers, excursions, and less formal gatherings going. This may have been simply a function of their particular personalities, of course, and may have had nothing to do with their homosexuality, but for whatever reason, only Sherwood and Elizabeth Anderson rivaled Spratling and Saxon as hosts and organizers. The French Quarter scene would have been very different—indeed, might not have existed at all—without the gay men who were a part of it.

Jews

Jews are another population often overrepresented among the literary and artistic, and they were so prominent in the cultural landscape of 1920s New Orleans that Sherwood Anderson was exaggerating only a bit when he observed, "Most of the intellectuals and the most interesting people here are Jews." Less than 3 percent of the city's white population was Jewish in 1920, but the Jewish community provided two of the five officers of the Arts and Crafts Club in 1925 and at least a quarter of the twenty women on the "Committee" of the Quartier Club. Two of the three women who founded Le Petit

Theatre—Louise Jonas Nixon and Rhea Loeb Goldberg—were Jewish, as was Harold W. Newman, chairman of the Theatre's board. Jews at the *Double Dealer* included three of the five founders—Paul Godchaux Jr., Albert Goldstein, and Julius Friend—as well as many unpaid helpers like Jimmy Feibleman, Adaline Katz, and Lillian Marcus, the magazine's managing intelligence. Marcus was one of five Jews among the Famous Creoles, along with Mrs. Nixon, Lucille Antony (Paul Godchaux's cousin), Moise Goldstein, and Harold Levy. This Jewish representation is especially notable since almost all were native New Orleanians, drawn from the roughly eight thousand members of the city's Jewish community. Unlike gay men, Jews were not attracted to New Orleans from elsewhere. Of the many artists and writers who came from other parts of the country to live the Bohemian life in New Orleans, few if any were Jewish. American Jews might go to Greenwich Village or Montmartre, but apparently not to the Deep South.

Jews had also long been conspicuous among the city's supporters and patrons of the arts. A notable example was sugar broker Isaac Delgado, who gave the money for the Delgado Museum (now the New Orleans Museum of Art) in 1910, and New Orleans Jews were no less generous in the 1920s. At least half of the eighteen advertisements in the first issue of the *Double Dealer* were taken by Jewish-owned businesses, including Jimmy Feibleman's family's department store and a men's clothing shop owned by another Godchaux cousin. In 1926, the magazine's last year, something between a third and a half of the "guarantors" listed were Jewish.

In short, New Orleans Jews seem to have been even more active in the cultural life of their city than Jews elsewhere, especially in proportion to their relatively small number. Why should that be? Anderson mentioned "several older Jewish families here with rather high intellectual standards," but many such families had lofty social credentials as well. Anderson referred to those who "came in here after the Civil War, dared to invest every cent when the city was in comparative ruins, and were made rich," which more or less describes the families of Moise Goldstein, Harold Levy, and Lillian Friend Marcus, but the families of their fellow Famous Creoles Louise Jonas Nixon and Lucille Godchaux Antony were older still, prominent in Louisiana since antebellum times. The same could be said of many more of the town's Jewish Bohemians and patrons of the arts. Jews from these established families, many of German or Alsatian origin, had been thoroughly integrated into the city's civic and political life. Before the Civil War New Orleans gave the United States its first openly Jewish senator, Judah Benjamin (also America's first Jewish cabinet officer, albeit in the Confederate cabinet), and after the War its second, Benjamin Franklin Jonas (Louise Jonas Nixon's uncle). "Newman," the elite private school that Caroline Durieux's son attended, was not a parochial school named for the Cardinal, but the *Isidore* Newman School, founded in 1903 to educate the children of the Jewish Orphans Home.

But in the 1920s there was one barrier that New Orleans Jews—no matter how distinguished, assimilated, and successful—could not break through. Social standing at the very top of New Orleans society was tied to membership in particular Mardi Gras krewes, the most prestigious of which were linked to exclusive gentlemen's clubs that excluded Jews. (In response, the Harmony Club, for the German-Jewish elite, had its own Mardi Gras balls for a time.) Although the first King of Carnival in 1872 was a Jew named Louis Solomon, there has not been another Jewish Rex. Looking back, a member of the Godchaux family observed, "We were an extremely prominent family, but of course when it came to the social clubs and Mardi Gras itself, we were left out. . . . It was very clear that in all other ways, we were major figures in the city. But in that way we weren't."

Consider the example of Solomon Wexler. A native of Natchez educated in Frankfurt and Zurich, Wexler had come to New Orleans in the early 1890s as a cotton broker, and then became a banker, instrumental in setting up the Federal Reserve system. A hardware and automobile parts business that he founded advertised in the *Double Dealer*'s first issue. He was civic-minded, president of the Orleans Parish school board, and he had married a Creole wife. In every respect but one he would have been an obvious candidate for the Boston or Pickwick Club, and then a member of Rex or Comus. But the only clubs he belonged to were the New Orleans Country Club and the Harmony Club. Eventually he left New Orleans for New York, where he became a partner in J. S. Bache and Company and died a millionaire.

These facts have led more than one observer to speculate that the prominence of Jews in the cultural life of New Orleans reflects, as Calvin Trillin put it, "the possibility that Jews, who are excluded from Carnival krewes despite their prominence in the cultural and philanthropic life of the city, constantly become more prominent in the cultural and philanthropic life of the city partly because they are excluded from Carnival krewes." This could come about by way of compensation for their exclusion, or simply result from the fact that they don't spend all their money on costumes, balls, and parades. In any case, for whatever reason, like gay men, New Orleans Jews were very much a presence on the French Quarter scene, which would have been quite different without them.

Sicilians

A third group that contributed to that Bohemian scene didn't contribute actual Bohemians, but it created a setting that Bohemians found congenial. In the thirty years after 1898 nearly one hundred thousand Italian immigrants came to New Orleans, and many settled in the French Quarter, where one estimate put them at 80 percent of the population by 1910. Nearly all were Sicilian, so many that New Orleanians had begun to call the Vieux Carré "Little Sicily" or "Little Palermo." Most of these immigrants were illiterate peasants who moved large families into overcrowded apartments, where they often kept livestock in the courtyard, or even in the apartment itself. (Flo Field claimed that one family kept a cow in their top-floor apartment: "carried

Sicilian dockworkers unloading bananas

it in as a calf," she said, "and it grew and grew.") The men found work on the docks or as laborers; eventually, many opened corner groceries, bakeries, fish markets, and butcher shops. By the time the Famous Creoles began to drift in, first- and second-generation Sicilians were the dominant group in the Quarter, and had largely created the atmosphere that Oliver La Farge described vividly: a life "largely conducted at open windows, on the balconies, and on doorsteps, and thence flow[ing] into the street," one where "there are never people lacking to advise you in any undertaking or to yell at a cop who is arresting a drunk. Start something that needs help or get into a fight, you'll soon have company."

What was it about these neighbors that so many artists and writers found attractive? (And not just in New Orleans: San Francisco newspaperman Herb Gold once pointed out how many Bohemian neighborhoods in American cities—Greenwich Village and his own city's North Beach, for example—began as areas settled by Italian immigrants.) Obviously, to begin with, noisy, illiterate, livestock-keeping, often non-English speaking neighbors did nothing for property values, contributing to the low rents that made the Quarter attractive to needy artists. They also provided an exotic and "continental" touch that may have appealed to artsy newcomers from the Midwest and small-town South. It was more than that, though. However rigid the codes that governed the new immigrants' relations among themselves, their attitude toward outsiders appears to have been live-and-let-live. They even seem to have had relatively easy relations with their black neighbors, at least compared to native-born whites.

There is also a factor that the Italian journalist Luigi Barzini was getting at when he wrote that Sicilians "long ago learned to distrust and neutralize all written laws (alien laws in particular) and to govern themselves in their own rough homemade fashion." It is difficult to discuss this without lapsing into stereotype—but if that's what it is, it is one shared by many Sicilians themselves. Barzini was Milanese, but a man styling himself "Il Siciliano" wrote in an essay on "What Makes a Sicilian?" that his people have long shared "a general dislike for the police and for the system of justice; a cautious disregard for laws; [and] a deep mistrust of governmental institutions and politicians." In New Orleans in the 1920s, this characteristic was most evident when it came to the recent immigrants' attitudes toward Prohibition. Alcohol was the drug of choice for Famous Creoles and their circle, an indispensable lubricant for their active social life. It was remarkably easy for them to obtain, as we saw, and it was their Sicilian neighbors who made it so. The underworld organization run by Sylvestro "Silver Dollar Sam" Carollo, a "produce dealer" on St. Philip Street, almost completely controlled the supply of liquor in the city and distributed it through Sicilian-owned groceries, which also sold incidentals like juniper essence for making bathtub gin.

No doubt other ethnic groups could have supported a burgeoning Bohemia in their midst, and even found a way to profit from it, but certainly there are also a good many that would not have tolerated it. The exotic, easygoing, and corrupt Sicilians of the French Quarter should share the credit—if that's what is due—for the Famous Creoles and their circle.

Why New Orleans?

So why New Orleans? And why, in the South, only New Orleans? Other cities might seem at first to have had possibilities. Why not Charleston, or Nashville?

One fact alone may provide the answer. New Orleans was the largest city in the South, with a population of over 400,000. It was three times the size of Nashville and roughly seven times as large as Charleston. New Orleans just offered more *room* for communities of every sort.

True, Charleston, like New Orleans, was a port city, with all that implies. It had suitably beautiful and run-down architecture and its African American population offered folk life as picturesque as its buildings. Consequently, like New Orleans, it had a preservation movement, an art scene, and local-color literature. But the Charleston Renaissance was more genteel than the Arts and Crafts Club, less Bohemian, more . . . Episcopalian. And New Orleans had a university that gave it a ready-made community of artistic students and salaried faculty Bohemians. Charleston had only its small municipal college.

Nashville had the university, which gave it a literary community, complete with its own little magazine, *The Fugitive*. But Vanderbilt had nothing like Tulane's architecture department or the art program at Newcomb College, and Nashville lacked the charming, often funky buildings that were such an asset for New Orleans and Charleston artists. Moreover, landlocked Nashville didn't have the others' easy commerce with Europe and Latin America (or their drunken sailors), and it was simply less cosmopolitan in general. Not that there weren't cosmopolitan Nashvilleans, but in the

French Quarter Sidney Mttron Hirsch, the bearded Rosicrucian mystic, play-wright, and etymologist who was such a fascinating and romantic figure for the young Fugitive poets, would have been just another oddball.

Neither Charleston nor Nashville had the competitive newspapers of New Orleans, with the employment and publicity they provided. The smaller cities had less appeal to gay men, and would have had a smaller number of them even if they'd had the same proportion. Just so, New Orleans Jews may or may not have contributed more per capita to their city's cultural life than other cities', but even if they didn't, there were simply far more of them to contribute: two and a half times as many as in Nashville and more than four times as many as in Charleston. And neither of the smaller cities had large, concentrated immigrant populations like New Orleans—much less a Sicilian one. Finally, Prohibition may have been ineffectual in Tennessee and South Carolina, but it wasn't a joke.

One more difference between New Orleans and the other cities is so im-portant that it deserves a chapter of its own.

Uptown, Downtown

FOR ANYONE FAMILIAR WITH other Bohemian scenes, one striking aspect of this one is the relative absence of rivalries, jealousies, backbiting, factions, and conspiracies. Cicero Odiorne was struck by the contrast with Paris, where, "underneath the brilliance, the spirit is that of the jungle." Elizabeth Anderson and Lillian Marcus were social rivals and disliked each other, and Flo Field resented her business competitor Helen Pitkin Schertz, but that seems to have been about it for hard feelings. Odiorne marveled that, "with us, in New Orleans, jealousy did not exist. If anyone had a small success . . . such as a story printed . . . the rest were delighted. We probably celebrated with a dinner party . . . with *vino pinto,* made by our Italian neighbors." Oliver La Farge also wrote of "delight"— "When one of us achieved anything at all, however slight, the other workers were delighted, and I think everyone took new courage"—and Basso, too, looked back fondly on an atmosphere of "mutual friendliness and good will." Even more remarkable is that this web of friendship and respect sometimes bridged the divide between Bohemia and Society, between "uptown" and "downtown."

Consider the case of Grace King. That genteel septuagenarian was a kind of figure that Bohemians elsewhere would have mocked. But that's not what happened in New Orleans. It may not be surprising that she and Lyle Saxon were close (Saxon had a weakness for dowagers), but she and the rumbustious Roark Bradford were also friends, and she even had a touching exchange of correspondence with Sherwood Anderson, in which the rough Midwesterner confessed that he had always hoped to merit acceptance by members of "the gentler tribe of the ink party" like her, and she wrote, in turn, "You have a pen of iron & use it like a giant." When the Louisiana Historical Society honored her at the Cabildo in 1923, flowers were piled up around her, the band played "Dixie," and her friend Dorothy Dix said that she "has not only given us back our past, but has stuck a rose in its teeth, and a pomegranate bloom behind its ear!" Surely Miss King belonged among the "lady fictioneers [from] the sodden marshes of Southern Literature" whose "treacly sentimentalities" the *Double Dealer* editorially deplored, but when King's *Creole Families of New Orleans* appeared in 1921, the *Double Dealer* reviewed it respectfully. And of course two young Bohemians less than half her age put her among the Famous Creoles.

Creole Families of New Orleans was illustrated by Ellsworth Woodward, an establishment figure with old-fashioned artistic tastes who might also seem an unlikely member of the circle. True, one or two of his more avant-garde students at Newcomb and more adventurous art-fanciers like Hunt Henderson grumbled about his conservatism, but Woodward seems generally to have been recognized as the kindly, avuncular elder statesman that he was, and Spratling and Faulkner honored him for his contributions. Just so, Mrs. James Oscar Nixon and Helen Pitkin Schertz, two distinctly un-Bohemian clubwomen, knew and were known by the more obviously "artful and crafty" and shared their interests. And there they are in *Famous Creoles*.

The respect and goodwill ran both ways. As we saw, moneyed and cultivated uptown people initiated and supported all of the circle's major institutions, enjoyed associating with the artists and writers of the Arts and Crafts Club and the *Double Dealer,* and invited the more presentable ones to speak at the Quartier Club and Le Petit Salon. Younger and more frivolous uptowners also liked to hang out with the Quarter's Bohemians, for other reasons.

The Campaign for Preservation

One of the most important of the interests shared by Society and Bohemia was the revitalization of the French Quarter. Most Famous Creoles contributed in one way or another to the nascent historic preservation movement. Grace King had been a pioneer; as early as 1884 she produced a display that celebrated the Quarter's charm at a time when it was far from obvious to most New Orleanians. Ellsworth Woodward and architects Moise Goldstein and N. C. Curtis were early and active preservationists, and their efforts received sympathetic newspaper coverage from, among others, Lyle Saxon and Keith Temple. Mrs. Schertz and Flo Field each claimed to have organized the Quarter's first guide service; William Spratling served on the Vieux Carré Commission, established in 1925; and Elizabeth Werlein would eventually become the city's most prominent preservationist. By the time *Famous Creoles* appeared, Saxon, Natalie Scott, Alberta Kinsey, and several others had restored and were living in historic properties in the Quarter, while Mrs. Schertz and Weeks Hall were living in historic houses they had restored outside it.

A popular version of the movement's history starts with the old French Quarter lying unappreciated until artists and writers recognized its neglected beauty, began to move in, and thwarted greedy developers and shortsighted business interests intent on its destruction. Certainly it's true that by 1900 the Vieux Carré was not what it had been. The old Creole families who had built it had gradually moved elsewhere and their gracious houses mostly went unrepaired. As Lyle Saxon lamented, "The French Quarter is now falling into decay, gracefully, it is true, but crumbling nevertheless. One by one the old mansions are destroyed, the iron balconies, that priceless art work that cannot be duplicated today at any cost, are sold as scrap iron." Many houses became tenements, and filled up with poor immigrant Italians (or worse: "There are negroes living in the Old Napoleon House at Conti and Chartres streets," Saxon reported). The first twenty years of the new century saw change and decay all around. Historic buildings were torn down for parking lots, an entire block was leveled to make room for a new courthouse, the old St. Louis Hotel was damaged by a hurricane and razed, a house (mistakenly) thought to be the oldest building in the city was demolished, and the old French Opera House, a center of cultural life since 1859, burned to the ground. And there actually were businessmen like William Schultz, who sneered in 1920 that the French Quarter "renders valueless a big slice of our commercial section," and that the "sentiment over [its] artistic and antiquarian aspects" expressed by "tourists and local art enthusiasts" should be ignored because "a general demolition [was] necessary for the expansion of the city."

But this appealing melodrama is a little too simple. For one thing, many New Orleans businessmen saw the money-making potential of a preserved Vieux Carré. The Association of Commerce went on record in 1917 supporting private preservation and restoration efforts, and two years later the association's president came forth with the first practical proposal for large-scale renovation in the Quarter when he suggested that the Pontalba buildings should be converted for use as artists' studios and living quarters. Ellsworth Woodward commented, "It seems too good to be true that leadership has been taken by a group of men who realize the practical side of the city's artistic development."

Moreover, although the Quarter was endangered, it was hardly unappreciated. Woodward's art classes at Newcomb had been using it for postcards, greeting cards, calendars, and illustrated maps since the 1890s. In 1895 Woodward's brother, William, helped to organize the successful opposition to a proposal to tear down the Cabildo, the old seat of government on Jackson Square. A decade later William and his architecture students at Tulane were busily engaged in documenting the Quarter's historic architecture, joined after 1912 by his Tulane colleague N. C. Curtis. One of William's students published *Pen Drawings of Old New Orleans* in 1916, about the same time Elizebeth Werlein's book of photographs, *The Wrought Iron Railings of Le Vieux Carré New Orleans,* appeared.

A good many artists had studios in the Vieux Carré well before the First World War, and there were even isolated instances of restoration before the Bohemians arrived. In 1915, for example, the Daughters of 1776–1812 bought

Interior of the restored Patio Royal.

an eighteenth-century house adjoining the Cabildo "occupied by a family without American traditions," because as "true patriots," the ladies "could not abide that oyster shells and bananas should drape the façade of this interesting building." Philanthropist William Ratcliffe Irby bought and restored the Seignouret-Brulatour house (later the Arts and Crafts Club's quarters) and the Paul Morphy house (later the Patio Royal, a favorite spot for debutante parties). Irby also paid for the renovation of St. Louis Cathedral after it was damaged by a storm in 1915, and he would later buy the lower Pontalba building and give it to the Louisiana State

Museum. (I have mentioned the part that gay men and Jews played in this story, but Irby is the only example I know of someone who was both.)

But most of these rehabilitations were for commercial or institutional use, and most of the artists with studios in the Quarter lived somewhere else. Respectable people largely avoided "Frenchtown" (some of the old Creole restaurants aside) after dark; they saw it, one journalist said, as "a den of thieves and cut-throats, of narcotics addicts, ladies of the evening, and simple sweet-tempered Italian storekeepers." When Alberta Kinsey was looking at a place on Toulouse Street, she asked Saxon, "Is it all right?" He replied, "As much as any place down here."

What really changed in the late 'teens was that people like Kinsey, Saxon, and their friends began actually to *live* in the Quarter. In the early days of the preservation movement, it's fair to say, Society provided most of the money and political influence, while Bohemia provided the shock troops. A great symbolic victory in the struggle came when the city established an advisory Vieux Carré Commission in 1925, with both sorts of preservationists as members. A *Times-Picayune* cartoon by Keith Temple titled *No Admittance* showed the "Commission for Preservation of Our Vieux Carre" [sic] in the

guise of a painter with smock and palette blocking the entrance of "The Un-sympathetic," with a cigar and "Plans for Inharmonious Modern Buildings," to "New Orleans' Picturesque and Historic French Quarter—Mecca of Tour-ists." It was not one of Temple's most inspired cartoons, but it made the point.

The Smart Set

Looking back, William Odiorne observed that in the 1920s "the revival of the old Quarter was a sort of civic project," and "Society . . . with a capital S" was interested in "French Quarter Bohemianism" because "we were useful." The Quarter's Bohemians were useful in other ways, as well. Many younger uptowners shared their enthusiasm for parties and alcohol. Consider some newspaper accounts of the 1927 Arts and Crafts Club ball. Under a head-line announcing that "Literati Rub Elbows With 'Low-Brows'—and Like It!" a story reported that "the art-folk were out in full force but the small band of 'intelligensias' [sic] were only a small wave of spirited enthusiasm in a sea of debutantes, newspaper reporters, bank presidents, and what have you?" Another story observed that while "the artists costumed themselves as any-thing but artists, . . . the bond salesmen of real life were triumphant in be-

Esther DuPuy dancing.

rets, open throat, and tight trousers," and everyone agreed that "one of the high spots of the evening was the pony ballet of Junior League girls."

This sort of mixture was not unique to New Orleans—the cos-tume balls of the Chelsea Arts Club at the turn of the century were said to have been "the moment when ar-tistic and high society London united to let its collective hair down"—but it was certainly unknown elsewhere in the South. Other Southern cities had no artists' balls to begin with, but if they had, would bank presidents and bond salesmen have put on costumes and joined in? It's hard to imagine the Junior League of any other Southern city providing a chorus line. But in New Orleans, a society-page writer judged this bacchanal to be "one of the most interesting events on the social calendar."

This is the sort of promiscuous mixing of the worlds of art and fashion that Faulkner found distasteful, but his roommate Spratling positively enjoyed it. Spratling's girlfriend Esther DuPuy, who chaired the invitation committee, had been a featured dancer at an earlier ball. DuPuy was also "one of the stars of the Junior League Review," an annual event that involved a good many Famous Creoles, one way or another. Like DuPuy, many crossed comfortably from Society to Bohemia and back. Natalie Scott was a Junior Leaguer, too; she performed in two sketches at the review, one of them with her acting buddy and fellow Famous Creole Sam Gilmore. Gilmore's father had been a congressman, and several other Famous Creoles had impressive social credentials, as a reading of their individual biographical notes will reveal. Olive Leonhardt, who did the program cover for the 1925 review, also did covers for the *Double Dealer* and chaired the publicity committee for an Arts and Crafts Club Ball. Pops Whitesell, yet another Famous Creole, photographed the League's officers for the program; Pops would never be high-

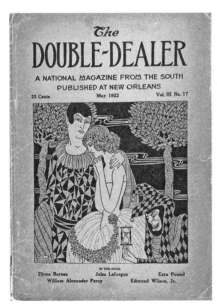

Leonhardt cover for *Double Dealer*

Leonhardt cover for Junior League Review program.

society himself, but he mingled easily with those who were. His fellow photographer William Odiorne mused in the 1970s that "I'd have to say that [New Orleans] was the only city I ever lived in where I had a social standing."

The easy familiarity between uptown and downtown impressed young Oliver La Farge. His "close friendships in the art colony," he said, "did not conflict in any way with my relations with the 'uptown' people, for your New Orleans débutante associates in entire simplicity with the artists on the elementary basis of likings and friendships between people of an age. The two communities were at home with each other." He thought this a refreshing change from prim New England, but it wasn't just New England where a "Bal des Artistes" that promised "unmentionable" features would have raised eyebrows in respectable society. That advertisement would not have attracted the beau monde of Nashville or Charleston either.

But New Orleans's smart set was drawn to the Quarter by more than parties. At the Green Shutter Tea Room on St. Peter Street, Lyle Saxon wrote, one could find both "artists in smocks discussing this business of life as they sip their coffee in the courtyard" and "a sprinkling of 'uptown' people who have come to see just what these artists are up to." Apparently the uptowners liked what they saw of the artist's life, because as early as 1921 the *Item* was reporting that "the French Quarter . . . is now humming with the advent of Orleanians who have taken up the study of art." In the introduction to *Famous Creoles,* Faulkner wrote (in the style of Sherwood Anderson) that "as one walks about the quarter one sees artists here and there on the shady side of the street corners, sketching houses and balconies. I have counted as many as forty in a single afternoon, and . . . as I walked onward I mused on the richness of our American life that permits forty people to spend day after day painting pictures in a single area comprised in six city blocks." After the Arts and Crafts Club's art school opened, the pace really picked up. "Someone always seems to be rushing off to a sculpture class or a life class or to a lesson in oil," a society columnist observed. She reported that a reception at the Club for a student art exhibit attracted "a large gathering of society," adding that "Helene Stauffer was presiding at the tea-table in the reception room, all in green, with a large green hat[,] Betty Fenner was in pink, looking very pretty, and Dot Sharp wore a brighter pink."

Lionel and Lucette Johnston, a shipping board engineer and his fashionable French wife, a childless couple in their early thirties, moved from Uptown to a place across from the Green Shutter, and became fixtures of the local society pages. Lyle Saxon reported that Lucette wrote "poems in prose" and her husband was "the perfect host," so "one always finds a group of art-ists and writers in her apartment." An "impromptu studio party" at their place led a reporter to gush, "That's one of the advantages of being an artist . . . , you can give such wonderful parties!"

Sometimes, to be sure, this playing at art produced a clash of uptown and downtown cultures. Soon a few downtowners were complaining that the Quarter was filling up with the kind of people "who rent an ordinary furnished room and call it 'my studio.'" Others came to share Faulkner's impatience with those who were not serious artists, what the *New Orlea-nian* called "the dilletante [*sic*] gang." Occasionally some unease about the genial coexistence of Society and Bohemia was expressed by the Society side, too, especially by the older generation. "Czarina" Elizebeth Werlein banned Faulkner from her house after he showed up barefoot, for instance, and the visiting Edna St. Vincent Millay drew some disapproving glances when she wore remarkably short skirts and very tight sweaters around Jack-son Square. The *New Orleanian* told of a party at the Baroness Pontalba Tea Room where "a dignified matron" was mortified when her prospective son-in-law "threw off his overcoat and then, calmly, stripped off his trousers and threw them wildly in the air, revealing himself in the guise of Apollo." (The magazine added that he was wearing "a flesh-colored bathing suit.")

By and large, though, as La Farge observed, the two worlds rubbed along happily together. In any other Southern city a "Junior League Bohemian" would have been something very odd indeed, but that combination seemed natural enough in New Orleans, and in fact the connection with Society made the French Quarter's Bohemia possible. But that link may also have led to Bohemia's demise.

The End of an Interlude

IT MAY SEEM ODD TO ATTRIBUTE transformation and decline to a successful campaign for preservation. But in fact that's a large part of what changed the French Quarter in ways that largely snuffed out its Bohemian aspirations. The common effort to preserve the Quarter papered over a cultural fault line. Just as Le Petit Salon's desire to bring back the cultivated life of Creole New Orleans appealed more to Society figures like Grace King and Helen Pitkin Schertz than to Bohemian sorts like Bill Spratling and Ham Basso, so those who wanted to see the Quarter restored to its antebellum elegance were not entirely in accord with those who loved the picturesque place pretty much as it was, with low rents and even dilapidation part of its attraction. Mrs. Schertz was delighted when respectable New Orleanians began buying and fixing up French Quarter properties for their own use ("Women are putting their bridge-winnings into the Vieux Carré and petting the old mansions into beauty, utility, and revenue"), but Basso grumbled that "in the days of its decay, when the houses were ramshackle and falling down," it was "one of the loveliest places in the world." While the Quarter's new haute bourgeoisie took satisfaction from new regulations that meant "hereafter the Italian vendor of garlic will be prohibited from propping an unsightly shed against a century-old building," other residents felt, rightly, that the vendor's presence made the Quarter more Continental. The ladies of Le Petit Salon disliked it when "tattered clothes fluttered from the iron balconies of the once proudly fashionable Pontalba buildings," but Spratling put just such a scene on the title page of *Famous Creoles*. The two sorts of preservationists didn't argue in public—in fact, they seldom had to confront the fact that they were in disagreement—because both were opposed to tearing

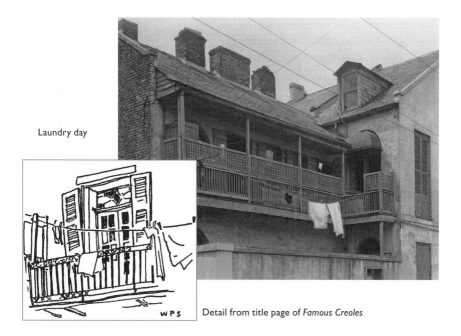

Laundry day

Detail from title page of *Famous Creoles*

down old buildings and replacing them with new ones, which was the major battle of the day. But the Quarter that had attracted Basso and Spratling and their Bohemian friends was doomed, in part by the success of the uptown ladies' vision.

What happened in the French Quarter has happened and is still happening elsewhere. Like all living creatures, Bohemias have a natural history, and a life span:

(1) Artists and writers discover a place where the living is cheap and the neighbors tolerant, or indifferent—ideally one that gives them material for their art.

It didn't cost much to live in the French Quarter in the early 1920s. An attic room in one of the Pontalba buildings went for $5 a month, and Lyle Saxon rented a sixteen-room house on Royal Street for $16. James Feibleman knew a painter who "got along very well on a quart of milk and fif-

Spratling drawing of Lyle Saxon's courtyard (note cracked stucco).

teen cents worth of red beans and rice a day." And there were less tangible attractions for Bohemians. Feibleman, who saw the French Quarter change as he grew up in New Orleans, said that it offered a "sensually pleasant and socially tolerant atmosphere" like that of Montparnasse and Greenwich Village. The sultry climate and the "Latin population" made for a "leisurely pace" of the sort "so necessary for the contemplative life." Its inhabitants were mostly "happy to be left alone just to be themselves."

As for material, the Quarter may have offered almost too much. The *New York Times* observed that it was "a polyglot bottom of the melting pot, . . . redolent of garlic," with "motley doorways and courtyards whose charms were not entirely erased even by the weekly wash" hanging from the galleries. As we saw, many of the artists had a hard time transcending the merely picturesque—some never did—and writers like Anderson, Faulkner, Roark Bradford, and Emmet Kennedy were fascinated by the local color, particularly the city's vibrant African American culture.

(2) The newcomers fix up decaying houses and apartments, or nonresidential properties like lofts and factory buildings—maybe not to bourgeois standards, but enough to make them places where one can work.

As early as 1919, Lyle Saxon had foreseen a sort of domino effect. Fix up the Pontalba buildings for artists, he predicted, and "artists from all over the United States" would converge on the Quarter. "In the trail of the artists would come the writers—they always do—and soon we could boast of our Place D'Armes as New York does her Washington Square." And, in fact, that is more or less what happened. Three years later, the new *Double Dealer* magazine published what amounted to a walking tour of "this ancient French Quarter," which was "gradually by new travail being rediscovered, restored, and re-exploited." In the lower Pontalba building, readers' attention was directed to the Quartier Club and Le Petit Theatre (not yet relocated to St. Peter Street), while across Jackson Square were "the Upper Pontalba Flats with numerous shops and studios: [William] Odiorne's print-room, Atelier Pontalba, Moses' studio, a plastic artist, etc." Around the corner was one of Natalie Scott's rental properties, "the quaint four-story home of a group of regulars—Bohemians who like the atmosphere sufficiently to pay it the tribute of residing there in the shadow of the Cathedral."

These living quarters were not always elegant. When Sherwood Anderson's young friend Adaline Katz rented a place on the corner of Bourbon and St. Ann previously occupied by an Italian family and their chickens, Anderson helped her haul out trash and wash the place down. (Still, Katz was one of the few in her circle with hot water: She let her friends come to take baths.) When Anderson had a visit from Weeks Hall's aunt at his Pontalba apartment, he reflected as she left that she was "a southern lady and no doubt one of the real ones" and hoped that the rats who lived on his staircase "would realize with whom they had to deal" and leave her alone.

Nevertheless, beginning in the blocks around Jackson Square and working outward, the Quarter was being transformed, physically and demographically. Although there were "still immigrants in the quarter," the *New York Times* observed, they were "slowly giving place, and newspaper men, artists and writers occupy the dwellings that were once the ancestral homes of creoles with mellifluous names." The new "Creoles," the Famous ones, had begun to assemble.

(3) *Some of the newcomers open cafés and bookshops and galleries, or attract entrepreneurs who open them.*

A 1922 *New York Times* article, "Greenwich Village on Royal Street" (how that title must have pleased New Orleanians!), observed that the Vieux Carré sported "the usual teashops and antique shops and bookshops," and the *Double Dealer*'s stroll through the Quarter that same year pointed out its "restaurants, auction marts, antique shops and book stalls," including such Bohemian hangouts as John and Grace McClure's Olde Book Shoppe and the Arts and Crafts Club's galleries. Oliver La Farge and Roark Bradford had joined with visiting author Carl Carmer to bankroll the Green Shutter Tea Room, mostly just as a place to sit and chat, although it doubled as a bookshop. Authors could sell their books on consignment at The Quarter's Book Shop, founded by a group of artists and writers, which also offered a subscription library, a poste restante service, and coffee for a nickel if you had it (free if you didn't). It seemed as if new businesses were opening every week, and soon one observer was exclaiming,

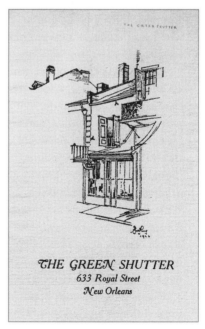

THE GREEN SHUTTER
633 Royal Street
New Orleans

Spratling drawing of the Green Shutter Tea Room.

"Studios and more studios, art shops and tea rooms! Good Lord, there's no end of them."

(4) The revitalized neighborhood begins to draw less serious people—poseurs, "fauxhemians," those who just like the "atmosphere"—first as visitors, then as residents.

Some of the new shops were not seeking the patronage of artists and writers, however. When the changes in the Quarter captured the attention of the uptown smart set, people Helen Pitkin Schertz swore had been "rather proud of the fact that they did not know that Toulouse, St. Philip, and Orleans streets were on the local map" ("This is no exaggeration") began to visit the Quarter to shop and to lunch. The *Double Dealer*'s walking tour pointed out antique shops and interior decorators, as well as the Paul Morphy Book Shop in the stylish Patio Royal, "the walls of which are hung with *objets d'art*," and which incorporated "a French lingerie corner presided over by Madam Ida Burgueires with a Parisian grace." Even late-night visits became common, as postscripts to uptown parties. Although high society had once "picked up its skirts when it passed [the French Market's] dingy old group of buildings," one reporter remarked, the coffee stands were now thronged until 3:00 or 4:00 in the morning with "folks in evening clothes who sit on stools alongside moderately drunken sailors or nondescript unfortunates" partaking of "Coffee and doughnuts, ten cents."

A magazine called *New Orleans Life* soon appeared, specializing in news of "the smartest new shops," like one at Royal and Toulouse "where the gay awnings hang out," and the "handy tearooms . . . filled every noon with shoppers and friends of the Quarter." Two Famous Creoles and the husband of another were on the masthead: John McClure (still an editor of the *Double Dealer*) as contributing editor, Cicero Odiorne as "Paris correspondent" (although there is no sign that he ever contributed anything), and Helen Pitkin Schertz's husband as business advisor. The magazine published Pops Whitesell's photographs and art from William Spratling, Alberta Kinsey, and Louis Andrews Fischer, poems by Richard Kirk, a Lyle Saxon short story, and a couple of articles by Helen Pitkin Schertz on the Quarter's architecture. At least fourteen more Famous Creoles were mentioned in articles or society news, with major features on Mrs. Schertz, Ellsworth Woodward, Flo Field, and Tulane cheerleader Marian Draper, "the ideal American girl." But the magazine was an odd sort of Bohemian-booster hybrid. News of the Arts and Crafts Club appeared side by side with news of uptown women's clubs.

A Chamber of Commerce official argued in one issue that "the growth of the art colony has been the dominant factor for greater cleanliness," and compared artists to benzene: "Wherever the hand of an artist touches the Old Quarter . . . an ugly, dirty spot disappears and in its place appears an 'atmospherous' studio." When the magazine folded in 1928, one critic was not sorry to see it go. "No tears need be shed for . . . the 'arty' New Orleans Life," he wrote, since it offered only "saccharine gushings about the beauty, the charm, the atmosphere of New Orleans." But while it existed it served to demonstrate that a *New York Times* article was right to observe that "the French Quarter has suffered the fate of such quarters. It has become a fad. It has become, in a way, fashionable."

Young uptowners were coming to the Quarter both to do the shimmy in its clubs and to go slumming among its Bohemians, and soon some of the more artsy and daring began to move into the Quarter themselves. They were joined by aspiring Bohemians from elsewhere. William Odiorne spoke of the "floating population of young geniuses" who "would come down from

Chicago or New York, rent an attic for five dollars a month and stay until their money was spent." He called them "attic poets." The *Times* asserted that, "as in Greenwich Village, the most ardent of the poseurs, the youths with the longest and the girls with the shortest hair, hail from Peoria and Oshkosh."

The original Bohemian inhabitants viewed the coming of these newest newcomers with mixed feelings, at best. Lyle Saxon was delighted to see some of them buying and restoring his beloved historic buildings, but he complained to a friend in 1924, "The whole quarter is filling up with artists and writers; I didn't know there were so many funny people in the world. They yell and scream all night long—like cats." New York writer Carl Carmer, a frequent visitor, wrote a mocking piece for the *New Orleanian* about "our little group in the artist colony": "It's very intimate—our little circle— one drops in any time he feels like it—takes a bit of time off from creating things, you know—to have some coffee—and to hear some clever conversation. . . . So many of our members have been pronounced promising by the very best critics. If I've seen the word once I've seen it a dozen times on the backs of returned manuscripts." But Hamilton Basso was less amused. He complained that "everybody we know talks about literature. Even the waiters in Gluck's talk about literature." As a writer himself, Basso said, "when I think of a whole world going about with a smudge of typewriter ribbon on its fingers, I become so ashamed I want to go off somewhere and hide." He wrote that "the crowd . . . who sit around the book-shops and swap ideas" made him feel as if he "ought to hurry home and take a bath." When an amateur poet paid to have a book of his verse published, Basso sneered at the title, *Just Thoughts*—"Isn't that cute? Isn't that just too goddamned cute?"— and complained that the man was "typical of the people who mess up the French Quarter."

Looking back, Oliver La Farge drew a "sharp distinction" between artists and writers who were there "because it was a good place in which to carry on the struggle, where living is cheap and one has the stimulus of one's own kind," and those—more numerous—who were just seeking "a slack, easy way of life." Another observer insisted on the distinction between "the cultural antics of the boys and girls who reside in Bohemia for Bohemia's sake and pursue art because it is a nice tea-room accomplishment" and "the life of the serious artists of the quarter." As a "definite step" to dissociate their work from "the 'studio life' of the 'Arty,'" fifteen men, including Famous Creoles Weeks Hall and Conrad Albrizio—men "who view their painting and sculpturing as seriously as Henry Ford views the manufacture of automobiles," Meigs Frost wrote in the *States*—formed the New Orleans Art League in 1927.

(5) Tourists and daytrippers come to visit the fashionable and picturesque neighborhood, and "old-timers" (many of them newcomers just a few years back) adopt an elegiac tone, complaining that the place isn't what it was.

As the 1920s wore on and the restored French Quarter became a popular tourist destination, Spratling complained about sightseeing buses that "bustle people through the quarter in ever increasing numbers," and a writer in the *New Orleanian* lamented that the place had become "a curio for wintering visitors from the North and East" and "sight-seeing old ladies." Eventually even Saxon, who had played a large part in making it happen—by publishing an early walking tour in his newspaper column, for example—wrote that the Quarter had become a "mad house," with "a horde of tourists everywhere, and people riding around with horses and buggies, sight-seeing." The *New Orleanian* reminisced about the old days a decade earlier when "the vogue of the French Quarter was not what it is; there were not hundreds of tourists streaming up and down Royal street." Hamilton Basso warned that the Quarter "won't be the same place in ten years. Take my word for it." In this judgment he echoed Sherwood Anderson, who had written in *Vanity Fair*, "I'm going to tell you it won't last long. . . . The end of New Orleans— the old town, the sweet town, is already in sight." Basso blamed the changes on "a flaxen flood, coming from the north and the east and the west, from Kansas, from Pennsylvania, from Iowa, Goths and Visigoths waving the American flag," and Roark Bradford observed wryly that "too many country boys and girls are coming in to be Bohemians and immorality lacks that calm, professional dignity it held in the corrupt era before 1927." "Some way or other," Bradford sighed, "the old quarter ain't what she used to be" (which of course could have been said when Bradford arrived, by some of the Sicilians already in residence.)

(6) Housing is rehabilitated to higher standards and demand for it increases; housing prices and rents go up and artists who support themselves by their art begin to be priced out of the market.

"There is an unmistakable smell of paint throughout the Quarter," *New Orleans Life* reported in 1925. "Fallen down buildings are being restored, new shops are opening, smart folk are finding it convenient to live so near town and once again, the Old Quarter is taking on the respectable air it used to have in ante-bellum days." This sprucing-up was not to everyone's taste: a visiting graduate student named C. Vann Woodward wrote a friend in dismay that since he had last been in town someone, "no doubt imbued with civic pride has replaced those priceless old gas street lamps which simply *made* the quaters [*sic*] by night with glaring, unblinking electric globes." Moreover, "they have painted those old pillars which supported the French market orange and Green!!" This sort of thing may not have done much for the Quarter's Bohemian ambiance, but it did good things for property values. Schertz reported that the value of Le Petit Salon's clubhouse had gone from $8,000 to $30,000 in six years and observed that a house that had sold for $2,500 in 1915 was "surrounded by buildings of less importance [selling] for twenty and twenty-five thousand dollars." In 1925 Natalie Scott bought a house on St. Peter Street and tripled her money when she sold it after sixteen months.

Finally, developers and speculators get into the act. *There's Been Murder Done* is a novel that Cicero Odiorne thought "gives a better picture of the physical French Quarter than anything I have ever read." (Alberta Kinsey said, "you could almost smell the Quarter" in its pages.) In it, Kenneth Knoblock described a new building knocked together as "a yokel-yanking residence for the neararty [near-arty]," for "uptowners seeking 'party' quarters." Its appearance owed something to the Pontalba apartments, "a cheap attempt to achieve something similar, something like the rich, antique glow of the older buildings." Three stories high, it had a half-story above that which was "sometimes skylighted and rented to the impecunious practitioners in oils who haunted the neighborhood, rented cheap at first for the atmosphere they gave the place, almost essential before the uptowners could be attracted, tolerated thereafter because they could not be evicted."

(7) Although some vestiges of its Bohemian days (and perhaps a few actual Bohemians) remain, the neighborhood becomes primarily housing for the upper middle class, a tourist destination, a center for nightlife, or—as in the case of the French Quarter—all three. The serious artists and writers begin to move on, looking for someplace that hasn't been "discovered" yet, where they can afford to live and where they can get some work done.

As the 1930s began, the *New Orleanian* complained, the Quarter had become "a tourist camp," offering "nightlife [for] those who live their best hours sometime between evening and dawn." The magazine added sadly that "as an artists' colony the spirit of the place grows more lethargic every year," and genuine Bohemians were indeed losing whatever centrality they might have had to life in the Quarter, as higher rents, tourists, and seekers of night life had begun to push them out. It seemed to Vann Woodward, writing in 1930, that "the whole colony in the Vieux Carre, who made up all my acquaintances and friends, have bodily migrated to cooler or more lucrative climates," and he was almost right about that. Some blocks had become too expensive, and maybe too precious (also on Vann Woodward's "list of my disappointments" was that his favorite bookshop had "been taken over by a crew of homosexuals and rabid intellectuals who disgust me"); other areas had become uninhabitable for more obvious reasons. "Let us stroll down into the picturesque Vieux Carré, dripping with romance and color and stale beer," wrote one disgruntled old-timer. "Oh, lovely! Oh, divine! What poetry, what music! . . . What romance! ('Come on in, Daddy.') Ah, the old Absinthe House! . . . What quaint characters, these drunks, these perverts. . . . So nostalgic, the bar fights. So profuse the garbage!"

L'Envoi

Some Famous Creoles stayed on in New Orleans. The activist clubwomen had families and social positions to keep them there (and most didn't live in the Quarter anyway). Some of the newspapermen and academics were immobilized by their salaries. A few of the literary and artistic remained and adapted quite successfully—Marc Antony became a prominent society decorator, for instance, and his wife, Lucille, went into real-estate sales. But most of the serious writers and artists left, and with them most of those who kept the social circle spinning. When the Andersons decamped for the mountains of Virginia and Spratling for the mountains of Guerrero, only Saxon was left in the role of perpetual host and tireless social organizer. When Freddie Oechsner and Ham Basso moved north and Natalie Scott joined Spratling in Mexico, the circle lost most of the journalists who had chronicled its activities. Meanwhile, Faulkner had returned to Mississippi and Oliver La Farge to New York; Caroline Durieux and Virginia Parker Nagle and Fanny Craig Ventadour had married and left town. Emmet Kennedy and Genevieve Pitot were in New York, Cicero Odiorne in Paris, and Ronald Hargrave somewhere in southern Europe. Eventually Marian Draper, Roark Bradford, and Conrad Albrizio would leave New Orleans as well. The final irony is that when people left the Quarter for a place like the Quarter used to be, they often had to watch the same process of evolution repeat itself. Spratling, Scott, and Elizabeth Anderson saw it happen all over again in Taxco, Roark Bradford and Oliver La Farge in Santa Fe. Maybe Faulkner had the right idea, going back to Oxford, which wasn't much like the Quarter at all.

Although "there was a time when the fame of New Orleans was based for the most part on gin-fizzes and brothels," the first issue of the *Double Dealer* proudly proclaimed, soon the city would be known for "the concerts, the lectures, the art associations," for Le Petit Theatre, and "the various clubs and coteries whose apparent purpose it is to nourish the traditions of the old ground." And indeed there was a brief interval between gin fizzes and hurricane cocktails, between brothels and strip clubs, when that looked possible. But the Bohemian moment was short-lived. In the early 1930s a local journalist noted that Keith Temple and his wife were part of a general migration uptown by "decent people who have been driven out of the Quarter." By then, he said, you could only find something like the old days—ten years earlier—"at two o'clock in the afternoon when the beer parlors and honky-tonks are too sleepy to turn on the loud-speakers." Even Lyle Saxon eventually moved across Canal Street to a suite at the St. Charles Hotel. Flo Field still guided her flocks of tourists through the Quarter's streets, but at the end of the day she rode the streetcar home to the Garden District.

Field wrote once about the days before 1920, when it seemed that Alberta Kinsey was almost the only artist living in the Quarter: "Came then the dawn—and perhaps the beginning of the end—artists, writers, tourists who found it cheaper than Europe." She wrote "the beginning of the end" because she had seen the artists and writers come, and flourish for a time, and then mostly move on (leaving the place to the tourists, who remained). It almost seemed that the one constant was "little, fragile, prolific Alberta Kinsey": by 1936, a decade after *Famous Creoles* appeared, a local journalist was exaggerating only a bit when he wrote that without Kinsey "New Orleans couldn't even have an art exhibit." Five years later, in 1941, the WPA's guide to Louisiana could refer to 1926 as "a time when the French Quarter was a second Greenwich Village"—could refer to it, that is, as history.

The Annotated
Sherwood Anderson and Other Famous Creoles

herwood Anderson and Other Famous Creoles is a good starting point for exploring the social circle around Spratling and Faulkner, but it is far from an exhaustive catalog. I kept running across people who could well have been in the book, including a few who seemed more suitable than some of those who made the cut. But no doubt Spratling and Faulkner had their reasons for the omissions. Being dead, for instance, seems to have been an implicit disqualification. Basil Thompson, the Byronesque figure generally agreed to have been the life of the *Double Dealer,* would have been a fine addition, had he not essentially drunk himself to death two years earlier. The tobacco millionaire, philanthropist, and pioneer preservationist William Ratcliffe Irby would also have been a likely candidate, except that the month before the book appeared he visited an undertaker, made arrangements for his funeral, picked out his casket, lay down in it, and put a bullet through his head. Some sort of at least potentially lasting connection to New Orleans also seems to have been required. A number of literary folk passed through the city in these years, for instance, and a few like Edmund Wilson, John Dos Passos, and Carl Carmer lingered long enough to have been part of the circle. Stories about them entered the lore, but they weren't picked as Famous Creoles, possibly because, unlike Sherwood Anderson, who came initially with the intention of staying, they were plainly birds of passage, headed back to where they came from.

Fortunately, if the point is to talk about the *kinds of people* in the circle rather than particular individuals, the omissions are less troublesome than they might be, because nearly all of the plausible candidates for Famous Creole status are represented in the book by someone similar. For instance,

Adaline Katz and Lillian Friend Marcus were both Newcomb College graduates, both came from prosperous New Orleans Jewish families, and both were involved with the *Double Dealer*. Katz took long walks with Sherwood Anderson and appeared as a character in his novel *Many Marriages*; Marcus went on his Lake Pontchartrain cruise and wound up in Faulkner's *Mosquitoes*. Katz was not a Famous Creole, but Marcus was.

This kind of substitution could be done so often that I found myself playing a sort of game that went, "Do we really need _____ if we have _____?" Thus: Do we really need artist Olive Leonhardt if we have Caroline Durieux, or Josephine Crawford if we have Virginia Parker Nagle? If we have Ellsworth Woodward, do we need his brother William, or his Newcomb colleague Will Henry Stevens? Do we need architect and preservationist Richard Koch if we have Moise Goldstein and N. C. Curtis? (And, besides, Curtis was Spratling's boss.) Sam Gilmore's sister, Martha Gilmore Robinson, was a formidable activist in the cause of historic preservation, but do we really need her if we have Elizebeth Werlein? And surely John McClure can stand in for Julius Friend and Albert Goldstein, his fellow editors at the *Double Dealer*. Young Jimmy Feibleman was always around, pleased to be part of the crowd, but Famous Creoles Ham Basso and Freddie Oechsner were just a little older and almost as star-struck. Dorothy Dix was very much a presence, too, a pioneering journalist and a woman of parts, but similar parts were shared between her friends Grace King and Helen Pitkin Schertz. Dancer and party-girl Esther DuPuy would have been a great addition, but Marian Draper was those things and an architecture student, too. Illustrator Olive Leonhardt linked the Junior League to the *Double Dealer*, but so did Natalie Scott, who was a newspaperwoman and a real-estate investor as well. It's not that Faulkner and Spratling were filling quotas, but the results were almost as if they had been.

Olive Boullemet Lyons

Still, some of the omissions do seem capricious. For instance, brother and sister Hunt and Sarah Henderson committed their energy and inherited wealth to keep the Arts and Crafts Club going and stockbroker-artist Gideon Stanton was an interesting and important figure, too—yet none was a Famous Creole. Olive Boullemet Lyons was the elegant, cultivated, Creole wife of a wealthy cotton broker whose family owned a pharmaceutical business. Edmund Wilson told his friends back in New York that she was "the most charming woman in the South," and put an admiring sketch of her in his book, *The Twenties*. She kept one of the city's most beautiful gardens, furnished her house with exquisite taste, and was an accomplished cook. She also smoked and drank heavily, bobbed her hair, drove a Stutz Bearcat, published poetry, and worked on the *Double Dealer*. Sherwood Anderson thought she looked "like a Russian prostitute," and gossip linked her romantically to Lyle Saxon (although he was gay). A portrait by Charles Bein shows her in a gold gown and tiara. I would have put her in *my* book—in fact, just did.

Only one omission strikes me as truly inexplicable, however—and it is almost inexcusable. Elizabeth (Mrs. Sherwood) Anderson wasn't an "artful and crafty one" herself, but as a hostess and a sort of den mother she was

Portrait of Olive Lyons by Charles Bein

absolutely central to the French Quarter scene, and Spratling had even done a sketch of her that he could have used. I'm going to give her an entry just like the others, at the very end.

Otherwise, what follows are the original Famous Creoles, in the order that Spratling and Faulkner presented them, each with an approximate age in 1926 and Spratling's drawing. I have not reprinted the front matter or Faulkner's facetious introduction, and I have taken the liberty of giving separate pages to John McClure and Roark Bradford, who were paired in the original (see page 33), and to Faulkner and Spratling, who were, too (page 14). But somehow it seemed appropriate to leave Louise and Marc Antony together. Call me romantic. Spratling and Faulkner could assume that people who bought their book were familiar with its characters, but I can't, so I have tried to tell what each Famous Creole was doing in 1926 and what each had done before. At the end of each entry, set off from the rest, I've said a bit about what became of each one in later years.

"The Locale"

THE FRONTISPIECE TO *Sherwood Anderson and Other Famous Creoles* is a sketch of the neighborhood near Jackson Square where Spratling and Faulkner lived. "Leonardi Studios," at the lower left, is the decorating business that Elizabeth Anderson undertook with Marc and Lucille Antony. The "decorator" at his window is Marc. The "writer" in the attic apartment is Faulkner, and the "artist" climbing out the apartment window is Spratling. Faulkner's bootlegger, "Le Pret Mauvais" (Creole French for "the bad priest"), is relieving himself against a wall in Cabildo Alley. "Alberta," at her easel, is Alberta Kinsey, and the "painter (C.A.A.)" is Conrad (Alfred) Albrizio. "Literature and Less," the title of John McClure's *Times-Picayune* column, marks

McClure's apartment in the house he and Natalie Scott owned and lived in. It's not clear who the "Creole" is, but Le Petit Theatre du Vieux Carré was indeed "opposite." There were in fact "more artists, writers, etc. on Jackson Sq—also on Royal St," and St. Louis Cathedral was built in 1793. Finally, Spratling drew Flo Field ("Our Flo") *in situ,* wearing her trademark brimmed hat and showing some tourists through the neighborhood.

Frontispiece to *Famous Creoles*

THE LOCALE, WHICH INCLUDES MRS. FLO FIELD

Flo Field, 50

Detail from frontispiece

IN LATER YEARS, FIELD SAID that her friend Spratling made her portrait minuscule as "a spanking and an insult and a compliment at the same time," after she told him that his first two sketches of her were "hideous." Certainly her presence on the French Quarter scene was bigger than her picture.

By the 1920s, Flo (nobody called her "Flora," her actual name) worked at an undemanding day job with a city agency that left her free to write lengthy letters to her son on official letterhead. But her real calling was as a French Quarter tour guide—the first, she claimed—whose tours were enlivened with colorful stories like one about a beautiful Creole maiden who fell in love with a mulatto footman and threw herself from a particularly attractive balcony. She also liked to point out one derelict Quarterite as a former premiere danseuse at the French Opera House driven insane by the loss of her baby. She and her friend Lyle Saxon "not only studied the legends," she recalled, "but if there were any missing, we supplied them."

Flo's widowed mother had been a pioneering newspaperwoman, a popular columnist and the first woman staffer on the *Picayune*. "Little Flo," as her mother called her in print, had spent many hours sitting in her mother's office, watching her write, so journalism was in her blood. In the early 1890s she made her debut, dropped out of school, and published her first article in the *Times-Democrat*. She spent the next several years car-

Spratling drawing of Field (maybe one she disliked).

ing for her mother, who had Parkinson's disease, but continued to write in her mother's sickroom, with such success that she was included in a *Leslie's Weekly* article, "Southern Women Who Have Made Their Mark in Journalism." The article noted that she was "petite, blond, and pretty," and praised the "wit and quaint philosophy" of her writing.

After her mother's death, Field moved to Greenwich Village to pursue a literary career. *Cosmopolitan* published her first short stories, and there were rumors of a romance with O. Henry, but he was already married. In 1905 she married another, but that marriage failed after a few years and she returned to New Orleans with her maiden name, a young son named Sydney, and a pressing need for income. (She sometimes intimated that her son's father was O. Henry, although the baby was conceived some four years after her marriage.) She joined the *Times-Picayune,* where she wrote a daily women's column called "Eve Up to Date" and a variety of feature stories, including one in 1916 on Ellsworth Woodward's program to document the old ironwork of New Orleans. She supplemented her $15 weekly salary by writing verse and short stories for magazines like *Harper's Bazaar* and the *Delineator* (for which she wrote several "darky" stories based on an old Negro

man she had known as a child) and working as a press agent for the Philharmonic Society. When the *Double Dealer* got going, she wrote for it and served on its advisory council, although it did nothing to address her chronic insolvency.

For $10 a month, Field rented the slave quarters of the old Morphy house, just a two-minute walk up Royal Street from Lyle Saxon's place. Saxon and George Favrot, *Times-Picayune* reporters like her, were "years younger than I, as all men always seem to have been," but the three were inseparable friends, eating 35-cent suppers at a small restaurant in the Quarter, "swing[ing] down Royal Street, singing La Boheme, ecstatic over every dim and dusky fanlight," and retiring to her second-floor gallery to swat mosquitoes and talk until all hours. It was Saxon and Favrot who talked

1920s portrait by Pops Whitesell

her into the guide business; Saxon told her all she had to say was, "Oh, my God, look at that balcony!"

When Field's play *A la Creole* premiered at Le Petit Theatre in March 1927 (see page 38), the author was one of several Famous Creoles in the cast or otherwise involved. The play also featured four "negro waif musicians" called the Tin Pan Kings, who had been playing on Royal Street when Flo discovered them. When a visiting Philadelphia millionaire engaged the group for his New Year's Eve party and hired Flo to go north with them, it made the national news.

Field's activities brought her recognition—as early as 1927 she was made an honorary member of the prestigious Orleans Club, like Grace King and Mrs. James Oscar Nixon before her, and later she was made a life member of Le Petit Salon—but her letters reveal her constant, and well-founded, worry about money. She tried unsuccessfully to book the Tin Pan Kings at New York's Palace, and she arranged a Philadelphia try-out for *A la Creole,* hoping for commercial success, but the play apparently didn't travel well, although Louisiana community theater groups revived it several times and it was staged by a community theater in Pasadena, of all places. (A limited-edition publication of the script in 1953 was dedicated to Sydney.) In 1931, she visited Spratling at his new Mexican home, returning with silver and dance masks to sell, and Spratling was helping her financially as late as the 1960s, when a letter said he would be sending some "folding money." She kept a typewriter near her bed (she said she couldn't think in longhand) and she continued to write, everything from an article accepted by the *New York Times* to a short story rejected by *True.* Her 1930 booklet, *Rue Royal,* gives a taste of her style as a guide.

In the early 1930s she moved to George Washington Cable's former house in the Garden District, but continued to lead tours of the Quarter for clients including Bertrand Russell, Fiorello LaGuardia, the German ambassador, and often scores of nonpaying tourists who simply attached themselves to paying groups. "Whole conventions would turn their women and children over to her," her son reported, and she was such a hit with one group that she was made an honorary mail clerk for life. She stayed active in historic preservation, speaking to community groups on its importance and working often with her friend Clay Shaw. (When Shaw was falsely accused of conspiring to assassinate President Kennedy, she stood by him staunchly.) And the honors, if not the money, continued to come in. In 1950 Alberta Kinsey and Natalie Scott (visiting from Mexico) were among a couple of dozen sponsors of a luncheon in Flo's honor, and in the 1960s Mayor Victor Schiro named her the city's "official historian." When the New Orleans Pharmacy Museum opened on Chartres Street, she worked as its assistant curator.

She took great pride in Sydney's literary career, which she had promoted as early as the 1920s by sending his teenage poetry to magazine editors she knew. He went on to work at *Esquire* and *Reader's Digest,* and in 1953 published *The American Drink Book,* dedicated "To Flo Field, a great woman— and to all the others who care about the charming and beautiful things." By the late 1950s, Flo was dividing her time between New Orleans and Sydney's place in Manhattan, enjoying being a grandmother. She died in a New Orleans nursing home shortly after her ninety-sixth birthday party, where she drank champagne with relatives and old friends, and made a ten-minute speech. For an epitaph she would have been content with what she once told an interviewer: "I never had any sense except a sense of humor."

Sherwood Anderson, 50

SHERWOOD ANDERSON FIRST CAME to New Orleans in 1922, on the run from a failing marriage. He took an apartment on Royal Street and immediately went to the *Double Dealer*'s offices, where the editors were taken aback when this "shaggy looking man" walked in. "His long hair fell in strands over his florid face. His apparel: a rough tweed suit with leather buttons, a loud tie on which was strung a large paste finger ring, red socks with yellow bands, a velour hat with a red feather stuck in it. He carried a heavy blackthorn stick."

Anderson was at the peak of his career. His path had not been easy, but he had made it. He grew up mostly in Clyde, Ohio. After a spotty education and service in Cuba in the Spanish-American War, he married, and fathered three children. Working at a number of jobs, including writing advertising copy, he began writing fiction on the side. After a breakdown of some sort in 1912, he moved to Chicago, where he fell in with Theodore Dreiser and Carl

MISTER SHERWOOD ANDERSON

Portrait by Pops Whitesell

Sandburg, divorced his wife, and married the former mistress of Edgar Lee Masters. By the time he got to New Orleans he had published three novels. *Winesburg, Ohio* had assured his place in American letters, and a story collection, *The Triumph of the Egg,* had been a triumph itself. His work often appeared in the *Dial,* which gave him its first annual $2,000 award. Phrases like "dean of American literature" would soon be thrown around. So the boys at the *Double Dealer* were even more startled when Anderson stuck out his hand, grinned, and introduced himself.

He found the editors "as pleasant a crowd of young blades as ever drank bad whiskey" and the French Quarter "surely the most civilized spot in America." Where else could one pass a day, as he had, working all morning, watching an oyster-opening contest after lunch, walking on the wharfs among singing Negro dock workers after that, and going to a prize fight in the evening? "And at that I missed the horse races." Soon he settled into a pattern of morning work, frequent lunches and dinners with Lyle Saxon or his *Double Dealer* friends, "loafing on the wharfs" with Roark Bradford, and long walks with Adaline Katz, the Bohemian daughter of a local banker. "As for the girls, my dear," Natalie Scott wrote in her newspaper column, "in two days he was 'Sherry' to them, and now I hear it is Cheri." When he left after a few weeks, he told a friend he'd been "hopelessly vamped by New Orleans, the sweetest town on this continent" and that he was "going to live there sometime and be an old son of a bitch." In fact, he added, "maybe I'll go whole hog and be a nigger."

A year and a half later he did come back, with his new wife, Elizabeth, and soon the daily *Item* was hailing him as "the Lion of the Latin Quarter." He resumed his practice of writing all morning and "loafing" all afternoon, this time with his young neighbor Lucille Antony or an aspiring young writer named Bill Faulkner, an acquaintance of Elizabeth's from her New York days. Faulkner remembered that "we walked and talked in New Orleans—or Anderson talked and I listened"—but Anderson fell for Faulkner's made-up war record and wrote him into a short story: "I noticed he was a cripple. The slight limp, the look of pain that occasionally drifted across his face, the little laugh that was intended to be jolly but did not quite achieve its purpose. . . ."

Maybe the two hit it off because Anderson was a fantasist, too. He admitted once that sometimes things he imagined became so real to him that he couldn't remember whether they'd actually happened. He was like his father, he wrote, always "playing some role, everlastingly strutting on the stage of life in some part not his own." Elizabeth agreed. Her husband "could be a struggling, poor writer at one time and then the grand old man of letters at another. He could be the simple, honest American workingman who insisted on having at every meal 'brown, white and green'—meat, potato and vegetable—with no fancy asides [sic], and then later pride himself on being a polished connoisseur of world cuisine at the restaurants we went to." Sometimes he presented himself as a Southerner, claiming that his father (a Union army veteran) came from a Southern family. (But he didn't fool Faulkner: Once, when Faulkner claimed that mulattos can't reproduce and Anderson laughed at him, Faulkner called him "a damn Yank.") Other times, he wrote, "for whole days, I try being a black man." He told readers of *Vanity Fair* that he'd acquired "the nigger craze." He envied blacks what he thought was their spontaneity and lack of neuroses, and he liked to watch black dockworkers and "the play of their muscles in the sunlight." He still dressed flamboyantly. Faulkner recalled a "bright blue racetrack shirt and vermilion-mottled Bohemian Windsor tie," and James Feibleman remembered "a corduroy shirt, a loud green one," a brown suit with a green pinstripe, and high-button shoes. (Spratling's sketch shows argyle socks, the shoes, and his cane, along with a copy of his recently published memoir.) Anderson thought that the dockworkers admired his clothes: "I can see the looks of approval pass from eye to eye."

Many Marriages had just been published, and although the Women's Club of New Orleans found it immoral and declined to ask Anderson to lecture, no less a personage than Grace King invited him to address Le Petit Salon. He got a respectful review from the *Times-Picayune,* and he basked in the admiration of local literati like Lyle Saxon, who wrote him to say that he was "astounded" by his work: "God, what a man! It makes me feel like a puny child beside you. . . . such virility and so much strength." Anderson was taken up by the Arts and Crafts Club, giving an address to open the Club's 1925–1926 season and serving on the committee that gave the 1926 Benjamin Prize for landscape painting to Weeks Hall, and he good-naturedly gave interviews to the local newspapers, although he didn't take them very seriously. When Saxon asked him why he wrote, for example, he replied, "It's the ink—that way it smells! It's a kind of perversion."

Anderson was extraordinarily generous with his time and advice. "What he had, he shared. What was his to give, he gave," Hamilton Basso wrote later. Cicero Odiorne said Anderson "had a heart as big as his frame," and Faulkner recalled him as "warm, generous, merry and fond of laughing, without pettiness." In return, though, the master expected to dominate conversations. Elizabeth said that he "enjoyed hugely his position as the center of attention," and Spratling remembered that, although "Faulkner and Sherwood enjoyed each other, . . . if Faulkner spoke out of turn or distracted Sherwood's listeners from the conversation, Sherwood would become annoyed."

A typical evening at the Andersons' found Sherwood surrounded by young people, many of them would-be writers like Basso and Freddie Oechsner who might be literally at his feet. Sometimes he and Faulkner would spin yarns about Al Jackson, their creation, who herded half-sheep/half-alligators in the swamp, but Elizabeth said that often "he would take over the floor to tell a long, rambling story and no one would dare interrupt him." She added that usually no one wanted to, because he was so entertaining. Feibleman said years later that Anderson was one of only two men he'd met who could tell a story properly. The monologues continued on Anderson's afternoon walks, at the Quarter's cheap restaurants, and, notably, on board a boat that he engaged for an ill-starred Lake Pontchartrain cruise (see page 22). Anderson's help for young writers didn't end with advice. In 1925 he wrote publisher Horace Liveright that "young Bill Faulkner" was "the one writer here of promise" and that "I think he is going to be a real writer." Even after he and Faulkner fell out over something—Anderson said he discovered that Faulkner had lied about his war record, Faulkner believed that Anderson was hurt by the parody in *Famous Creoles*, scholars suggest other explanations altogether—Anderson wrote Liveright that although he didn't like Faulkner personally, the young man was "a good prospect." (For his part, Faulkner dedicated *Sartoris* to his mentor, "through whose kindness I was first published," and almost thirty years later wrote appreciatively about Anderson's tutorial method and sound advice.)

In the summer of 1925, however, the Andersons spent a month in the southwest Virginia mountains, near the town of Marion, and Sherwood found himself thinking, "What an ideal place for an American writer." Soon he wrote his brother that he was going to build a house and that he and Elizabeth were "planning to spend the rest of our lives there." He bought some property, and in May 1926 he left New Orleans as abruptly as he'd come. In 1924 a percipient interviewer had reported her "feeling [that] if things, including people, get in his way, he will go away and leave them. He has work that must be done." He wrote at one point that he had "my little hidden hole where I go to work every day [because] people are so very social down here that, at any time someone may drift in to interrupt," and after he'd left town the *New Orleanian* recalled of his last months that "lion-tamers and social folk had got at him, while he fought back at them savagely like a lion fighting fleas, wanting only to eat the lotus and write a little." Perhaps the social obligations that came with being the Great Cham of the New Orleans literary set had started to wear on him. Or maybe it was simpler than that. Anderson himself said, "The heat and mosquitoes drove me out."

Anderson built the house (although neither he nor his builder could understand the plans that Spratling had drawn for him). He bought Marion's two weekly newspapers, one Republican and one Democrat, and wrote for both of them, often under the pen name "Buck Fever." He continued the grueling but lucrative schedule of lectures that he had begun in New Orleans; Elizabeth sniffed later that she didn't care for his lectures herself, but "the people who attended such affairs seemed to love them and women flocked around him adoringly when they were over."

In time he concluded that one of the things in his way was Elizabeth. In 1929, when she was visiting her family in California, he wrote and asked her not to return, then three years later filed for divorce on the grounds of desertion. In 1933 he married the daughter of a prominent local family, a much younger woman who had studied social work at Bryn Mawr and worked in the industrial division of the national YMCA. She encouraged him to write the articles about labor conditions during the Depression collected in *Puzzled America* (1935), but unfortunately there was no denying that, as a writer, Anderson was in decline. The critics turned on him, often savagely. As one friend put it, he had begun "to write parodies of his own work. . . . His friends remained with him, but it was a broken Sherwood, striving desperately to keep up the old optimism and courage and enthusiasm, that they saw."

By all accounts, however, his fourth marriage was happy and successful. The Andersons traveled extensively. They vacationed in Texas, the Southwest, and once in Mexico, sometimes accompanied by Sherwood's old friends like Marc and Lucille Antony. Almost every winter they came to New Orleans for a month or two, driving down in a half-ton white truck. They were on their way to South America in 1941 when Anderson swallowed a toothpick from a martini olive, which perforated his colon. He died of peritonitis, and his body was returned to Marion for burial.

Nathaniel Cortlandt Curtis, 45

SPRATLING'S DRAWING SHOWS N. C. Curtis "irrigating the Sahara of the Bozart" [Beaux Arts]—H. L. Mencken's contemptuous label for the South. Curtis's watering can is labeled "Property School of Architectur T. U. [Tulane University]." Curtis came from Auburn University in 1912 to help get Tulane's architecture school going, and he promptly fell in love with the Vieux Carré. His drawing of the Cabildo and the cathedral appeared in the school's 1913 yearbook. He wrote a scholarly article on the Quarter's ironwork and another entitled "Some Thoughts on the Architectural Beauties of Old New Orleans; Their Proper Preservation," and got involved in the nascent preservation efforts of the American Institute of Architects' local chapter. He published his drawings of the derelict old St. Louis Hotel and laid out strikingly prescient plans for converting it to a convention center. (The building was pulled down anyway, in 1916.) He showed his drawings and watercolors in

NATHANIEL C. CURTIS, *Architect*
IRRIGATOR OF THE SAHARA OF THE BOZART

the annual members' exhibits of the Art Association of New Orleans and in a show of local work at the Delgado Museum.

While teaching at Auburn, Curtis had met and married the president's daughter. In 1917, with a growing family, he couldn't resist the offer of a higher salary from the University of Illinois, but after three years in Urbana (which he later described, not quite approvingly, as "spick and span in the Mid-Western sense") he jumped at the chance to return to New Orleans. There he resumed his affiliation with Tulane, joined Moise Goldstein's architectural firm as chief designer, and picked up where he had left off with the local arts scene. He was an early supporter of the Arts and Crafts Club and by 1921 he and his Tulane colleague Charles Bein were teaching classes there. He had done some painting in Urbana, and showed it at the Club. (One critic remarked, "It is hard to imagine anyone's desire to go to Urbana, Illinois. It is even harder to imagine painting cow-barns there. But Mr. Curtis did.") Later in the decade he chaired both the Club's "Lectures and Entertainments" committee and the committee that awarded the Benjamin Prize to Bein. In 1927 the Club showed his French Quarter scenes in a joint exhibit with Spratling's Mexican drawings and "negro studies" by a Richmond artist.

Appointed to the AIA's "Committee on Preservation of Historic Monuments and Scenic Beauties," Curtis reported in 1923 that New Orleans architects were planning to preserve and redevelop the plaza at the foot of Canal Street, had rehabilitated the Royal Street house occupied by the Arts and Crafts Club, and had moved a plantation house from an insalubrious neighborhood to a site near the country club. Tulane students were making systematic measurements of old buildings, and a prize had been established "to encourage the study and proper recording of historic buildings." Curtis published a monograph with Spratling, *The Wrought Iron Work of Old New Orleans*; wrote the preface to Spratling and Natalie Scott's *Old Plantation Houses in Louisiana*; and continued the drawing and sketching that would culminate in his 1933 magnum opus, *New Orleans, Its Old Houses, Shops and Public Buildings* (which also included photographs, some of them by Pops Whitesell).

Curtis's designs in the 1920s ranged from a twenty-three-story downtown skyscraper for the American National Bank to the gardens at the New Orleans zoo, for which he later designed the Elephant House and other buildings. At his alma mater, the University of North Carolina (Class of 1909, with a thesis entitled "The Relation of Mathematics to Music and Poetry"), he designed a house for his old fraternity and a "castle" for a secret society. He had also taught at Chapel Hill after his graduate work at Columbia, before he went to Auburn, where he designed three other buildings.

In the 1930s Curtis worked with Moise Goldstein on the Dillard University campus and designed both the Art Deco Flint-Goodridge Hospital and the first Modernist house in New Orleans (commissioned by the *Times-Picayune* to celebrate its centenary). He served as the vice-chairman of the Vieux Carré Commission. In 1941 he designed the Tulane library building that now houses the university's special collections, which include his own papers, including pastel and watercolor sketches, many architectural drawings, and two unpublished novels. His son, Nathaniel "Buster" Curtis Jr.—a distinguished architect in his own right, who designed the Superdome and Rivergate—recalled fondly that his father was also "a sailor and fisherman [who] built furniture and three boats with his own hands." He died in 1953, on his way to work.

Frans Blom, 33

FRANS BLOM CAME TO NEW ORLEANS in 1924 to join Tulane's new Department of Middle American Research, although he left almost immediately on a research expedition to the Mayan ruins of Mexico and Guatemala. There he and his young colleague Oliver La Farge made a number of significant discoveries, which they reported in their joint publication *Tribes and Temples* (1926–1927). After his return Blom was made head of the department, a position he held for the next fourteen years. (The label on Blom's portrait in *Famous Creoles*, "the Tulane Champollion," refers to his continuing attempts to decipher the Mayan writing system: Jean-François Champollion was the scholar who decoded the Egyptian hieroglyphs.)

Blom was born in Copenhagen in 1893, the son of a wealthy businessman. After a conventionally misspent youth, the college dropout was sent to Mexico in 1919 by his family to make his own way. While doing odd jobs in the oil industry, Blom became interested in the remains of Mayan civiliza-

FRANZ BLOM
THE TULANE CHAMPOLLION

Blom on an expedition

tion scattered across southern Mexico. He found work with a Mexican government archeology office and started sending drawings and reports to a leading American Maya scholar, who was so impressed that he helped Blom get a scholarship to study at Harvard. There he wrote his thesis on Mayan ruins and participated in a 1924 expedition to Guatemala. When he came to Tulane he was a newly minted M.A., but one with considerable experience, several publications, fluency in five languages, and one remarkable discovery (that a group of buildings at the Uaxactun site are aligned with seasonal changes in the position of the sunrise).

Blom could be a dapper dresser when he felt like it, but at work he wore the baggy cotton shirt and trousers of a Mexican peasant, with a red sash at his waist. He also insisted that his colleagues and staff call him "Don Pancho." A friend recalled that he enjoyed "several daily drinks" and was a heavy smoker of Turkish cigarettes. He cut a swath on the social scene: *New Orleans Life* magazine included him in a list of the city's "popular bachelors," observing that "debutantes prefer blondes." Blom was largely responsible for introducing the Quarter's artistic and literary crowd to Mexico. The audience at a 1925 Tulane lecture on his recent expedition included Famous Creoles William Spratling, Natalie Scott, and Caroline Durieux—who would all eventually live there—as well as Charles Bein and Virginia Parker Nagle. He soon became part of that crowd himself, especially after he moved in 1927 from an apartment near Tulane to one in the lower Pontalba building. He recalled "good talk and claret" at Lyle Saxon's after a dinner party with Sherwood Anderson and Spratling, and he was one of the passengers on the famous Lake Pontchartrain boat ride.

As a Tulane department head, Blom continued to mount expeditions to Mayan country. In 1929 photographer Pops Whitesell went along, and Blom took casts of an impressive structure in the Yucatan that were used to reconstruct the building at the Chicago World's Fair. He showed casts, photographs, and movies from his travels at the Arts and Crafts Club. In 1932 he took a group of tourists to Mexico, and married one of them, a Long Island heiress whose money he used to buy an Italian sports car. Blom remained involved with the artistic set. The *Item* reported in 1934, for example, that work by Mexican painter and sculptor Enrique Alférez could be seen "in the gallery of the studio of Frans Blom."

But in the late 1930s Blom's marriage broke up and his drinking became excessive. In 1940 he was eased out of his position at Tulane. He sold his books, and his possessions were seized for unpaid rent. Having hit bottom, he moved to Mexico. But there he met Swiss photographer Gertrude Duby, married her, and dried out. He and Trudi began to do archeological research for the Mexican government and turned their large house in San Cristóbal de las Casas into a research center for visitors. After Blom died in 1963, Trudi continued to operate the center until her own death thirty years later.

Mayan temple at the Chicago World's Fair

Ellsworth Woodward, 65

ELLSWORTH WOODWARD AND HIS older brother, William, came to New Orleans in the 1880s, but in 1924 William, confined to a wheelchair by cancer of the spine, retired and moved to Biloxi to concentrate on his etchings. That left Ellsworth as the unquestioned elder statesman of the New Orleans art scene. Although he was an accomplished watercolorist and printmaker, he was even more important as a tireless promoter and teacher of art. *The Encyclopaedia of New Orleans Artists* takes nearly two full pages of small type to summarize his career. When *Famous Creoles* appeared he had been director of the Newcomb College School of Art for forty years, since the school's founding. The school offered instruction not only in painting and sculpture, but in everything from clay modeling and furniture design to text illumination and art embroidery—and Woodward taught many of these subjects himself. Perhaps his best-known enterprise was Newcomb's art pottery operation, founded in 1895 and winning medals at international expositions five years later. He also taught evening and weekend adult classes, traveled in Europe in the summers, and was probably the first Famous Creole to work

ELLSWORTH WOODWARD

1920s portrait by Wayman Adams

in Mexico, painting Aztec ruins there in the summer of 1898. Woodward was a forceful lecturer and a memorable personality, known for his use of the expression "Jumping Jehoshaphat!" He and his wife (also an artist) had no children, and his students were his family. They returned his affection: In 1912 the Tulane yearbook was dedicated to him, and illustrated with artwork reflecting his teaching.

He and his brother complemented one another. William taught oil painting to Ellsworth's students at Newcomb, and Ellsworth taught art history at Tulane's architecture school, which William had founded in 1907. William's architecture students were drawing the French Quarter's historic buildings, and so were Ellsworth's Newcomb girls. Both "Will" and "Ell" (as they called each other) were early and active preservationists. Shortly after Ellsworth arrived in New Orleans in 1885 he recognized in a scrap yard an ironwork panel from a café that George Washington Cable had written about, took it home, and, years later, installed it in Newcomb's new Arts and Crafts building. Around 1915 he undertook a project to photograph the Quarter's balconies, galleries, and fences for the archives of the Newcomb museum, and when a proposal was floated to turn the Pontalba buildings into artists' studios, the *Times-Picayune* naturally turned to him for comment: "For years, the restoration of the old French Quarter has been the dream of a large number of Orleanians," he told the newspaper.

Ellsworth founded and was first president of the Art Association of New Orleans. He helped to found the Delgado Museum of Art and served it as president and trustee. He founded the Southern States Art League, and seemed to be president-for-life of that organization. He helped to set up the Natchitoches Art Colony, at the instigation of a couple of his Newcomb students. The arts organizations in which he was merely an active member were legion. He was particularly known for his watercolors, for which he won an award at the Brooklyn Museum in 1927. He also did book illustrations, notably for Grace King's *Creole Families of New Orleans* (1921). His subjects ranged from studio work to scenes from his summer travels abroad, but when he had a watercolor show at Newcomb, Lyle Saxon particularly praised his pictures of "bits of the Vieux Carre of New Orleans [and] scenes along Cane river near Natchitoches"—ironic, given Woodward's belief that "no Yankee artist, however skillful, can paint the South" (as he told a meeting of the Southern States Art League). "I think what masterpieces I could paint," he added ruefully, "if only I were a Southerner-born!"

But he wasn't. The Woodward brothers were Yankees from Seekonk,

Massachusetts, both of them graduates of the Rhode Island School of Design. After William went on to study in Paris and Ellsworth studied in Munich, William came to New Orleans and Ellsworth soon joined him there. The arts and crafts ethos that the brothers had absorbed at their Rhode Island alma mater was soon evident in the range of classes they offered both at the newly founded Newcomb College and, for adult students, through the Tulane Decorative Art League for Women. When Ellsworth founded the Delgado Museum he made sure that it displayed handwork as well as fine arts and pioneered its decorative arts collection.

Both brothers were early members of the Arts and Crafts Club and showed their work there. Ellsworth was one of the painters whose work the Club sent to Jackson, Mississippi, for a show there, and in 1927 he served on the selection committee for the Club's Benjamin Prize. But the Woodwards were hardly Bohemians. Both lived exemplary bourgeois lives uptown. (Ellsworth left his house every morning at 6:45 to buy groceries before he walked to work, and his principal diversion was having his wife read to him.) Moreover, the Woodwards' commitment to the applied arts sometimes put them at cross purposes with more "arty" members of the community and, by the 1920s, both Ellsworth's Impressionism and William's Beaux Arts approach to architecture had become somewhat old-fashioned. Finally, Ellsworth's commitment to promoting Southern artists working on Southern subjects meant that the Delgado under his direction largely ignored the avant-garde art movements of the 1920s. "No doubt I am an 'old fogy,' as the young folks think," he remarked. Some undoubtedly did think that, but the not-so-young members of Le Petit Salon elected him an honorary life member for his contributions to the cultural life of their city.

Woodward retired from Newcomb in 1931, and two years later Tulane awarded him an honorary doctorate. Although his career seemed to be winding down, he was appointed director of the Gulf States Public Works of Art Project in 1934 and accepted a commission to design a mural for New Orleans's new Criminal Courts building. Meanwhile, he continued to paint—in 1936 the Fine Arts Club of New Orleans established a watercolor prize in his name—and he helped his brother, William, by printing his etchings of French Quarter buildings, some of which were published in 1938, with a foreword by N. C. Curtis.

Ellsworth and William Woodward both died in 1939, within months of each other.

Meigs O. Frost, 44

MEIGS FROST WAS BORN IN Connecticut, went to Andover, played football at Haverford, and talked his way into a job reporting for the *New York Times*. ("I quit school, got a job, and got married, all in the same day.") After a year at the Gray Lady he moved to the *Galveston News* for seven years, then briefly to the *New Orleans Item* before switching to the competing afternoon paper, the *States*. In his early days Frost covered six revolutions in Latin America, fought in the campaign against Pancho Villa, lost an eye to "a jungle fever," and took some shrapnel that put a silver plate in his leg for the rest of his life. (You have to wonder what he made of Bill Faulkner's "war wounds.") He later ate an entire suckling pig, to win a bet with his city editor.

Frost's interviews were always worth reading. His subjects in the 1920s included a white Unionist from "the Free State of Jones" (Jones County, Mississippi); two aged Creole sisters who objected to plans to locate "a jazz cabaret" across Royal Street from their 1831 ancestral home; and a New Orleans physician who claimed that the pirate Jean Lafitte was Napoleon's

MEIGS O. FROST
SKETCHED ON THE SIDE LINES

Another Spratling drawing of Frost

cousin and John Paul Jones's nephew and that all three were buried in Jefferson Parish. In the 1920s Frost reported on the French Quarter cultural scene for the *States,* with a review of an Arts and Crafts Club exhibit of work by Spratling, Virginia Parker, and Will Henry Stevens; a story on the formation of the New Orleans Art League; and a tongue-in-cheek account of the Lady Godiva episode at the Arts and Crafts Club Ball (see page 27). He moved with his wife (the mellifluously named April Frost) and their two children from the Audubon Park area into the lower Pontalba building, and the Frosts became part of that scene themselves. In 1925 Lyle Saxon wrote that a portrait of Mrs. Frost on exhibit at the Arts and Crafts Club was "attracting considerable attention by its air of quiet distinction and its beautiful handling."

Frost was a reporter's reporter, but he also wrote fiction on the side. One of his six hundred or so short stories won the *New York World*'s prize for best short story published in 1924. In 1913 he published a poem—not very good, but widely reprinted—in the *Galveston News.* If he wrote verse after that, it has not survived.

In the late 1920s Frost began to write books as well. His name appears as co-author only on his first, *A Marine Tells It to You* (about the Boxer Rebellion), but he was also the uncredited ghostwriter of at least three other books, including one for the captain of the rum-runner *I'm Alone,* about the Coast Guard's sinking of his ship. Notable interviews in the 1930s included one with Henry Ford. His reporting of a homicide case got him honorable mention for a 1933 Pulitzer Prize, and Loyola gave him an honorary degree that same year. Probably the high point of his Louisiana journalism career came in 1940 when a series of his stories sent the president of Louisiana State University to prison, led Louisiana's governor to resign, helped to bring down the remains of the Huey Long machine, and won the Sigma Delta Chi "Courage in Journalism Award" for the *States.*

During World War II, Frost served as the Southern public relations officer for the Marine Corps, working out of Atlanta and retiring as a lieutenant colonel. But his always precarious health caught up with him. Crippling arthritis kept him from writing for his last few years, and several strokes left him unable to speak for the year and a half before his death in 1950.

Natalie Scott, 36

SPRATLING'S SKETCH THAT SHOWS "Peggy Passe Partout" on horseback, jumping the hurdle of a building on Royal Street, refers to Natalie Scott's column for the *States* newspaper, her love of horseback riding (she was a founder of the New Orleans Equestrian Club and perennial city champion), and the famous old Court of Two Sisters, one of her real-estate holdings.

Scott was more central to the French Quarter scene than almost anyone else. In 1921 she and John McClure bought a building on Orleans (now Pirate's) Alley and told a newspaper that they intended to convert it to studios for artists. They lived there themselves, and when Spratling came to town the next year he moved in as well. Subsequently, Scott bought a Creole cottage on St. Peter Street, where her tenants included Oliver La Farge and Sam Gilmore, and the Court of Two Sisters, where a tenant started a tearoom in the ground floor. At another of her properties, on St. Peter, Spratling converted the attic into an apartment where he and Faulkner moved in 1925.

PEGGY PASSE PARTOUT TAKES A HURDLE

Downstairs, Marc and Lucille Antony lived above their ground-floor shop. (Scott made a lot of money when she sold these places; unfortunately, she put much of it in the pre-Crash stock market.)

The heroine

The journalist (by Pops Whitesell).

The socialite (by Pops Whitesell)

She turned up everywhere in those years. With Helen Pitkin Schertz and Mrs. James Oscar Nixon, she helped to get Le Petit Theatre established. She wrote and acted in plays there, often with Sam Gilmore, and the two performed skits at the country club and for the Junior League Review. She and Gilmore also worked alongside Flo Field and Lillian Marcus (her former basketball teammate at Newcomb College) as unpaid staff members at the *Double Dealer,* and Scott supported it with enough of her own money to make her the magazine's fourth largest investor. Her column for the *States* often dealt with fluff about the Famous Creoles and their doings, but she also reported such hard news as a sensational murder trial. (In 1929 Sherwood Anderson called her "the best newspaperwoman in America.") Meigs Frost, her colleague at the *States,* wrote once that Scott "poured the 'T' that puts the finishing touch to ART," and her efforts for the Arts and Crafts Club included working with Charles Bein and Elizebeth Werlein to arrange the program for one of its annual balls. She sat (or, rather, stood) for a society portrait by Pops Whitesell and, naturally, she was one of the dozen or so Famous Creoles who went on Sherwood Anderson's hapless Lake Pontchartrain excursion. She also went with Spratling, Caroline Durieux, Virginia Parker, and

Charles Bein to hear Frans Blom's lectures on Mexico at Tulane, a decision that was to have major consequences for her a few years later. She traveled the back roads with Spratling to write their book, *Old Plantation Houses in Louisiana,* which was praised in Lyle Saxon's column for the *Times-Picayune* when it appeared in 1927 (with a preface by N. C. Curtis). Almost incidentally, she wrote *Grand Zombi,* a "tragic mulatto" drama based on the life of voodoo priestess Marie Laveau, which won a national playwriting contest in 1927, went on to win other prizes, appeared in a "best plays" anthology, and was staged at Le Petit Theatre.

Throughout the 1920s she traveled abroad extensively, often for months at a time, sending her column back to the *States,* where her activities were often front-page news. In 1924 she went to Greenwich Village and three months in 1926 were her first exposure to Mexico, but most of her travels were in Europe, where she had been before, in the vastly different circumstances of World War I.

Raised in New Orleans, the daughter of a railroad contractor, she went to Newcomb College on a scholarship and was graduated with honors. After a year of Greek studies in Washington, she returned to join the Newcomb fac-

Publication announcement for book by Scott and Spratling

ulty and took a master's degree at Tulane in 1914. With skills in French, German, Italian, and Spanish, as well as Greek, she seemed to be headed for a quiet academic career. But when the United States entered the First World War, she went to France as a Red Cross worker, and she came back as a heroine, the only American woman to receive the Croix de Guerre (for rescuing wounded soldiers from the rubble of her hospital during a bombing raid). In other words, Natalie Scott was famous before she became a Famous Creole.

As the 1920s drew to a close, she began to loosen her ties to the French Quarter, then to New Orleans itself. Her mother, father, and brother had all died during the decade, her circle of friends was breaking up, and there was less reason to stay. In 1928 she resigned from the *States,* left the Quarter for a house near Audubon Park, and sold the St. Peter Street cottage to her tenant Sam Gilmore. Although all her previous investment properties had been within a few hundred feet of Jackson Square, she used some of the money to buy two rental houses uptown. Also in 1928, she visited Sherwood Anderson at his new home in Virginia and worked steadily on a cookbook, published the next year as *Mirations and Miracles of Mandy,* with illustrations by Spratling. In 1929 she and ten others, including Lyle Saxon, Grace King, Roark Bradford, and Dorothy Dix, were honored at a "New Orleans in Song and Story" banquet, but she and Spratling had already begun to discuss a move to Mexico, and in the fall she went back to explore the country—on horseback. When the stock market crash wiped out most of her savings, she had yet another reason to make the move. She returned to New Orleans long enough to appear in Le Petit Theatre's production of *The Devil's Disciple,* but early in 1930 she joined Spratling in Taxco.

She threw herself into the life of the town with her usual gusto, working to preserve its historic architecture, opening a *pensione* for artists and writers, riding her horses through the wilds of Mexico, pursuing anthropological research on the native peoples, and joining the staff of the magazine *Mexican Folkways.* She introduced a proper sanitation system for the town and brought in its first physician. Most important, she founded and ran a nursery school that provided education, health care, and nourishing meals for local children. She also continued to write: first *The Gourmet's Guide to New Orleans* (foreword by Dorothy Dix); then *Your Mexican Kitchen* (foreword by Spratling); finally *Cocina to You: Mexican Dishes for American Kitchens.*

By 1940 Taxco was her home. But her story took one more turn. After Pearl Harbor, she went overseas with the Red Cross once again, serving with mobile evacuation hospitals in North Africa, Italy, France, and Germany. (The *Times-Picayune* published her letters to Martha Robinson, her Newcomb friend and Sam Gilmore's sister, as a war diary.) She was on her way to the Pacific front when the Japanese surrendered, but she stayed on with the Red Cross in the Philippines, Japan, and Korea until 1948. She came back to New Orleans long enough to lead a national fund-raising campaign for Newcomb, but then returned to Taxco, her school, and her friends. She died and was buried there in 1957.

Oliver La Farge, 25

OLIVER LA FARGE STOPPED BY NEW ORLEANS in 1925 on his way to join Frans Blom on an expedition to investigate Mayan ruins in Mexico and Guatemala. La Farge (his full name was Oliver Hazard Perry La Farge) was from Newport, Rhode Island, and had a family tree full of distinguished Yankees, a grandfather who was a well-known artist, and an uncle who was a prominent architect. While at Harvard, he had edited the literary magazine, been elected class poet, and gone on several anthropological field trips to the Southwest. He had just begun graduate work when Blom met him, liked him, and hired him.

Despite some friction, the two men made a number of remarkable discoveries. Blom's testy note in his diary that La Farge "is somewhat of a weak sister and seems to hate hard work" was belied by the results of their explorations, soon published in their joint book, *Tribes and Temples*. When they returned to New Orleans (with a Mayan informant, "Prince Tata," in tow), Blom got the approval of Tulane's president, Albert Bledsoe Dinwiddie, to

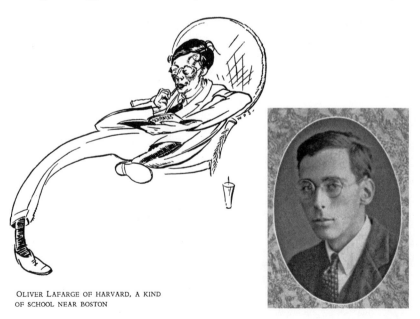

OLIVER LAFARGE OF HARVARD, A KIND OF SCHOOL NEAR BOSTON

La Farge, Blom, and "Prince Tata"

hire La Farge as a regular member of the Department of Middle American Research, and sent him and a colleague back to Central America the next year to look into the survival of the Mayan calendar, with success reported in La Farge's book *The Year Bearer's People*.

On La Farge's first visit to New Orleans, Natalie Scott, who knew his family, took him in hand and introduced him to some young people who invited him to join them on a Mardi Gras float. La Farge was enchanted: "The gang on the truck were delightful, *and they liked me*. On my merits only, coming out of nowhere as if dropped by the stork, they liked me. Harvard was nothing to them, Groton they had not heard of. . . ." (Note the caption on his picture in *Famous Creoles*.) He found the "free-speaking and free-acting" style of his new friends a refreshing change from prim New England, and before long he was wearing an Indian headband and dancing his "Eagle Dance" on the tabletop at parties. His St. Peter Street apartment—one of Natalie Scott's properties—became known as the Wigwam. Shared for a time with *Times-Picayune* cartoonist Keith Temple, it was, he said, "a place in which we could laugh and sing without causing parents to protest or scandalizing the neighbours." There was a good deal of laughing and singing—and exploring the pleasures of alcohol and sex, both abundantly available in the Quarter. Faulkner and Spratling were amused when La Farge came by one night having apparently just discovered the latter, but he was a fast learner and quickly became known as a ladies' man. (One friend recalled a costume party where La Farge needed help to remove his gladiator costume before heading upstairs with his date.) He also picked up a thirst for bootleg absinthe, which may have sealed the fate of a dozen expensive glasses Spratling borrowed from Marc and Lucille Antony: La Farge dropped them out a dormer window, one by one, to hear the sound. No doubt drink also accounted for the spectacle (reported by John McClure) of La Farge and Faulkner walking down the street singing the obscene ditty "Christopher Columbo" at the top of their lungs.

Appearances were deceiving, however. Between parties and research expeditions, La Farge was writing: an article for *Scribner's* (the magazine shown in Spratling's drawing), a story in the *Dial* (chosen for *Best American Short Stories of 1927*), and the beginnings of a novel about a young Navajo couple. Things seemed to be going well for him. But then, while he was visiting Harvard in 1928, his paycheck did not arrive and he learned that Tulane had fired him, without notice. At a masked ball two years before, he had quarreled with the son and daughter of a university trustee, and the father had taken his revenge. (This was not President Dinwiddie's finest hour: he forgot to tell La Farge that he no longer had a job, but gave him $75 severance to compensate for his absent-mindedness.) La Farge came back to the French Quarter and worked full time on his novel, but when *Laughing Boy* was finished in 1929, he sent it to his publisher, packed up his belongings, bade the Wigwam adieu, and headed for New York.

The book was a triumph. It was a selection of the Literary Guild, and it won the Pulitzer Prize in 1930. (Le Petit Theatre du Vieux Carré staged a dramatic adaptation in 1932.) The *New York Telegram* said, "La Farge has done for the Indians in this book what 'Porgy' did for the Negro." La Farge went on to write a couple of dozen books (the best of them dealing with American Indian life and culture); scores of his articles and short stories appeared in the *New Yorker, Atlantic Monthly, Esquire,* and elsewhere; one of the stories won the O. Henry Award in 1931. But he never again had the success that he enjoyed with *Laughing Boy.*

After leaving New Orleans, La Farge married a New York heiress, the daughter of a wealthy broker turned publisher. (Both parents-in-law were active in promoting interracial cooperation and traveled extensively to spread the tenets of Baha'i.) In 1937, after seven years, two children, two less-successful novels, and a move to Santa Fe, his marriage broke up. In 1939 he married Consuelo Pendaries y Baca, from an old ranching family in northern New Mexico. La Farge was increasingly active in advocacy and charitable work affecting Indians, and was president of what became the Association on American Indian Affairs for thirty years beginning in 1933, interrupted only by service in the Army Air Corps during World War II.

Spratling's drawing portrays La Farge accurately, with a pipe and a drink: he had recurring problems with alcohol, and he was always a heavy smoker. He died from emphysema in 1963, and is buried in Santa Fe.

William C. "Cicero" Odiorne, 45

Spratling drew Cicero Odiorne seated at the Café du Dome in Paris, a Left Bank gathering place for the expatriate literary colony. (In the background is a *pissoir,* an inexhaustible source of amusement for Americans in Paris.) In 1925 Spratling and Faulkner had been sitting at the café with him.

Spratling had known Odiorne since the early 1920s, when the gay, club-footed photographer had a studio in the upper Pontalba building. As a youth Odiorne had gone from Barry, Illinois, where his father ran a clothing store, to Chicago, where he worked as a stenographer while he studied photography with the accomplished portraitist Eugene Hutchinson. He had also worked in Boston and New York before coming to New Orleans in 1917, where he supplemented his studio income by doing society photographs for the newspapers. He got his nickname when his Pontalba neighbor Louis Andrews (later, Fischer) asked him what his middle initial stood for. He told her to guess, and when she suggested Cicero he told her she was right. Although

Odiorne of the Cafe du Dome and
New Orleans

134

in fact it stood for Cunningham, he was Cicero forever after (so much so that I haven't put the nickname in quotation marks).

When Spratling and Faulkner went to Paris in 1925, Spratling took Faulkner by Odiorne's cold-water flat in Montparnasse, a sort of New Orleans consulate in Paris, with friends and friends of friends from the Quarter constantly dropping in. Odiorne was doing fashion photography for the Fairchild Magazine Company to pay the bills, and discovering that the murky, atmospheric style he had honed in the courtyards of New Orleans worked just fine with Parisian subject matter. (Harold Levy—another New Orleans friend who dropped by—found the results so striking that he urged Cicero to exhibit his work in New York.) Odiorne and Faulkner hit it off. Faulkner posed for a portrait in the Luxembourg Gardens looking like an Im-

Odiorne photograph of Lyle Saxon's Royal Street courtyard

pressionist painter, and the two took long walks together. "We used to roam the streets at night, from one end of Paris to the other," Cicero recalled in 1950. "We discussed many things (books mostly)."

The Fairchild Company went under in the Depression, so Odiorne came back to the United States in 1932 and opened a commercial studio in New York, where he also worked for the Metropolitan Museum. But things did not go well for him. By 1942 he was back in Chicago, sixty years old and taking pictures for the portrait studio in Goldblatt's Department Store. In the late 1940s he moved to San Francisco, and then, in the mid-1950s, to Los Angeles, where he settled into a furnished room and worked as a retoucher for a Beverly Hills photographic studio. Faulkner was working in Hollywood at the time; one day he and Odiorne ran into each other on the street and found that they didn't have much to say to one another.

Odiorne did stay in touch with a few of his New Orleans friends, although in the 1960s his letters (many of them to Sam Gilmore) began to wander off into strange byways populated by Bilderbergers, Zionists, and "international bankers" (his quotation marks). He worked on his memoirs, but had no luck finding a publisher. It must have been gratifying when, in 1977, his ninety-fifth year, a respected Los Angeles gallery put together an exhibit entitled "Odiorne's Paris." He died the next year.

Louise Jonas Nixon, 70

LIKE GRACE KING AND ALBERT BLEDSOE DINWIDDIE, Mrs. James Oscar Nixon (as she wished to be called in public)—"Mother Nixon" to her younger admirers—was very much an Establishment figure, but one who helped to make the French Quarter Bohemian scene of the 1920s possible.

Louise Jonas was born in 1856, before the War, in Pass Christian, Mississippi, to a distinguished Jewish family. Her grandfather was a Republican assistant postmaster in Quincy, Illinois, and a personal friend of Abe Lincoln, but her father, a cotton factor, served in the Confederate Army, as did four of his brothers (another was a Union officer). Captain Charles H. Jonas, her father, was captured with his unit at Port Hudson in 1863 and imprisoned at Johnson's Island, Ohio, but he was paroled for three weeks by Lincoln himself to visit his dying father. After the War, he returned to his cotton

LE PETIT THEATRE OPENING

MRS. JAMES OSCAR NIXON

business in New Orleans. Her uncle Benjamin Franklin "Frank" Jonas was elected senator from Louisiana in 1879 (the *New York Times* story described him as "a man about 46 years of age, with a well-pronounced Hebrew expression"), and her uncle Samuel wrote "Lines on the Back of a Confederate Note," a poem that became a staple of Lost Cause piety ("Representing nothing on God's earth now, / And naught in the waters below it, / As the pledge of a nation that's dead and gone, / Keep it, dear friends, and show it").

In 1878 Louise married James Oscar Nixon Jr., a promising young lawyer. His father, a New Jersey-born newspaper editor, alderman, and Confederate cavalry colonel, had also been imprisoned at Johnson's Island, although it is not clear whether he met Louise's father there. (Oddly enough, near the end of the War, Colonel Nixon had been paroled as well, to the house of his brother, a bank president in New Jersey.) The young Nixons had four children in rapid succession. When James Oscar died after little more than a decade of marriage, Louise and the children joined a number of other relatives living with her mother-in-law in the Garden District. In 1916, she, Helen Pitkin Schertz, and Rhea Loeb Goldberg began collecting amateur theater-lovers to put on plays in Mrs. Goldberg's Seventh Street house, the Drawing Room Players who became Le Petit Theatre du Vieux Carré when they moved to the lower Pontalba building in 1919. By moving there at that time, and by constructing its new home at the corner of St. Peter and Chartres streets in 1922, "Le Petit" played a role in the revitalization of the Quarter as important as its contributions to the cultural life of New Orleans. "Mother Nixon" was the organization's first president. (About the same time, her daughter Rosalie opened the Paul Morphy Book Shop in the old Morphy house on Royal Street.) In 1925–1926 she was elected one of the first honorary life members of Le Petit Salon, along with Ellsworth Woodward.

Mrs. Nixon was an indomitable spirit. Her career of civic and artistic involvement had almost been interrupted in 1918 when she volunteered, at the age of sixty-two, for war service abroad with the Red Cross. When the American Protective League investigated her loyalty, Elizebeth Werlein was one of her references and gave her a sterling report, but in the event, she did not go. In 1935, aged eighty, she undertook a trip to South America with her daughter and granddaughter, and she continued to serve as Le Petit Theatre's president until her death at ninety.

Her contributions were recognized by more than her selection as a Famous Creole. In 1919 she won the *Times-Picayune* Loving Cup, awarded annually to "men and women who have worked unselfishly for the community without expectation of public recognition or material reward." In 1935 Tulane gave her an honorary doctorate, and in 1947, the year of her death, the New Orleans Federation of Clubs named her a "Woman of the Year."

Richard R. Kirk, 49

RICHARD KIRK LIVED IN A boarding house in the Touro neighborhood, roughly a third of the way from Tulane to the French Quarter. That was just about right: Kirk was an academic with Bohemian connections, not the other way around. His only notable eccentricity was the cane he always carried ("strictly for atmosphere," the *Item* reported). In the mid-1920s Kirk was just hitting his stride as a poet. He was a frequent contributor to the *Double Dealer* and sufficiently part of that scene to have gone on Sherwood Anderson's star-crossed Lake Pontchartrain cruise. His *Penny Wise Verses* (1924) and *A Tallow Dip* (1926) were both were published in minuscule editions but well received by reviewers. One praised what he said was Kirk's unique "sardonic whimsy"; another called him "a craftsman in epigram and gentle irony." In the *Times-Picayune* John McClure (to be sure, an easygoing critic when it came to his friends) said that Kirk was the "one good epigrammatic poet in the United States." A typical example of his verse: "Thrice blessed are our friends: They come, they stay; / And presently they go away."

Kirk was born in St. Clair, Michigan, in 1877, and his English immigrant father died soon after. Kirk and his mother lived with various relatives until

RICHARD KIRK

Kirk left to go to the University of Michigan. He seems to have flourished there, writing verse for the campus humor magazine and the lyrics for the song "A Toast to Michigan" ("Fill your tankards deep with wine, Drink a health to Michigan!"), still sung occasionally by the Michigan Men's Glee Club. Kirk was graduated with the Class of 1903 and stayed on in Ann Arbor for graduate work in English literature. When the United States entered the First World War, he was living in Atlanta and teaching at Georgia Tech. He enlisted in the American Ambulance Corps and served in France, where he won the Croix de Guerre and a Silver Star. He joined the English department at Tulane in 1921.

Although Kirk published another slim volume of poetry, *Short Measures,* in 1943, he spent most of his career as a teacher. He published a textbook and a reading list for undergraduates. As a good teacher should, he encouraged talent when he encountered it, as in the case of the black poet and novelist Margaret Walker (see page 60).

Kirk never lost his ties to his native state. In 1937 Fred Waring and His Pennsylvanians sang "A Toast to Michigan" in the Dick Powell movie *Varsity Show,* giving its lyricist a small film credit and presumably a small fee. At some point Kirk acquired a Michigan summer place that he called "Half a Loaf." He lived there after his retirement until his death in 1951.

Moise Goldstein, 44

THE 1920S WERE BUSY YEARS FOR Moise Goldstein. In uptown New Orleans, the architect designed new gates for Audubon Park, a couple of Mediterranean-style houses, a "Spanish Eclectic" apartment building, and Temple Sinai, in a style described as "Stripped Classical," with Art Deco elements. His firm had done a new Elizabethan science building for Tulane. (N. C. Curtis, his principal designer, would work with Goldstein on many other projects.) On the outskirts of town, Goldstein designed Long Vue, a Colonial Revival estate for philanthropists Edgar Bloom Stern and Edith Rosenwald Stern (a Sears and Roebuck heiress); in the countryside north of Lake Pontchartrain he did an extensive Craftsman-style remodeling of a lodge owned by some Chicago industrialists; and on the Mississippi Gulf Coast, the grandiose, Romanesque, $1.5 million Pine Hills Hotel loomed to his specifications near Pass Christian. While he was at it, he picked up an antebellum cottage in Pass Christian for his family and added a number of cabin outbuildings, including a "pout house" where he could escape when his wife had visitors.

As the variety of styles in that catalog suggests, Goldstein was nothing if not versatile. Earlier he'd built everything from a house described as combining Art Nouveau, Spanish Mission, and Secession-style (one of his very

MOISE GOLDSTEIN

first buildings) to a simple Nantucket cottage (for a Newcomb College potter). When *Famous Creoles* appeared, construction was about to begin on his first skyscraper, a twenty-three-story, $3.5 million, Gothic-Art Deco number for the National American Bank, and he had been retained by the Rosenwald Fund to design a housing project for black New Orleanians (although the Depression came before it could be built).

Goldstein's rise had been a rapid one. He had grown up as the son of a wholesale "notions" merchant, in a household filled with various relatives on St. Charles Avenue. He studied architecture at Tulane, then went north for graduate work at MIT. In 1906 he returned to New Orleans from a *Wanderjahr* in Europe and set up his architectural practice. Not much more than a decade later, he was president of the local chapter of the American Institute of Architects, working with President Dinwiddie and Charles Bein to keep Tulane's financially troubled architecture school afloat, and beginning to receive the important commissions that would turn him from an accomplished architect into a distinguished one.

But his professional achievements are probably not what put him in *Famous Creoles*. Yes, Spratling may have been angling for a job, but Goldstein had actually earned his place among the "artful and crafty." Although he lived with his wife and infant son (and another on the way) out by Audubon Park, he was active in the Arts and Crafts Club, serving on its Executive Committee for a time, and, as an avid amateur painter who had studied (briefly) at the Academy of Rome, he was good enough to show his work at the Club in 1925 in the very good company of William Woodward. Most importantly, he was an early and fervent preservationist. His senior prize essay at Tulane was entitled "The Architecture of Old New Orleans," and in 1915, as head of the local AIA chapter's Preservation Committee, he had suggested that a "vigilance committee" of local residents be recruited to sound the alarm when historic structures were threatened. (And that's precisely what Flo Field did when she noticed a man removing bricks from the Patio Royale. As she recalled it, she immediately telephoned: "Moise, they're taking down the French Quarter!") He also proposed a systematic survey of all the old buildings in New Orleans, although that had to wait. In 1927 a prospectus announced that a volume about the early buildings of New Orleans by Goldstein and Curtis was "shortly to be issued" by the AIA Press; it never appeared, but Curtis's *New Orleans, Its Old Houses, Shops and Public Buildings*, published in 1933, may have originally been intended for it.

Goldstein's first actual architectural work in the Vieux Carré came only in 1929, when he oversaw the restoration of the 1833 Pierre Soulé House. Later he would work on two other antebellum properties in the Quarter. His major projects in the 1930s were for the Sterns, his old clients, who were major benefactors of the new Dillard University. With their support, Goldstein designed the university's Flint-Goodridge Hospital (Art Deco) and its main campus (Beaux Arts). His firm also built the first International Style building in New Orleans, a "New American Home" for the *Times-Picayune*'s centenary. Although Curtis designed that house, Goldstein himself would later do a number of notable Modernist buildings. He and his firm also did extensive work on the Audubon Park zoo, largely paid for with WPA funds he obtained in his role as park commissioner. He continued his association with Tulane's architecture school, teaching part-time and chairing its advisory board, until his retirement in 1961. In 1966, Tulane held a show of sixty years' worth of art by him and his wife, Lois. Most of his work was from his time in Europe, but a 1925 pencil sketch of "Old Man River" recalled his days as a Famous Creole. He died in 1972, and is buried in a tomb of his own design in Metairie Cemetery.

Virginia Parker Nagle, 29

VIRGINIA PARKER WAS ONE OF WHAT Elizabeth Anderson disapprovingly described as "several young girls Sherwood had casually asked along" on his unlucky 1925 Lake Pontchartrain excursion. Sam Gilmore recalled that she and William Faulkner left the party for a while to go "skirmishing around at Mandeville," and Faulkner later wrote her into his novel *Mosquitoes* as the character Dorothy Jameson. The year before, she had returned to her native New Orleans from a season in Europe, after some years of study at the Pennsylvania Academy of the Fine Arts, where she won two prizes, one a traveling scholarship that had paid for an earlier European trip. While a student at PAFA, she had been showing work at the annual spring shows of the Delgado Museum in New Orleans, and as soon as she came back she put her work in a group show (with six other Famous Creoles, among others) at the

VIRGINIA PARKER NAGEL

Arts and Crafts Club. Beginning in 1924, she taught a very popular Saturday morning life class at the Club, and a joint exhibit with Spratling and Will Henry Stevens was, one newspaper said, "the talk of the town." The New Orleans papers extensively reviewed her work, for the most part very favorably (especially her portraits, figure work, and European landscapes—her more "modernistic" compositions puzzled some reviewers).

As the niece of Louisiana's governor, Miss Parker frequently appeared in the society pages as well. Her mother was a woman with some artistic credentials herself—the author of a book-length "dramatic poem" and a history of Louisiana—whose father had helped to erect the statue of Robert E. Lee on Lee Circle (the Lee daughters had been visitors in their home). Virginia's father, the governor's brother, was in the grocery business and did well enough to support the family in the Garden District, but he killed himself in 1908, and his widow had to take in boarders for a time to make ends meet. The hard times didn't last, however; Virginia's mother went with her on a trip to the Far East in 1920, as well as on her two European visits. By 1924 this eligible young lady had found an admirer, a young artist named Edward Pierce Nagle, who had been at Harvard with Harold Levy and moved in the same circles there (although he dropped out before graduation). In 1925 the couple visited Edward's mother and stepfather at their country place in Maine, and by the next year they were married, just in time for Virginia's picture in *Famous Creoles* to be labeled with her married name.

The marriage was an unfortunate one. When Nagle was a boy, his mother, Isabel, had left her husband to become the mistress, model, muse, and eventually the wife of the French-American sculptor Gaston Lachaise—but that's another story. In the early 1920s, Edward had shown some promise, placing a few drawings in the *Dial* and his paintings in various exhibitions, but he was never able to make a living. Lachaise was barely a decade older than Edward, but he was a devoted stepfather, writing scores of letters, offering sound career advice, and sending a great deal of money to a young man described by one of his own friends as having "very little talent but plenty of temperament."

After their marriage, the couple lived in Washington, New York, and Philadelphia. By 1932, however, they had settled in Charlottesville, Virginia. Soon after that, Edward began to show signs of mental instability. He would

Portrait of her husband, by Virginia Parker Nagle.

be institutionalized several times, the last time for good. (He died in 1963.) In 1936, Virginia started divorce proceedings. After the divorce, she returned to her maiden name and she apparently worked in drafting to support herself. She had a solo show at a respected New York gallery in the late 1930s and later contributed to a group show in Washington, but she never fulfilled her early promise. She died in 1976 in Alexandria, Virginia, but it is nice to think that she might still have been in Charlottesville when Faulkner came to the University of Virginia in 1957 as a writer in residence, and that the two got together to reminisce about "skirmishing around at Mandeville."

Frederick Oechsner, 24

FREDERICK OECHSNER'S FATHER WAS A physician, the son of German immigrants who had settled in the French Quarter, and his middle name was Cable because his mother was kin to novelist George Washington Cable and proud of it. Frederick went to prep school in New England, then came back to Tulane, where (as the yearbook put it) he "withstood the attack of the law and emerged still holding great enthusiasm for the arts." After graduation he passed the bar, but took a job reporting for the *New Orleans Item* and later the *Morning Tribune* as well, where his beat came to include the Vieux Carré cultural scene. One roundup of artistic news in 1926 mentioned the activities of five Famous Creoles and was illustrated with a sketch by another.

The cub reporter became part of that scene himself, a regular at the Andersons' evenings and one of Sherwood's admiring acolytes. His role as leading man in Flo Field's play *A la Creole* (which he also plugged in a newspaper

Portrait by Pops Whitesell

FREDERICK OECHSNER
YOUNG LOCHINVAR WITH A CAP PISTOL

story) may have sparked his lifelong interest in drama: the *Time-Picayune* said his performance "leaves nothing to be desired," adding, "He's a young man with a very genuine sense of the poetry of acting, a romantic touch light and charming." But Oechsner's ambitions lay elsewhere. As a seventeen-year-old he had worked his way to Europe on a tramp steamer, the start of an international career that would eventually take him to fifty-two countries and teach him to speak five languages and read several others.

In 1927 he jumped at the chance to report on Central America for the *Item-Tribune*. He went on to Italy, then France, then back to Washington, then Berlin. Working for the United Press in London in 1933, he picked up an English accent, which he kept, and an English wife, which he didn't. He went on to head the UP bureau in Berlin, where he interviewed Hitler and other top Nazis. His fellow Tulane alumnus Howard K. Smith worked for him and described him as "an unreconstructed Southern rebel" who agreed to be president of Berlin's Foreign Press Association only after Foreign Minister von Ribbentrop made it clear that he didn't want him in the job.

By 1941 Oeschner was running all of UP's Central European operations and reporting the war from Berlin for the *New Yorker* and other publications. When Germany declared war on the United States, he and four of his colleagues were interned for several months. They used the time to write *This Is the Enemy,* a book published after their release in 1942. Oechsner returned to the United States as an expert on Hitler and the Nazis and he shared with the readers of *Time* the news that Hitler's nose had been cut down by a plastic surgeon and that a doctor close to the führer said that he exhibited "strong homosexual traits." These assertions should probably be taken with a grain of salt, since Oechsner's next job was working for "Wild Bill" Donovan as director of the "black" propaganda division of the Office of Strategic Services. He served in Europe, North Africa, and Egypt, and wound up in charge of psychological warfare under General Eisenhower.

In 1945 he was married again, to Olga Said-Ruete, daughter of an anti-Nazi German journalist and great-granddaughter of the Sultan of Zanzibar by a Circassian concubine. He returned briefly to journalism, but interviewing Juan Perón and covering the Nuremberg trials (where Ribbentrop and some of the other defendants recognized him from the old days) lacked a certain frisson, so he joined the Foreign Service and served in a series of suspiciously interesting postings in eastern Europe and Latin America, possibly putting his enthusiasm for acting to work in a different sphere until he retired in 1962.

In retirement he kept up an active schedule of traveling and lecturing. He moved to Florida in 1969, where he resumed his involvement with community theater, married for a third time in the mid-1970s, and died in 1992.

Joseph Woodson "Pops" Whitesell, 50

EVEN IN A SETTING KNOWN for characters, photographer Pops Whitesell stood out. Newspaper and magazine articles invariably described him as "tiny," "elfin," "a gnomelike little fellow," "barely over a hundred pounds," "a leprechaun." In cold weather he might wear a half-dozen shirts, jackets, or sweaters at once, and he didn't trust banks: "My bank account is always on my hip," he said. He was a great fan of mystery novels, and also of western movies, which he went to see as often as several times a week—although he usually fell asleep before the previews were over. An inveterate tinkerer, he was always looking for different ways to do things (Spratling showed him pulling his camera on a wagon) and he devised everything from a shower bath to soles for his shoes. His studio on St. Peter Street was full of ingenious contraptions, including one that let him see from the toilet who was at the door, and his fellow photographers looked with wonder at his complicated, jury-rigged enlarger. Once a day he had a roast beef sandwich (one

MR. WHITESELL
THE ROYAL STREET PHOTOGRAPHER

thin slice) and a 7-Up with salt at a restaurant a few yards from his studio; other than that, having read something about yoga, he ate nuts. Pops didn't smoke or drink, but he had an aspirin habit.

Miss Elinor Bright, in the Junior League Review.

His bread and butter work was portraits of Mardi Gras royalty, brides, and socialites like the Junior League officers he photographed for Junior League Review programs in the mid-1920s. "He could carve thirty pounds of heft off a Mardi Gras queen effortlessly and imperceptibly," a profile after his death explained. Pops also shot portraits of his friends, including at least ten Famous Creoles, visiting celebrities like mystery writer Erle Stanley Gardner (who put Pops in two of his novels as "Gramps Wiggins"), and some dreamy young men of the Quarter. He did street scenes, landscapes, and "tableaux" (carefully posed humorous shots or Norman Rockwell-like scenes) both commercially and for his own amusement. His technique was unorthodox, but he was an expert manipulator of prints—dodging, burning, retouching, cutting and pasting. After someone pointed out that the subjects of one tableau were smoking but had no ashtrays, he put some in.

Pirate's Alley

Pops was born and grew up on an Indiana farm, which he didn't like to talk about. As a teenager he paid a studio photographer in Terre Haute to teach him the craft, and then set out on his own, working in a dozen or more Indiana and Illinois towns in the next few years. When he was in his forties, in 1918, he moved to New Orleans, where he had been offered a studio job. He liked the town, but not the job, and went into business for himself, trying several locations before he set up his apartment and studio in the slave quarters behind a charming old building, where he filled the courtyard with flowering plants and ferns, and goldfish in an old sugar vat (which he took inside one day "because it was raining").

Pops stayed in his St. Peter Street quarters for nearly forty years, until his death. He continued his portrait work in the 1930s, and began to receive some recognition as an art photographer. In 1929 he went to the Yucatan with one of Frans Blom's Tulane expeditions, and took some photographs that he showed at the Arts and Crafts Club. He also showed his work at the Delgado Museum. But real success came after Pops announced in 1943 that in ten years he planned to be one of the world's top-ranking "salon photographers." (Salon photographers were ranked by the number of their pictures shown at officially recognized "salon exhibitions.") Five years later, he was ranked number nine. He had a one-man show at the Smithsonian, was named a "Master Photographer" by the Professional Photographers Association, and was sent on a twenty-three-city lecture tour by the Photographic Society of America.

Always unconventional, Pops grew more eccentric with age. His upstairs neighbor, a fellow photographer who was his protégé, benefactor, and friend for nearly three decades, stepped in when unpaid bills and unfinished commissions reached critical levels. In 1953, Pops lost his leg after he treated a sore himself (with sandpaper). Although his friends chipped in to buy an artificial leg, Pops tinkered with it until it was virtually useless. He died in 1958 and was buried near his family in Indiana.

Fanny Craig Ventadour, 29

FANNY CRAIG WAS BORN IN YAZOO CITY, Mississippi, where her father was a cotton broker. One of his great-uncles had been a U.S. and Confederate congressman, another was a Confederate general, and her mother's father was a Confederate colonel, although he'd been born in Pennsylvania. (His name, Eshleman, common among German Jews, has led to speculation that his granddaughter was among the Famous Creoles of Jewish descent, but it is found as often among the Pennsylvania Dutch and, in any case, the man was on the vestry at Christ Episcopal Church for twenty-seven years.) Fanny's mother was also named Fanny and was an artist and writer, too.

When young Fanny was six, her father committed suicide and her widowed mother moved the family to live with *her* widowed mother (yet another Fanny, as was *her* mother) in the Garden District, which later made it convenient for the youngest Fanny to attend Newcomb College, where she studied art with Ellsworth Woodward and won two prizes for her work. She went on to join the New Orleans contingent at the Pennsylvania Academy of the Fine Arts, but she was back in New Orleans by 1921, teaching and paint-

MADAME FANNIE CRAIG VENTADOUR

Portrait by Pops Whitesell

ing portraits in her studio on the top floor of the old Presbytere on Jackson Square, and showing her work in shows at the Delgado Museum and the Artists' Guild gallery on Royal Street. "Her work belongs in the extremely modern school," one commentator observed, but it was to become even more modern after 1922, when she went to visit Paris and stayed on to study at the Montparnasse atelier of the Cubist painter and sculptor André Lhote. When she returned briefly to New Orleans and showed some new work at the Arts and Crafts Club, the *Item*'s society columnist was "startled" to encounter "a large brown woman scantily clad (to speak guardedly) and holding in one hand a broken papia [*sic*] or some such South Sea fruit." (When the reporter ventured that "the head is so small and sort of pointed—out of proportion to the large stout legs—there's the suggestion of a pyramid—" her companion remarked, "It's a new school, you know.")

Fanny soon returned to Paris, where three of her pictures had been accepted for the annual Salon exhibit and where, six months later, she married Jacques Ventadour at the American Church. Before Fanny came along, Ventadour had taught a Sorbonne student named Cornelia Otis Skinner to tango; a few years later, he became a stalwart in the Comintern-inspired League Against Imperialism. (Fanny's marriage may have ended some sort of romantic relationship with Weeks Hall.) Although Fanny took French citizenship immediately, she stayed a part of the Vieux Carré scene for the next few years, returning for three visits, bringing her new daughter with her in 1925, and showing several pictures in the 1927 Arts and Crafts Club show.

In the 1930s Fanny sent a few more pictures to be shown at the Club, but she herself did not return until 1937, after her husband died. Although she sent her two children to stay in safety with her mother during World War II, she remained in France throughout the Occupation. Given that she shared her late husband's left-wing politics, one might wonder why. She never said anything about working for Allied intelligence, but she did have useful language skills—fluency in French, Spanish, and German—and the man who was later her boss in the North American service of Radiodiffusion Française, the poet Pierre Emmanuel, was active in the Resistance.

Somewhere along the way, she stopped painting and took up writing. Besides working for French radio, she turned her hand to journalism, covering the world of postwar haute couture. In the mid-1950s, she returned to the United States, where she married playwright Howard Southgate, settled in Winter Park, Florida, and pursued a new career as a poet. Her poems appeared in a great many little magazines, and she published two collections of them. She also became a peace activist, proud to have been threatened with arrest (in her seventies) for protesting the Viet Nam War at the Winter Park Sidewalk Art Festival. After her second husband died in 1971, she lived on in Winter Park, the last surviving Famous Creole, until her death (at 101) in 1998.

Roark Bradford, 30

AFTER HIS DISCHARGE FROM THE ARMY in 1920, Roark Bradford went to work for newspapers in Georgia and Louisiana and married his former high school English teacher before coming to the *New Orleans Times-Picayune,* where he soon became editor of the Sunday edition. On the side, he had been writing fiction, and not having any luck selling it. His stories tended to be set in exotic places he'd never been, but when he wrote one about a Negro fisherman he'd seen sleeping on the riverbank, with a bell on his line to wake him up if he got a bite, it sold immediately. So he started cranking out "darky" stories. When one published in *Harper's* won the O. Henry Award in 1927 (Ernest Hemingway came in second) Bradford's New Orleans friends threw a "Bringing-Home-the-Bacon Party."

Bradford said he based his fiction on what he'd heard from three of his childhood playmates and from old "Uncle Wes," back on his family's cotton plantation near Nankipoo, Tennessee. He also studied (after a fashion) black life in Louisiana, spending many hours standing on Rampart Street, just

ROARK BRADFORD
Story-Teller

Detail from *Famous Creoles*

"Bringing Home the Bacon"

Keith Temple cartoon on party invitation.

watching, and going to services at a Baptist church across the river in Algiers where the preacher was an evangelist widely known as "the Black Billy Sunday." When Bradford wrote some of what the *New York Times* called "charmingly garbled episodes from the Old Testament," the *World* was eager to publish them. He had hit on a popular formula—a good thing, because about this time he lost his job at the newspaper. Of necessity, he became what he'd wanted to be all along: a full-time writer of short stories and novels.

Bradford and his wife, Lydia, lived in the Pontalba apartments and Bradford became particular friends with John McClure and Lyle Saxon, his coworkers at the *Times-Picayune*. In Lafayette, he had written newspaper stories about Hy Boudreaux, a Cajun who could charm fish and hypnotize hens to lay double-yolk eggs. (When an LSU professor wrote the editor to protest that this was impossible, Bradford said that Hy threatened to hypnotize the prof and make *him* lay a double-yolk egg.) This sort of tall-tale-telling continued in New Orleans: Saxon and Bradford enjoyed making up stories about Annie Christmas, a legendary giant river woman Saxon claimed to have invented out of whole cloth and presented deadpan as "Louisiana folklore" in his newspaper column. (The deception, if that's what it was, continues on the Internet to this day.)

Bradford struck pay dirt in 1928 when some of his Old Testament dialect stories with titles like "The Adulteration of Old King David" and "Nigger Deemus" were published as *Ol' Man Adam an' His Chillun.* Playwright Marc Connelly adapted the book for a Broadway play, *The Green Pastures.* (Connelly changed De Lawd's race: In Bradford's stories, he was an old-time white planter.) The play opened in 1930, ran for 640 performances, won a Pulitzer Prize, and was made into a movie in 1936.

Just as Bradford was becoming a wealthy and famous author, however, Lydia contracted tuberculosis, and the Bradfords moved to the Southwest for her health. A few years later, in 1933, *Time* magazine took notice when Bradford got a Mexican divorce from Lydia, a "longtime tuberculosis patient in Arizona," and married Mary Rose Himler, a former editor at Bobbs-Merrill and "mother of his year-old son." After Bradford and his new wife returned to New Orleans, the couple ran a salon of sorts in their house on Toulouse Street (although Mary Rose's opposition to alcohol meant that they served only coffee) and Bradford wrote a play called *Lousy with Charm,* about the French Quarter scene. When it was staged in 1937, the *Times-Picayune* reviewer observed, "Into his series of sketches, strung upon a meager plot, he threw garbage cans, art, marihuana, tourists, balconcies [*sic*], race horse tips and absinthe frappes." Among the characters were a termite exterminator, a WPA rat catcher, two Negro nuns, an art instructor and six students, a tour guide, and six Midwestern tourists (one played by Mary Rose).

But Bradford's ties to New Orleans were wearing thin. He was doing much of his writing in a cabin on his brother Richard's plantation near Bossier City (the setting of some of his later stories), and he and Mary Rose began to spend more and more time at a place they had bought in Santa Fe as a summer home. After Pearl Harbor, Bradford served with the navy in French West Africa during World War II, where he contracted a parasitic disease from which he died in 1948. His ashes were scattered over the Mississippi.

Bradford's attempts to write serious novels—one about white mountaineers and two about black life—were commercially unsuccessful, although he was elected to the National Institute of Arts and Letters shortly before his death. For obvious reasons his literary reputation has not fared well since then. The critic Lewis Simpson got it just about right when he observed that Bradford's stories "are clearly now significant only in the historical sociology of American literature."

John McClure, 33

WHEN JACK MCCLURE GOT OUT OF THE ARMY in 1919, he and his wife, Grace, moved to New Orleans, where they opened Ye Olde Book Shop on Royal Street, in the not-yet-fashionable French Quarter. McClure also took on the editorship of the *Southerner,* a new "magazine of the New South" that folded after only four issues. Undiscouraged, he tried the magazine business again in 1921, joining Julius Weis Friend and Basil Thompson as a founding editor of the *Double Dealer,* where he contributed verse, book reviews, at least one short story, a number of essays, three "dramatic fantasies" set in classical Cairo, and an element of literary seriousness—although Friend commented later that the "facetious note" he and Thompson favored was "patiently unvetoed by McClure." He also accepted one of William Faulkner's poems—Faulkner's first publication—and reviewed a collection of Faulkner's poetry, *The Marble Faun*—probably Faulkner's first review. McClure thought the volume of poems "failed, but with real honor," and that Faulkner was "a Southern poet from whom we shall hear a great deal in future."

To make ends meet, McClure also took a day job as a copyreader at the *Times-Picayune,* where he soon became editor of the Sunday book page and took over the book review column from Lyle Saxon. He prevailed on the newspaper to print some of Faulkner's stories and sketches, and the young

JOHN MCCLURE
Ballad-Maker

Detail from *Famous Creoles*

Mississippian started hanging out with McClure and his *Times-Picayune* colleague Roark Bradford, often going with them to a cabaret to hear the jazz clarinetist George "Georgia Boy" Boyd or for Roquefort cheese sandwiches and Cuban beer at a place on Rampart Street run by Tom Anderson, a man reputed to control the city's red-light district. When H. L. Mencken came to visit, McClure took him to Anderson's café. McClure and Natalie Scott were among the pioneers in French Quarter real-estate investment, turning a building near the cathedral into studios for rent and apartments for themselves.

McClure had a genuinely winning personality. A sketch in the *New Orleanian* called him "the kindest man that ever wielded a pen," and the Harlem Renaissance writer Jean Toomer, who corresponded with him at the *Double Dealer,* wrote something in a letter to which Sherwood Anderson replied, "You are right about McClure. He is the real thing—one of the most fundamentally sweet men I've seen." He was especially gentle and encouraging with beginning writers. A young colleague at the *Times-Picayune* remembered him as "free of cant and jealousy," adding, "I never knew anyone so eager to encourage a cub by putting his byline on a story at the slightest excuse," and James Feibleman recalled sitting for hours on the McClures' balcony, drinking Mrs. McClure's eggnog and discussing poetry, while McClure smoked his corncob pipe. By the time *Famous Creoles* appeared, McClure had become an important figure in New Orleans literary circles. But literary journalism, however distinguished, was something of a letdown for someone from whom greater things had been expected.

Born in Ardmore, Indian Territory, in 1893, McClure was the grandson of a Confederate captain on one side and a Methodist college president on the other. His mother died when he was three, and he grew up under the influence of a stepmother who had studied voice in Italy and wrote a volume of verse about her childhood that led her obituary to call her "the poet historian of rural Arkansas." McClure worked his way through the University of Oklahoma, his college career marked by a campus romance with Muna Lee (later well known as a poet, feminist, and Latin Americanist) and a year off tramping in Germany and France. After his graduation in 1915, he continued his tramping, logging over two thousand miles in the Southwest (a sketch said that he belonged to "the national hobo fraternity, 'Quo Vadis'"). He also worked in the university library, where he met Grace, a librarian from the Midwest a few years older than he, whom he married after he was drafted in 1918. (The war ended before he got overseas.)

Meanwhile, McClure was writing poetry, some of which came to the attention of Mencken, who praised it extravagantly—McClure, he said, was "the best lyric poet the United States has produced in fifty years"—and published much of it in the *Smart Set*. In fact, McClure had more poems in Mencken's magazine than any other author. (His college flame, Muna Lee, was second). In the preface to *Airs and Ballads*, a 1918 collection of his poems, McClure thanked Mencken for his friendship, and he dedicated a selection of "convivial and merry verse" called *The Stag's Hornbook* to the Sage of Baltimore.

Not everyone shared Mencken's enthusiasm. A 1918 survey volume called *Our Poets of Today* put McClure in some very good company, but called him a "youthful writer of modest airs," and damned him with faint praise for his "lyrical charm," calling him "a singer, a 'troubadour'—and perhaps well content to remain one." Nevertheless, as the 1920s began, McClure was not just promising, but already accomplished.

In 1930, an article about McClure lamented the fact that someone who was possibly "New Orleans' greatest literary man" had stopped writing poetry, but reported that "for years, the tale goes, he has been writing at seven books" and "now, at last, one of these is completed and on its way to publication." But it never appeared.

McClure treasured his wife, Grace, as "a thoughtful and heroic helpmeet" (although he recalled that she was "not very literary"), and when she died in 1933 at the age of forty-three he was devastated; twenty years later he wrote, "I love her as much in death as I did in life." In 1937, he was remarried, to an old friend, interior decorator Joyce Stagg, an Orleans Alley neighbor since the days when she used to visit Spratling and Faulkner for breakfast and was in love with Conrad Albrizio. Toward the end of his life McClure claimed to have stopped reading just about everything except the racing news, which he read for the horses' names ("Desert Battle, by Canter, out of Tremendous, by Shifting Sands," for instance, or "Ardent, by Broomstick, out of Heart's Desire"). He also claimed that he had never read *Mosquitoes*, which seems at least equally unlikely. McClure continued to work for the *Times-Picayune* in various capacities until two years before his death, at age sixty-two, in 1956. The pallbearers at his funeral included his old colleagues from the *Double Dealer*, Julius Friend and Albert Goldstein.

Charles Bein, 35

CHARLES BEIN WAS A BLOND six-footer who was listed among the "Popular Bachelors of New Orleans" by *New Orleans Life* in 1927. The magazine's one-line comment, however, was, "Preoccupied with the arts." As director of the Arts and Crafts Club's New Orleans Art School, "Uncle Charlie" (as some of his students called him) was very much a part of the French Quarter scene, but every night he went home to a house near Audubon Park that he shared with his mother, his sister, and his aunt, as he'd done since his days as a Tulane student, when the family boarded a couple of other students as well. (Bein's father, a freight agent, had died a few years earlier.)

Bein was a New Orleanian, born and bred. At the centenary celebration of the Battle of New Orleans, he had been one of the dancers who performed a "Varsouvienne" in period costume. (Caroline Wogan—later, Durieux—was another). Since there was no art program for men in New Orleans at the

CHARLES BIEN

time, he studied architecture at Tulane, then went on to Columbia University School of Architecture and classes at the Art Students League, before heading to Munich and Paris to study, then to Spain, Italy, and Tangiers to paint. (While he was abroad, he was joined by his mother and sister. They were also with him—so was his aunt—a decade later when he returned from a working trip to Europe and North Africa.) Along the way, Bein studied privately with William Woodward.

In 1917 Bein took a job as assistant professor of architecture at Tulane (replacing N. C. Curtis, who had left for a position at Illinois). Bein acted as head of the school for three years, very difficult ones for it financially. He began to teach classes at the Arts and Crafts Club before it was even officially organized, and when its art school opened he became director of an institution with finances even more precarious than those of his former employer. When enrollment exceeded expectations in 1931, an officer of the school wrote, "For the first time in years I find Mr. Bein in a good humor."

Over the years Bein taught everything from architecture to advanced commercial art, watercolor to art history and appreciation. After he showed some of his Mediterranean work at the Club, he sent it on to a New York gallery for an exhibit in 1924. A show at the Club the next year included work from a return visit to the Mediterranean, but also recent pictures from Louisiana, where he was beginning to concentrate his attention. He spent the summer of 1926 in the Teche country, probably at the plantation house of his colleague Weeks Hall. The work he did then is among what the *Chicago Daily News* was referring to when it said Bein's work showed the "peculiar heavy luxuriance of the bayous" and "nature's own setting for the simple and emotional Negro." The luxuriance was certainly evident in *Cypress Swamp*, the Blanche Benjamin Prize winner in 1927, and the Negro probably figured in one called *Baptism* exhibited at the Arts and Crafts Club the next year. But it wasn't all work and no play. The *States* correspondent covering the 1927 Bal des Artistes reported, in a run-down of memorable costumes: "Charlie Bein was a baby. Can you imagine that lanky Charlie as an infant?"

Bein was one of the many Famous Creoles attracted to Mexico, and he took two trips there, including one in 1930 with some other New Orleanians to the budding artists' colony in Orizaba. In the mid-1930s his mother and his aunt died, and his sister moved to a place of her own. Soon after, he stepped down from his directorship at the art school, and he seems to have lived quietly thereafter. Unlike some artists, he wasn't afraid to pack it in; in 1959 he listed his occupation on a British entry document as "retired." He died in New Orleans in 1966.

Marc Antony and
Lucille Godchaux Antony, both 28

MARC ANTONY AND LUCILLE GODCHAUX were secretly married in Paris in 1923. The marriage thrilled New Orleans newspaper readers when it was revealed a few months later. It was literally front-page news in the *Item,* which gushed, "They met and longed in the old quarter, and the Paris moon, reminding them of the bronze glory above the Pontalba buildings, did the rest."

But Miss Godchaux's parents were less delighted with this Vieux Carré romance. Lucille's father was a wealthy man who had inherited several sugar plantations (one about thirty miles upriver from New Orleans was home to the largest sugar refinery in the United States), a Jewish philanthropist honored with a stained glass window in a Roman Catholic church that he had paid to renovate. The Godchaux family lived on St. Charles Avenue with a butler and chauffeur. Marc Antony's father was a mere building contractor, who lived in 1920 with his family in a rented

Front-page photos in the *Item*

By
THE LEONARDI STUDIOS, SAINT PETER STREET

168

house in a lower-middle-class neighborhood of Covington. By the time of the clandestine marriage, Marc himself had moved to a shotgun house in the Gentilly Terrace neighborhood of New Orleans.

Both young people were aspiring artists. Lucille had studied art at Radcliffe and briefly at the Art Students League in New York, while Marc had attended the Art Institute of Chicago and worked with the stage designer for the Chicago Grand Opera. He came back to New Orleans as stage designer for Le Petit Theatre and by 1922 he was teaching at the Arts and Crafts Club. Lucille and Marc moved in the same circles and it was inevitable that they would meet. Both went to Europe in the summer of 1923—she to study art, he to study stage design—and when they returned (on separate ships) they were man and wife. Sherwood Anderson's wife, Elizabeth, wrote that she and the Antonys opened a decorating shop together to make some money because Lucille "was completely cut off from the family fortune" (for a while at least)—although a 1921 story in the *Item* had already mentioned "the Mark Anthony [sic] man who has that fascinating batik shop down by the Cathedral" as among the interesting people one could meet at the Arts and Crafts Club.

In any event, by 1924 Elizabeth, Marc, and Lucille were running the Leonardi Studios and the Antonys were part of the Andersons' circle. Sherwood's biographer reports that Lucille and Anderson "took long afternoon walks, while he talked about his work in progress." The Antonys were on the famous Lake Pontchartrain boat ride that Anderson organized. In 1925 they were featured in an *Item-Tribune* story on artists' studios in the Quarter, and they had at least a couple of

The Leonardi Studios
INTERIOR
DECORATORS
Craftworkers

BATIKS—HOOKED RUG LAMPS
SHADES—ANTIQUES PURCHASED
RESTORED AND UPHOLSTERED
IN THE CORRECT PERIOD

520 ST. PETER STREET
NEW ORLEANS, LA.

Advertisement in 1923 edition of *A Walk through Frenchtown in Old New Orleans*, by Helen Pitkin Schertz.

joint exhibitions at the Arts and Crafts Club. Marc was on the Club's Executive Committee, he was teaching courses in "Color and Design (Commercial Art)" and wood engraving, and he joined a number of other New Orleans painters in putting together a collection for exhibit in Jackson, Mississippi. He also ran tours of the French Quarter for conventioneers and once hired

Bill Faulkner for $10 to do one for him. Faulkner was a great success, Marc said later, because he made up gruesome stories about all the buildings.

Lucille's career as a painter may have been going less well—one reviewer said that "a rather cubistic picture of figures in oil [was] notable if only to give cause for wonder that one should bother to paint and preserve a thing so distressing"—but the couple's interests were moving away from painting anyway. The *Item-Tribune* reported in 1925 that Marc "has abandoned the-atrical work, devoting himself almost exclusively to interior decoration and craft work," and when the Leonardi Studios moved that year to one of Nat-alie Scott's properties, across from Le Petit Theatre, Marc was selling batik and "decorative work" while Lucille was showing "carved and painted wood, in trays, boxes and in wall panels," as well as some of her paintings. In the new quarters, the shop was on the ground floor, while Marc and Lucille lived on the third, with Spratling and Faulkner in the attic apartment. (The fron-tispiece of *Famous Creoles* shows the authors and Marc *in situ.*)

Detail from "The Locale":

THE LOCALE, WHICH INCLUDES MRS. FLO FIELD

By 1930 Marc was becoming established as an interior decorator, while Lu-cille—perhaps seeing where real opportunity in the Quarter now lay—listed her occupation in the census as "Saleslady/Real Estate." In the 1940s Marc helped to restore the eighteenth-century house on Royal Street that now houses the Historic New Orleans Collection and he painted murals of the old Cabildo and Presbytere for the Gumbo Shop when it moved into another eighteenth-century building on St. Peter Street. Eventually the couple came to run Marc Antony Interior Designers, on St. Charles Avenue (outside the Quarter), which the *Times-Picayune* called in 1972 "one of the most promi-nent interior design firms in the city."

The Antonys were among the few in their circle who maintained their friendship with Sherwood Anderson after his divorce and remarriage, vis-iting him and his new wife at their home in southwest Virginia and at least once vacationing with them. In 1958 their 331 Gallery on Chartres Street had a show of silver designed by William Spratling (who returned from Taxco for the opening).

Lucille died in 1967, Marc in 1979. They are buried together in Metairie Cemetery in New Orleans.

Elizebeth Werlein, 39

THE LABEL ON SPRATLING'S SKETCH of Elizebeth Werlein, "Czarina of the Movies," refers to her work as in-house censor for the Saenger theater chain, but that job didn't even begin to define her. Elizebeth's friends described her as "six feet tall, blonde, and cultural," a "soignée" woman with "a yen for intellectuals." Born in Michigan, she was the daughter of a wealthy Union army veteran who owned a dynamite factory. When she was fifteen, she was sent to Paris to pursue her interest in becoming an opera singer. She abandoned that plan, but in her eight years abroad she took up Theosophy, hunted in Russia and Africa, met royalty, was briefly engaged to an English nobleman, and ballooned around Europe. She took her first airplane flight in 1908 and went on to be one of the first women to be licensed as a pilot. About the same time, on a visit to New Orleans, she fell in love with one of the city's most eligible bachelors, Philip Werlein, who ran the New Orleans music store and publishing house founded by his grandfather, a Bavarian immigrant. (In 1861, P. P. Werlein had printed the first sheet music for "Dixie.") The couple were married in a matter of months.

CZARINA OF THE MOVIES

From a glass-plate negative by Pops Whitesell

With a husband who was a prominent businessman (and also state chair-man of the Democratic Party), Elizabeth threw herself into good works and civic activism with her customary energy. She hired an instructor to teach her to sew so that she could teach sewing at a settlement school; she raised money for a kindergarten to serve a poor white neighborhood; she helped to organize the Philharmonic Society and gave generously to the symphony orchestra. But she didn't limit her activities to those befitting her social standing. She also wrote articles and stories for newspapers and magazines, and worked tirelessly for the Louisiana Woman Suffrage Party. Her emancipation was evidenced by the ever-present cigarette that Spratling drew in her hand. (One of her rivals in the suffrage movement was distressed to see her not only light up in public, but blow smoke out her nose.) The lifelong activity on behalf of the French Quarter that put her in *Famous Creoles* had begun as early as 1916, when she wrote *The Wrought Iron Railings of Le Vieux Carré New Orleans,* calling for greater efforts to preserve "the sacred confines of the old quarter."

Philip's early death in 1917 left Elizabeth with four young children and a modest settlement (her mother-in-law, with whom she didn't get along, kept the business) but didn't slow her down. The First World War involved her in a great many new committees and campaigns, and after the passage of the Nineteenth Amendment she went hither and yon for meetings and conferences as first president of the state League of Women Voters. Her involvement with the Quarter intensified. In 1919 she founded the Quartier Club, which brought society women to its clubhouse in the lower Pontalba building for luncheons, dinner dances, and edifying lectures. She crossed paths with other Famous Creoles in Le Petit Theatre's productions and at the Arts and Crafts Club.

When ill-advised investments in German marks wiped out much of her savings in the early 1920s, she took the job as Saenger's censor, but she continued to live in a fashionable neighborhood near Audubon Park. In 1926, however, she bought and began to restore an old house on St. Ann Street in the Quarter.

In the 1930s Werlein was distracted from the French Quarter only briefly by her activities in opposition to Governor Huey Long and in support of FDR. In 1932 the *States* reported that she was "czarina" of an art show at Jackson Square, and for a time she worked in the Cabildo, restoring paintings owned by the Louisiana State Museum. But her real interest was in conserving and restoring the buildings of the Quarter. She organized a campaign to amend the state constitution to give the ineffectual Vieux Carré Commission (founded in 1925) enforcement powers. In 1936 she moved into her house in the Quarter, then founded and became president of the Vieux Carré Property Owners Association, which agitated to make the commission use those new powers. Her unceasing and successful efforts were honored when the American Institute of Architects made her an honorary member in 1942. Local businessmen, she said, had patted "me on the back, [telling] me I was a nice girl, who didn't know that 'progress' meant destruction of old buildings," but they had sadly misjudged her. It's not surprising that she found a kindred spirit in her son-in-law, the perennially crusading journalist Hodding Carter.

Werlein's cigarette habit finally caught up with her in 1946: she died of lung cancer and was buried in New Orleans.

Marian Draper, 20

MARIAN DRAPER WAS THE YOUNGEST of the Famous Creoles, but she had already led an eventful life. She was born in St. Louis in 1906, the only child of a hardware salesman and an aspiring artist. Within a few years her parents had separated, and by 1920 Marian had moved with her mother to Los Angeles, to live with her mother's parents, who had retired there. Somehow, three years later, the seventeen-year-old Marian was dancing in the Ziegfeld Follies. But she turned her back on Broadway and she and her mother moved to New Orleans where (although her parents did not reunite) her father was living. It was said in New Orleans that the New York critics had deemed her a worthy successor to Gilda Grey, the Follies dancer who had popularized the shimmy, but she told a New Orleans newspaper that "she saw in stage life only vapid, evanescent glory, inevitably unsatisfying," and enrolled in architecture school at Tulane.

The former showgirl seems to have been a good student. She won a scholarship awarded

MARIAN DRAPER

"The Girl Cheerleader of Tulane."

175

every year to the most promising sophomore, and a newspaper story noted that William Spratling, "well-known architect of N.O.," had praised her work, and added that "she is paying for college by dancing, having just finished a weekly engagement at a local club." She was also studying painting at the Arts and Crafts Club, and when it had an exhibit of student work from the summer program run by Daniel Whitney at the Ocean Springs Art Colony, in Mississippi, the *Morning Tribune*'s reviewer observed that "'Shady Lane' by Marian Draper is an excellent rendering of a difficult subject."

Meanwhile, at Tulane, Marian quickly became a star on campus when she was enlisted as a cheerleader. She was not the first female college cheerleader, as one historian claims—she wasn't even the first at Tulane—but females were unusual enough that when Marian led the Tulane cheers at the 1925 Northwestern game in Chicago (no doubt including the classic that begins, "A One, A Two, A Helluva Hullabaloo!"), the *New York Times* ran her picture, captioned "The Girl Cheer Leader of Tulane. Miss Marian Draper." Back home, the front page of the *States* carried a photograph of the "Daughter of the Regiment" getting off the train from Chicago and demonstrating how she had led cheers there, and a Keith Temple cartoon in the *Times-Picayune* showed a Tulane runner vanquishing would-be tacklers from Northwestern

Keith Temple cartoon

and Auburn, while a figure labeled "Marion" leads cheers in the background. The Tulane yearbook that year carried her picture, too, nominating her for the "Hall of Fame"—"Because she is one of the peppiest individuals on Tulane's campus [and] has made a name for herself and come to be known as 'Tulane's great little cheerleader.'"

Although her picture appears in the 1927 Tulane yearbook as a member of the Architecture Society, she did not finish her degree. It seems that she tried unsuccessfully to resume her show business career. (In 1928 she sang and danced in one musical's out-of-town tryouts, but she was not in the cast when it opened on Broadway.) The 1930 census found her living with her mother in a third-floor apartment in the commercial part of Bourbon Street. Both women listed their occupations as "artist."

Marian did not keep up with her New Orleans friends. In 1968 a club-woman trying to find the surviving Famous Creoles to help with a benefit for the New Orleans Symphony, wrote the *States-Item* to say that Marian Draper "hasn't been seen in 40 years," and asked if any readers might know where she was. In fact, she had married a New Orleans journalist, and she, her mother, and her husband had moved to the Washington, D.C., area, where, among other things, he wrote the narrative for a World War II movie about a Victory ship and worked in the Public Affairs division of the Treasury Department. Marian enrolled at George Washington University, took her bachelor's degree in botany in 1940, and worked in the GWU botany lab until 1947. In the 1970s, when her husband retired, the household moved to Savannah, where he edited the newspaper of the Episcopalian diocese. Marian's mother died there in 1982. Soon after that, Marian suffered a stroke, which left her unable to speak. She died in 1985.

Conrad Albrizio, 27

CONRAD ALBRIZIO WAS BORN in New York City, the son of a shoemaker and his wife, both Italian immigrants. After studying art at the Beaux Arts Institute and architectural drawing at Cooper Union, he found work as an architectural draftsman, an occupation that took him to New Orleans in 1919 to work on the new Hibernia Bank skyscraper. Soon after arriving, he was one of three students in the art class held in Alberta Kinsey's studio that was the germ of the Arts and Crafts Club. In 1923 he returned briefly to New York to study at the Art Students League with the Ashcan School painter George Luks, then went to the Académie de la Grande Chaumière in Paris, but didn't care for it. He joined his New Orleans friend Ronald Hargrave to paint in Majorca, until his mother's death required him to return to the United States.

Albrizio had a studio next door to Faulkner and Spratling, and continued his association with the Arts and Crafts Club, winning first prize for charcoal drawing at a student exhibition and exhibiting some of his Majorcan work there in 1925. At this time his work consisted mostly of conventional portraits of New Orleanians and views of the French Quarter and the Louisiana countryside. One of

CONRAD ALBRIZIO

Photograph by William Odiorne

CONRAD ALBREZIO AND
HIS PORTRAIT OF MISS
IRMA VON TRESCKOW
The portrait painter has a
studio in Orleans Alley, but is
spending the summer in New
York at the Students' League.
—Odiorne Photo.

1924

his landscapes got honorable mention in the 1927 Benjamin Prize competition, and a reviewer described a view of Grand Isle as "given over to the melancholy which Louisiana landscapes sometimes hold, always an opportunity for the painter." In 1927 Albrizio was one of the fifteen "male workers in the graphic arts" who founded the New Orleans Art League.

In the late 1920s Albrizio traveled for three years in Italy and France, where he studied fresco in Rome and Fontainebleau. His new specialty led directly to a commission in 1930 from Governor Huey Long to do six murals (of which, alas, only one remains) for the Kingfish's grand new capitol building in Baton Rouge. In the 1930s he took a position at Louisiana State University in Baton Rouge, did five major fresco projects for the WPA, added mosaics to his repertoire, showed his striking picture *Jordan* at the Whitney, and married novelist Imogene Inge, an Alabama plantation heiress twenty years his junior. A Rosenwald Fellowship in the 1940s supported two years of travel in New York, Alabama, and Mexico. He continued to do large murals—most notably those in New Orleans's Union Passenger Terminal (1954)—until a stroke confined him to easel painting. He died in Baton Rouge in 1973.

Lillian Friend Marcus, 35

LILLIAN FRIEND GREW UP IN NEW ORLEANS, the oldest of the four children of a cotton broker, originally from Wisconsin, and an energetic, philanthropic clubwoman from Mississippi. At Newcomb College she was active in drama and was captain of the basketball team her senior year. Two years after her 1911 graduation, she married Clarence Marcus, a cloth manufacturer from Cincinnati, and moved to his home state, but his death in 1921 left her widowed with two young sons, so she moved back to New Orleans to live with her parents near Loyola University. Eventually she rented a place that was a five-minute walk from them.

Although her younger brother Julius and some of his friends started the *Double Dealer* and graced its masthead, no less an observer than William Spratling insisted that the "guiding hand" behind the magazine was Lillian's. Julius put a good deal of his own money into the project, and Lillian may well have done the same; cer-

LILLIAN F. MARCUS

Newcomb College graduation picture

tainly she provided everything from the first typewriter to her (unpaid and uncredited) services as manager and fund-raiser. The young widow greatly admired editor Basil Thompson, an aspiring poet who received no sympathy from his father, a Philistine insurance agent, or his wife, an interpretive dancer and party girl who had never read a book. Thompson basked in Marcus's admiration, and the two formed an attachment that lasted until Thompson's death from binge-induced pneumonia in 1924.

Marcus befriended Sherwood Anderson when he first came to New Orleans, and when he returned in 1924 with his new wife, Elizabeth, and his teenage son, Robert, she found the family a three-room furnished apartment on the second floor of the upper Pontalba building. As manager of the "Modernist Lecture Bureau" (at the same address as the *Double Dealer*) she started lining up speaking engagements for Anderson. Later, she went on the famous Lake Pontchartrain excursion, and everyone agrees that she was the model for one of the characters in Faulkner's *Mosquitoes,* although they disagree about which one (see page 24). Gay men may have liked Marcus more than other women did. Although Sam Gilmore saw her as "brilliant and original, . . . powerful and determined," and Spratling said she had a marvelous personality with "no humbug" and would never let you down, a female relative by marriage told Faulkner's biographer that Marcus was "a bitch" and Elizabeth Anderson said that she "insisted on being the center of contention at all times" and "considered herself to be a social and literary arbiter and did not care to be challenged or corrected." "Miss Elizabeth," who had her own aspirations to arbitership, offered a catty description of Marcus's "birdlike face in which everything came to a point," adding that "whenever I talked to her I half expected her to peck at me." For her part, Marcus remembered Sherwood as "like a nice brown little bear . . . sweet simple and overflowing with the joy of life," and claimed that Elizabeth "was his undoing, as a writer."

When the *Double Dealer* ceased publication and the Famous Creoles began to disperse, Marcus seems to have been left at loose ends. After an impulsive and brief second marriage in 1931, she played with the idea of a career in social work, but soon retired into private life. She traveled with her grandchildren, summered in New England, and cared for her aging mother, whose example she may have found intimidating: Ida Weis Friend, sometime president of the National Council of Jewish Women and one of *New Orleans Life* magazine's "Women Builders of New Orleans" (along with Helen Pitkin Schertz, Mrs. James Oscar Nixon, and Dorothy Dix), remained, as one observer put it, "the presiding genius of the household" until her death in 1963. In any event, when Marcus died in 1974, the *Times-Picayune* listed her name under "Deaths," with no further elaboration. Over the years, when various Faulkner scholars sought her out, she insisted that Bill was "a very shallow person taken up mostly with the nasty details of life" and that his Nobel Prize was "a farce."

Daniel Whitney, 32

ART HISTORIAN JUDITH BONNER says that Dan Whitney brought Cubism to New Orleans when he came from his native Baltimore in 1924. Already an accomplished painter, he took a studio in the lower Pontalba building, started doing sketches for the *Times-Picayune,* and showed his work at the Delgado Museum and the YMCA. The next year found him teaching at the Arts and Crafts Club: a painting class in the morning, night classes in life drawing and composition, and a Sunday morning still-life class. Spratling's portrait parodies one of Whitney's own works (now apparently lost), a picture of two ballerinas. He also painted a portrait of an uptown student named Catherine Wainwright, and then married her. Like the mésalliance between Lucille Godchaux and Marc Antony (see page 168), this marriage was front-page news ("Vieux Carré Is Startled by Paint-Box Romance," in the *Times-Picayune*); unlike the Antonys', however, it was short-lived.

DANIEL WHITNEY
FROM THE PORTRAIT NOW AT THE ARTS & CRAFTS CLUB

Newspaper photo of Whitney at work

Whitney was very much a presence on the Quarter's art scene, serving as a judge for the Arts and Crafts Club's Benjamin Prize and as supervisor of the decorations for its balls. He and Caroline Durieux had a joint show at the Club, and a group exhibition that included work by Whitney and Charles Bein attracted notice in the *New York Times*. Eight of Whitney's students from the Ocean Springs Summer Art Colony showed their work at the Club in 1926, and presumably it was his experience teaching life classes that qualified him that year to judge both the "Most Beautiful Girl" in New Orleans contest and the Annual Biloxi Bathing Revue.

Painting right-handed, in a *Morning Tribune* illustration, circa 1927.

Whitney was born outside Baltimore in 1894. After the University of Maryland and the Maryland Institute of Fine Arts, he went to the Pennsylvania Academy of the Fine Arts, where he may have known some of the Louisiana contingent. At PAFA he won a scholarship to study in Paris. World War I found him back in France as an infantryman. When he was wounded in his right (painting) arm in the Meuse-Argonne offensive, he taught himself to paint left-handed; later he became ambidextrous when he recovered the use of his right hand.

For a time in the 1930s Whitney operated the Whitney School of Art, on Chartres Street. He married another of his students (lastingly, this time), and the couple moved to a place in the country, near Covington, where they lived and he continued to paint until his death in 1965, an idyll broken only by World War II service with the Coast Guard's Port Security Force (for whom Whitney designed a flag).

Helen Pitkin Schertz, 56

WHEN *FAMOUS CREOLES* APPEARED, Helen Pitkin had been Mrs. Christian Schertz for seventeen years. She and her husband, a native of German-speaking Lorraine and the prosperous owner of a drugstore chain, had restored the eighteenth-century "Old Spanish Customs House" on the Bayou St. John, where Mrs. Schertz's glittering dinner parties brought together actors, musicians, visiting celebrities, and local notables and made her one of the city's leading society hostesses.

"The Lady Helen" (as her friends called her) was almost a caricature of the benevolent clubwoman, active in a score of social, cultural, civic, charitable, and ancestry-based organizations, ranging from the DAR to the ASPCA, often as a founder or officer. But it was probably her zealous commitment to preserving the Vieux Carré that made her a Famous Creole. She started leading tours of the Quarter no later than 1917, and ten years after that had person-

HELEN PITKIN SCHERTZ
OF LE PETIT THEATRE

185

ally shown the place to at least ten thousand visitors. She said she gave her fees to charity, although Flo Field later hinted darkly that she didn't. (Field, who proudly claimed to have been the first French Quarter guide for hire, called Schertz a "scab guide," and resented the fact that Schertz didn't need the money and she did.) Schertz also organized an effort to put markers on historical buildings, wrote an early guidebook, *A Walk Through French Town in Old New Orleans,* and was very much a part of the effort to locate respectable activities in the Quarter, serving on the committee of the Quartier Club with her old friend Dorothy Dix, and then helping in the club's relocation and transformation into Le Petit Salon. After she helped to found Le Petit Theatre, she secured its first quarters in the lower Pontalba building, was active for years as everything from a benefactor to a set painter, played her

Mrs. Schertz (upper right), friends, and servant (lower left) at the "Old Spanish Customs House"

harp for many performances, and appeared memorably in one production as "Big Kate" (Catherine the Great). In 1927 she received a silver loving cup "From the Women of New Orleans" for her contributions to the Quarter's revitalization.

Perhaps Mrs. Schertz was overcompensating for having a "scalawag" father whose name had been sullied by scandal. John Robert Graham Pitkin read law in New England with a cousin, but returned to his native Louisiana in 1860. He served the Confederacy briefly as a private in Louisiana's Crescent Regiment, but when New Orleans fell he declared himself in a public speech to be a Union man. As a leading Republican during and after Reconstruction, he was appointed U.S. marshal for Louisiana by his friend President Grant, and put his oratorical skills to use at many public occasions. In 1888 Benjamin Harrison appointed him minister plenipotentiary to Argentina. Unfortunately for his reputation, the year before his death in 1901 he resigned his last political appointment—postmaster of New Orleans—under a cloud that involved his secretary's attempt to blackmail him.

Helen probably got her musical and dramatic inclinations from her step-mother, an accomplished mezzo-soprano and Shakespearean actress who had studied in New York and Paris, but her choice of the harp as her instrument may have come indirectly from her mother. The story is that after her mother died, Helen's black mammy showed the little girl a picture of an angel playing a harp, and she set her heart on playing one, too. She went to Newcomb College and then became a reporter, columnist, and "woman's editor" for the old *Times-Democrat*. A 1903 article in *Leslie's Weekly* named her one of five "Southern Women Who Have Made Their Mark in Journalism" (another was Flo Field, later her rival) and called her "the champion of the woman who works, [who] spares no pains to better the lot of shop-girl, factory-girl, and the rest of the toiling sisterhood." In these years she was engaged, briefly, to the patrician novelist Booth Tarkington, and began her lasting friendship with her fellow journalist Dorothy Dix. The two women shared a lunchtime oyster loaf on Royal Street, when they could afford the 25 cents, and later they often traveled together, notably on a six-month European excursion in 1924.

Meanwhile, Helen was writing and publishing fiction and poetry. Her first book was a long poem, *Over the Hills,* published in 1903, followed the next year by *An Angel by Brevet,* a novel in which voodoo plays a major role. Folklorist Newbell Niles Puckett later reprinted its accounts of voodoo séances as legitimate ethnography and even a century later a historian allowed that the book, despite its demeaning portrayal of Afro-Creoles, remains valuable for documenting how they spoke.

After Helen married, she devoted herself to her social and civic activities and to managing her household—for years, she and her husband ate dinner (not supper) at 11:00 p.m., after he returned from work—but she still found time to write a last book, *Legends of Louisiana,* published in 1922 and dedicated to "Captain James Dinkins C.S.A. and his Beautiful Lady." Dinkins was prominent in Confederate veterans' affairs as a writer, historian, and controversialist, and old wounds were obviously healing when the scalawag's daughter was friends with one of Forrest's cavalrymen.

Christian Schertz died in 1927, but his widow continued her philanthropic and civic activities—if anything, at an accelerating pace—and her devotion to the French Quarter was undiminished. In 1937 she and Dorothy Dix inaugurated the Quarter's annual Spring Fiesta, which included an artists' street exhibit off Jackson Square, and she kept up her work as a volunteer tour guide: in 1934, for instance, the program "for the ladies" at an insurance agents' national convention included "visits to points of interest in the Vieux Carre under the guidance of Mrs. Helen Pitkin Schertz, and Luncheon at the Patio Royal."

By all accounts Mrs. Schertz was a force to be reckoned with. After she died in 1945, her nephew told an interviewer, "I was very proud of Aunt Helen, because when she walked into a room, things began to pop."

Keith Temple, 27

BY 1926, KEITH TEMPLE HAD BEEN the *Times-Picayune*'s editorial cartoonist for three years and a naturalized U.S. citizen for one. The young Australian would get his law degree the next year—he had enrolled in law school at Loyola after the subject of one of his cartoons threatened a libel suit—and he was also taking art courses at the Arts and Crafts Club, where he had an exhibit of his cartoons and sat for his portrait by Dan Whitney, one of his teachers. He was serious enough about his art to join the New Orleans Art League after its founding in 1927. For a time, he shared the French Quarter apartment of Oliver La Farge.

Born in Glasgow, but raised in Sydney, Temple volunteered for the Australian Imperial Forces at seventeen and fought in France, where he was wounded (and his brother killed). After being discharged in Australia he decided to travel, but he'd had enough of Europe, so he headed for the United States in 1919, listing his occupation on the ship's passenger manifest as "artificial limb maker." When his war wound gave him trouble, he wound up in the Marine Hospital, in New Orleans. Two operations later, he was out of money and applied for a job with the *Times-Picayune,* which hired him as a utility reporter, doing "almost anything"—including sketches for the news

KEITH TEMPLE

Portrait by Dan Whitney

The "Bishop of Bucktown" and his date for an Arts and Crafts Club ball.

pages. After a brief switch to the *Item*, he was hired back by the *Times-Pica-yune* to replace its departing editorial cartoonist.

Temple fit right into the often antic world of New Orleans journalism. After he and Roark Bradford dressed as bishops for one Mardi Gras and found themselves treated as real prelates (policemen even fetched them chairs to watch the parades), Temple had cards printed up identifying himself as the Bishop of Bucktown, and appeared in that persona from time to time.

Temple was the *Times-Picayune*'s cartoonist for forty-four years, retiring in 1967, over twelve thousand cartoons later. In the mid-1930s he married a co-worker at the newspaper and the couple settled in the Garden District. (A magazine story numbered them among the "decent people who have been driven out of the Quarter.") Temple never practiced law, but he did serve for two decades as a notary. After his retirement, he began painting in earnest, turning out scores of city and river views, many of them imaginative reconstructions of historical scenes, like three of "Old Storyville." Before he died in 1980, he had seen exhibits of his work at a grand Canal Street department store and at the Downtown Howard Johnson's Motor Hotel. The owners of the Howard Johnson's subsequently put a "Permanent Collection" of his work on display in the hotel's Keith Temple Room, where, the *Times-Picayune* observed, "visitors using the meeting and luncheon room can get a tour of the area without stepping outside the doors."

Times-Picayune cartoon

R. Emmet Kennedy, 49

EMMET KENNEDY WAS BORN AND RAISED in Gretna, across the river from New Orleans. Both of his parents were Irish immigrants; his father was a blacksmith, fiddler, and Confederate veteran. Even as a boy, Emmet was fascinated by the songs and folktales that were all around him in the mostly black neighborhood where his family lived, and he was the first to write down the words and music of many of the spirituals he heard ("Free at Last" was one of them). Although Kennedy worked until his mid-forties as a bookkeeper for a local cooperage, he developed a sideline telling dialect tales and singing spirituals, accompanying himself on the piano. After he moved across the river to New Orleans about 1910, he became a popular entertainer for New Orleans high society. He was also known for the parties at his ornately decorated bachelor quarters in Mid-City, where he performed his tales and songs and recited "Irish" verse of his own composition. (This bardic angle was nothing new: he had been writing such poems since his teenage years, and as "Robard Emmet Ua Cinneidig" had self-published a collection of them.)

When the *Times-Picayune* started a radio station, it put Kennedy on the air regularly as a Negro impersonator, and he was engaged to entertain the Music Teachers' National Association when that organization met in New Orleans. By 1923, he had become something of a tourist attraction, and he

EMMETT KENNEDY

caught the attention of Edward Larocque Tinker, a New York philanthropist and man of letters who wintered in New Orleans. Tinker persuaded Kennedy to give up his day job at the cooperage and try his luck in Manhattan.

Kennedy worked briefly at a bookstore, then at a Park Avenue antique shop, but he found success in 1924 when he published *Black Cameos,* a book of dialect stories (with illustrations by his patron Tinker) that the *New York Post* hailed as "the very quintessence of the black people, with whom he has grown up, whom he loves. . . . uproariously amusing without departing from truth." After that he was in demand as a performer and a lecturer on Negro music and folklore. For "A Dixie Evening" at Town Hall, he told tales from his book and introduced the Yankee audience to New Orleans street vendors' cries. Some of those vendors' cries were included in his next book, *Mellows: A Chronicle of Unknown Singers* ("Mellow," he explained, "is the Negro word for melody"), but most of the melodies are spirituals, with piano accompaniment—many of them unfamiliar.

Kennedy published a collection of his Irish work, *Runes and Cadences, Being Ancestral Memories of Old Heroic Days,* but the market was plainly greater for Negro dialect material like his next book, *Gritny People* ("Gritny" being the Negro word for Gretna), comprising tales with titles like "Felo's White Folks," "Roving Rosey," "Scandalizin'," and "Upsetment."

In 1929, Kennedy tried his hand at a *Porgy*-like novel of Negro life in New Orleans called *Red Bean Row,* then two years later published *More Mellows,* which was exactly that. Meanwhile, he was studying Chinese folklore and poetry, attaining enough authority in that area to write three book reviews for the *New York Times,* although a planned collection of Chinese folk songs was never published and the manuscript went missing after his death. In the mid-1930s he visited Ireland for the first time, and returned to write *Songs of an Alien Spirit* (a second poetic stroll through Irish legends and mythology) and a life of St. Patrick (another fugitive manuscript).

During his years in New York, he often returned to visit friends and family in Louisiana. On one of those visits, in 1941, he died of a heart attack in a Camp Street drugstore. He is buried in his native "Gritny."

Ronald Hargrave, 44

RONALD HARGRAVE'S TIMING WAS good. When he came to New Orleans in 1921, hoping to work as a portrait painter, a group of investors had recently bought the upper Pontalba building. One of them, an uptown bachelor lawyer, offered Hargrave a studio there in exchange for fixing the place up and letting his patron use it for parties. The deal sealed, Hargrave joined the newly formed Arts and Crafts Club and was soon designing sets for Le Petit Theatre. He did a portrait of Sherwood Anderson on spec, after Anderson came to live in the neighborhood, and asked Anderson's publisher $250 for the rights to reproduce it, but the publisher didn't bite. (His Pontalba neighbor Harold Levy later acquired the portrait.)

Before Hargrave came to New Orleans, he had been painting in Brittany and Spain for several years. He was in Paris in 1915, at least long enough to get his passport renewed, with a passport photo showing him at his easel. (His sister believed that he was doing "undercover work" for the United

'EL DIA", MAJORCA

Passport photo, 1915

States during World War I, but there is no evidence that he was doing anything other than landscapes.) Before Europe, he had been in Peoria, of all
places, where he spent four years painting portraits of wealthy Midwestern-
ers and exhibiting his work at the Art Institute of Chicago. He had studied at
the Art Institute for seven or eight years (breaking off several times to work
his way to Europe) after leaving his home in Baraboo, Wisconsin, in 1901.
Baraboo was the winter home of the Ringling Brothers Circus, and Hargrave had been sketching elephants and painting signs and displays from the
age of fifteen. Other than that, though, Baraboo had little to offer him. His
mother had died when he was ten, and his father, a Congregationalist minister, had married a woman young Hargrave didn't get along with. He may
never have seen his father and stepmother after he left for Chicago, and he
is the only one of the five children not mentioned in his father's obituary.

Hargrave did sculpture, too

In New Orleans, though, he fit right in, designing costumes and decorations for the *Double Dealer*'s first fund-raising ball and holding memorable
parties of his own. His sometime apartment-mate Cicero Odiorne remembered gatherings enlivened by Hargrave's imitations of camels, monkeys,
burros, and muezzins, and characterized his friend as a man born in the
wrong century, someone who would have made a perfect courtier. Hargrave
and Odiorne were among those from the neighborhood—Conrad Albrizio
and Louis Andrews (Fischer) were others—who liked to stroll on the docks
at sundown, when a breeze usually started up.

In 1922 Hargrave married an art student some fifteen years younger; a
year later, sadly, she was living with her widowed mother in Beverly Hills,

with a baby daughter Hargrave apparently never saw. But his professional life was going better. The *Times-Picayune* reported that three of his paintings in the window of the Arts and Crafts Club had "attracted much attention," and when a wealthy patron offered the use of a studio attached to his house, Hargrave moved from the Pontalba building; his new quarters exposed him to famous visitors like violinist Jascha Heifetz, whose portrait he painted. In 1924 he showed a collection of pastel sketches of actresses and dancers, including Anna Pavlova and Ruth St. Denis, at the Arts and Crafts Club. About this time the Hotel Roosevelt commissioned ten etchings to decorate the hotel's rooms, showing "scenes in the old quarter, quaint streets, odd bits of architecture" and "scenes along the river, showing the great vessels in the docks and the men busy in unloading the cargoes," as Lyle Saxon described the project for readers of the *Times-Picayune*. One set was given to the Arts and Crafts Club for its collection, and another went on display at Arnaud's Restaurant. In 1926 Sazerac Ginger Ale offered a free copy of the Cabildo etching as a premium.

By then, however, Hargrave had left New Orleans. The *Times-Picayune* told its readers that Hargrave, "that man of uncanny talent, who exhibited such a tremendous influence when he lived three years in the Pontalba buildings," had "returned to his first love—Spain." He and Conrad Albrizio had settled into El Tereno, an American artists' colony on Majorca, where they were joined by William Spratling, who was touring Europe that summer. Although news of his doings got back to New Orleans—Harold Levy passed on to the New Orleans newspaper a review of Hargrave's work in a Spanish paper that hailed him as "the man who truly interprets the spirit of Spain" and in 1930 the *New Orleanian* magazine reported that he was "in Corsica among the brigands"—the man himself never returned.

Spratling drew Hargrave at his painting, with the caption "Ben dinat" (I have dined well), supposedly what King James of Aragon said when he was offered bread and garlic in a Majorcan cottage after a battle with the Muslims. The banner in the background, lower right, says "Fornalutx," the name of a mountain village on the island, but it's not clear why the drawing is signed "Icarus."

On Majorca Hargrave met the woman who became his second wife, and the two began a life of almost incessant travel—across France, Spain, and

Italy, to Corsica and North Africa, and ultimately to the Dutch East Indies. There—on either Java or Bali, in either 1934 or 1935 (accounts differ)—Hargrave injured his leg. Without proper medical attention it became infected, and he died. When a friend put together an exhibit of his work in 1948, the *Los Angeles Times* observed that Hargrave had led "an enviable, publicity-shunning life," which may answer his biographer's question, "how someone who did much in his life, having met and painted so many interesting, often famous people would . . . be so thoughtlessly consigned to obscurity."

Hamilton Basso, 22

HAM BASSO WAS THE SON and grandson of Italian immigrants and spent his first years in the French Quarter, but the Bassos were Northern Italian and middle-class, not poor Sicilians like most of their neighbors. After Grandfather Joseph Basso died, the family sold his shoe factory on Decatur Street and moved with young Ham from their place above it to the "American" Mid-City section of town. This was part of a larger pattern of assimilation: Mrs. Basso was a devout Catholic, but went to an Episcopal Church in the wintertime for the central heat, and Ham went not to Loyola but to Tulane, where he styled himself "J. Hamilton Basso."

At Tulane he was the editor of an award-winning yearbook and a BMOC,

Tulane BMOC (from the *Jambalaya*)

A HAPPY CONCEPTION OF THE ARTIST, THE SIGNIFICANCE OF WHICH HAS SLIPPED HIS MIND IN THE INTERVAL. PICTURE HAS TO DO WITH SUPERIORITY OF AGILE HEELS OVER THE KEENEST BRAIN IN CAPTIVATING THAT ELUSIVE FEMALE, SUCCESS. HAM BASSO AND THE MUSE DO THE CHARLESTON put in the annual "Hall of Fame" his senior year and elected to the most pres-tigious honorary society. A practical joker, a good dancer (hence, Spratling's drawing), and something of a dandy, who favored white suits and maroon ties, he was also, according to one profile, "the reputed and recognized champion of Tulane University at the scholarly custom of beating checks" (i.e., getting cash to the bank before his bad checks bounced). Later, Eliz-abeth Anderson would recall that Basso "had no money at all except what he could borrow here and there" and that "he rarely gave much thought to returning the borrowed money, but he was young and very excited about writing."

Like Freddie Oechsner, his near-contemporary at Tulane, Basso studied law but preferred literature—especially after the *Double Dealer* accepted a couple of his poems and he started hanging out with the French Quarter crowd. He was part of the group that met at the Pelican Bookshop after clos-ing for wine and sandwiches, and he met Bill Faulkner at one of the Ander-sons' regular Saturday suppers. (Still a prankster, he once arranged to have a brick covered in sauce, baked, and served to Sherwood at a restaurant.) He showed up for the Andersons' Lake Pontchartrain cruise with a "giddy young girl," and was mentioned in the society pages as part of "a notable gathering of the social world" to be seen at an Arts and Crafts Club ball. He and Faulkner took long walks together along the wharfs, talking about far-off places, books they'd been reading, "and, inevitably, the South," but their bond was cemented when Basso was assigned to write about the Gates Fly-ing Circus for the *Times-Picayune* and the two young men went up together a few times. "Nobody else in our crowd had gone looping-the-loop in a bucket seat and open cockpit over the Mississippi River." The whole scene, he said later, was "fun" and "something to be 'in' on," although he confessed that "I was bound, having just turned twenty and still enrolled at Tulane Univer-sity, to wonder occasionally if I had not been admitted into the ball park by mistake."

At the time Basso was writing for several New Orleans dailies. Shortly before graduation, he dropped out of Tulane—to ensure, he said, that he would never have to be a lawyer—and took a full-time reporting job with the *Tribune,* then one with the *Times-Picayune.* He wrote notable features on the waterfront and on crime. In June 1926, he left to seek fame and fortune in New York, but after less than six months of trucking freight and working in a department store, homesick and lonely, he came home to work seriously on his first novel.

To make ends meet, Basso worked as a reporter for the *Item,* then took a job with an advertising agency (which he came to hate), but he finished *Relics and Angels* in 1928 and it was published the next year. Meanwhile, he had been seeing Etolia "Toto" Simmons, a Newcomb graduate from St. Louis who worked for the Pelican Bookshop. He proposed to her over dinner at Galatoire's, and they were married in 1930. When Basso lost his advertising job—because of his "complete and even appalling lack of ability as a copywriter," he said, although the Depression probably contributed—the young couple moved to a $10-a-month cabin in the North Carolina mountains, where he worked on a biography of the Creole Confederate general, P.G.T. Beauregard.

The Bassos never lived again in New Orleans—they settled in suburban Connecticut in 1942—but Ham stayed in touch with friends like Lyle Saxon. He worked successively for *New Republic, Time,* and the *New Yorker,* and he published eight more novels before 1954, when *The View from Pompey's Head* spent forty weeks on the bestseller list and was sold to Twentieth Century-Fox. After that success, Basso was elected to the National Institute of Arts and Letters, and he wrote three more novels—*The Light Infantry Ball* was a finalist for the National Book Award in 1960—before his death from lung cancer in 1964.

Louis Andrews Fischer, 25

WHEN LOUIS ANDREWS WAS BORN in 1901 she was given the first name of her father, a Mobile ship broker. Louis Sr. left the family when his daughter was five years old, and his wife moved with the young Louis and her younger sister to New Orleans. As a child, Louis read avidly, especially poetry and fantasy—*Alice in Wonderland* was a particular favorite—and at sixteen she entered Newcomb College, where she became widely known for her coruscating wit. Impressed by her artistic talent, Ellsworth Woodward steered her toward Mardi Gras design. Carnival historian Henri Schindler reports that by 1926 she had designed "parades and costumes for Rex, Momus, and Proteus, and invitations for Comus and The Mystic Club." (Happily, the theme for the Momus parade in 1923 was "Alice's Adventures in Wonderland.")

Schindler notes that the Arts and Crafts Movement, Art Deco, and the Ballets Russes all influenced Louis's designs, but adds that "none of them shaped her style more than her lifelong loves, literature and nonsense." For instance, gender-bending was rarer in New Orleans a century ago than it is now, and Louis was a pioneer. The influence of her masculine name (which

LOUIS ANDREWS FISCHER

Louis at work (photograph by Pops Whitesell)

always caused confusion: newspapers referred to her as Lois, Louise, and Mrs. Louis Andrews) was augmented by her mother's tendency to dress the child in boyish clothes, a pattern that Louis continued on her own at Newcomb, where, according to Schindler, she was "usually attired in tweed jackets and neckties" (although, to be sure, she "also made dramatic appearances on campus in the costumes of various nationalities"). As a Carnival designer, she "relished the genial mischief and occasionally sublime comedy" of costuming prominent New Orleans businessmen as "Southern belles in hoop skirts, pioneer women in gingham and bonnets, queens Elizabeth, Antoinette, and Victoria," and the like. The 1924 Rex parade alone included gentlemen representing Salome, Jezebel, Joan of Arc, and Lucrezia Borgia.

Fischer's costume designs

Louis did not confine her work to Mardi Gras events. In one 1925 issue of the *Times-Picayune*, for instance, she illustrated a children's story called "Hiawatha's First Great Battle" ("As Retold by Lydia Sehorn"—Mrs. Roark Bradford), and Lyle Saxon reported that "in the Quarter these days, one hears much of the work of Miss Louis Andrews, delightful line drawings of vividness and charm," calling particular attention to some recently published in the *New York Times*. The next year, the *Morning Tribune* illustrated a story about the Arts and Crafts Club with her sketch of the courtyard at its Royal Street headquarters. Louis lived with her mother and sister in the Pontalba apartments, where her neighbors and good friends included Ronald Hargrave, Cicero Odiorne, and Harold Levy. Bill Spratling was another friend

Fischer and her sister, Martha Andrews, photographed by Pops Whitesell.

(Flo Field said that Louis and Spratling had pet names for each other, but didn't reveal what they were).

Louis made occasional appearances in the society pages—a newspaper story reported that "stunts" for the Arts and Crafts Club's 1925 Bal des Artistes would be under her "personal direction," and another article reported that she was present at an "impromptu studio party" in the Quarter and "did her part to make [it] a grand success"—but her social life really picked up after she married Lawrence Fischer in 1926. Louis and her husband (whose occupation was reported in the 1930 census as "manager/florist") moved to the lower Pontalba building, had a baby boy, and played frequent hosts to informal Sunday afternoon gatherings of the artistic set. Their apartment was also the scene of grander parties like one held to honor a (fictitious) young artist named Narkiss Nietzke, at which the hired policeman on the door turned away a good many prominent citizens who had been sent forged invitations by some practical joker.

The stock market crash put a crimp in the celebration of Mardi Gras. Louis's last Rex parade was in 1930. The Fischers opened a bookshop on St. Peter Street that became a popular meeting place for their crowd. Louis started working at Le Petit Theatre and spoke at the Arts and Crafts Club on "Stage Craft and Design." Although she kept her hand in, doing Mardi Gras costumes and settings for balls, she designed no parades until 1964. In that year, however, she returned to float design, staging a successful second act in a remarkable only-in-New Orleans career that continued until her death in 1974.

Alberta Kinsey, 51

THE CAPTION FOR SPRATLING'S SKETCH of Alberta Kinsey was obviously some kind of inside joke, now lost, but perhaps it referred to her general obliviousness. In any case, it's fitting that she's shown in her smock, at her easel. She was an oddity among the Quarter's scores of painters in that she actually made her living entirely by painting. Described by her friend Lyle Saxon as a "little Quaker artist . . . of uncertain age, very sincere, and very serious in her work," Kinsey specialized in views of French Quarter court-yards. "I won't tell you how many courtyards I have painted," she told the *New Orleanian* magazine. "If people knew, they might not buy them any more, thinking there were too many thousands of pictures like them."

Kinsey was a sixteen-year-old schoolteacher when she enrolled in a sum-mer art program and determined to be an artist. She joined the Cincinnati Women's Art Club, and found a job teaching china painting at a former nor-

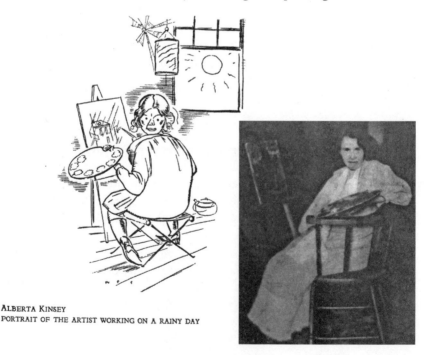

ALBERTA KINSEY
PORTRAIT OF THE ARTIST WORKING ON A RAINY DAY

mal school in Lebanon, Ohio. The college closed its doors in 1917, however, and she headed south the next year. She chose New Orleans, she said, because it was warm and the name pleased her. She won a scholarship to Newcomb College, although it seems she never actually matriculated there. But Newcomb art professor Ellsworth Woodward may have steered her to a residence for single young women, just off Lee Circle, called the Catherine Club ("The City's Big Sister to the Worthy Girl"), where his wife was the registrar. In any case, Kinsey took a room there, and set off to explore the French Quarter. "I saw that it was the place I had been looking for all my life," she recalled. She bought paints and an easel, and met an artist who let her paint the courtyard of the old building where he had his studio (he lived uptown). When she sold that painting, her course was set.

It wasn't easy. At first, she traded arithmetic lessons for dinners, and once she had to leave New Orleans to take a teaching job in Alabama, for the money. Somewhere along the way, she met Saxon, who was living in the Quarter and encouraged her to join him there. (In an article for the *Item* on a proposal to turn the Pontalba buildings into an artists' colony, he quoted "Miss Alberta Kinsey, Cincinnati artist" as writing to ask about reserving one.) When she returned from Alabama, she found a studio for $15 a month in the old Governor Claiborne house on Toulouse Street, just off Royal, becoming perhaps the first artist actually to live in the Quarter in years.

Kinsey was an unlikely pioneer in this still sketchy neighborhood. "See her en route . . . to a defenseless courtyard," a magazine profile suggested, "a tiny, timid, virginal woman, probably in a smock," almost certainly with paint in her hair, "naively unconscious of the dangers that hemmed her in" and "absolutely unconscious that she has done anything amazing." But she made herself at home. A reporter who visited her said she could be found "almost every evening, working at her easel, while the fire crackles cheerfully in the grate nearby." In one of Flo Field's plays, "an artist from Ohio" was obviously based on Kinsey: "In what she fancifully decided had been the billiard room of Louisiana's first American governor, [c]ooking on a one-burner oil stove . . . , she painted like mad to fill every home in the country with the courtyards and balconies, the arches and Spanish windows of the old New Orleans."

Kinsey's studio was the site of the 1919 art class that led to the formation of Arts and Crafts Club. She was one of the Club's founding members and her work was almost perpetually on display there. She had a joint show with Spratling in 1923 and showed her landscapes in 1924. The next year she

Le Petit Theatre

showed plantation scenes and French Quarter pictures ("painted with her usual sincerity and straightforwardness," Lyle Saxon wrote). In 1927 she showed paintings from a summer in Europe, but in 1928 reverted to views of the Quarter, evoking some purple prose about "by-gone splendor" and "ghostly spells" from the *Times-Picayune*'s reviewer. Kinsey claimed that when she came to New Orleans she knew no more about painting than "the average person who paints china," and that "most of the time I've just taught myself," but in the 1920s she did go twice to Europe, and she went away most summers to study. (She took courses at both the Art Institute of Chicago and the Cincinnati Art Institute.)

She wasn't exactly the life of the party (she left one of her own early to go to bed), she didn't drink, and, as Cicero Odiorne put it, "It was difficult for Alberta to tell a falsehood, even when politeness required it." Nevertheless, she had a lot of friends, most of whom seemed to feel protective about her. She must have been an incongruous figure at Arts and Crafts Club balls, but at one of them she and Bill Spratling did what the *States* reporter said was "a very clever take-off" on Flo Field's play, *A la Creole*. And, as Odiorne observed, although "there was always something a little absurd about Alberta," there was "something charming at the same time, also something very solid."

Since Kinsey painted "in a manner that is not above the head of the average person who wants a picture to beautify his home," as one reviewer observed, "and she depicts scenes that are friendly and kindly and close to earth," her work became popular enough—with locals and visitors alike—to pay for those summers studying art and visiting relatives in Ohio, with trips to Europe and (in 1929) to Mexico. Her savings allowed her to buy the historic Daniel Clark house on Royal Street in 1927 ("to save it from destruction, or from remodeling, which is sometimes worse"), and this seemingly impractical woman surprised everyone by fitting it out with a ground-floor studio and living quarters for herself and rental units on the upper floors. A decade later, she was serving as vice president of the Vieux Carré Property Owners Association.

Unlike some other New Orleans artists, she never complained about having to do picturesque paintings for the tourist trade, but when a 1936 show of her work at the Arts and Crafts Club included no views of courtyards, she remarked, "Everyone has seen those—no one wants to see something over and over again." She started spending a good deal of time at Melrose Plantation, doing landscapes and flower pictures—some paints she left behind at Melrose led to the career of famed folk artist Clementine Hunter—and a summer in Woodstock inspired her to attempt modern art. "But I don't seem able to do it," she told an interviewer. "Things I paint always look like the things I paint." In time, through sheer persistence, Kinsey became something of an institution. The Arts and Crafts Club marked its reopening after World War II with an exhibition of work by "the quarter's most beloved artist."

She died in New Orleans in 1952, and was buried in her native West Milton, Ohio.

Lyle Saxon, 35

SPRATLING DREW HIS FRIEND Lyle Saxon in characteristically natty attire, reclining on a lacy pillow and reading Lytton Strachey's *Eminent Victorians*. Saxon must certainly have caught the implications of the caption, "The Mauve Decade in St. Peter Street." Like several other Famous Creoles—Spratling and Faulkner, for that matter—Saxon wasn't exactly as he presented himself. For starters, he wasn't strictly heterosexual. He also wasn't a Louisiana native, a Southern gentleman with a plantation background, a graduate of Louisiana State University, or a jovial bon vivant. Although his

parents were from Louisiana, Saxon was born in Washington state—not his fault, to be sure, but a fact he later elided in biographical statements. His father immediately left the family and went off to be a bit player in Hollywood, so Lyle was raised back in Baton Rouge by his mother and two maiden aunts, and he let people assume he'd been born there. He spent much of his childhood in his grandfa-

Portrait by Pops Whitesell

LYLE SAXON
THE MAUVE DECADE IN SAINT PETER STREET

ther's bookstore, not, as he sometimes implied, on his family's plantation (there wasn't one). He did go to LSU, but dropped out (or was expelled—there was a rumor about a cross-dressing scandal) shortly before graduation; although he never claimed to be a graduate, he didn't correct anyone who said he was. As for the joviality, his letters and diaries make it clear that he was often unhappy, even anguished, and subject to profound depression.

When *Famous Creoles* appeared, Saxon had recently left his job at the *Times-Picayune* and moved to New York. (He'd even sold his house on Royal Street, although he kept a rented pied à terre on St. Peter, just in case.) He had been a newspaperman for a decade and he was good at it, but he wanted to write "serious" literature. He told Sherwood and Elizabeth Anderson that "this New York move is absolutely essential if I am ever going to amount to anything." Newspaper work felt like prostitution—"And I'm tired of street-walking. I want to be a good girl, I do." He'd just had his first success as a fiction writer, with a local-color short story published in the *Dial* (Grace King wrote, "*You have arrived,*" and it subsequently won an O. Henry Award), and he hoped to finish a novel he'd been trying to write for several years.

But more than his day job had kept Saxon from writing his book. He was a busy man. His biographer observes that he had not only become the "official spokesman of Frenchtown" through his many newspaper articles on the Quarter, but its "unofficial host," constantly entertaining both visitors and residents. As the *New Orleanian* observed, "he has thousands of friends who take up quantities of his time, but he doesn't mind"—or so it appeared. Privately, he sometimes complained about it, but he enjoyed being seen as "a *bon vivant* in the old tradition," who lived "in indolent elegance on Royal street," waited on by "stylish and snobbish Negro servants."

Ham Basso once unkindly described Saxon as "maybe a little old ladyish" (though "not such a bad guy"). As a matter of fact, old ladies were among his greatest fans—and he theirs. He kept up a busy schedule of speeches to groups like the Alliance Française, which met at Le Petit Salon (when he lingered at one of their meetings, Faulkner strode in demanding, "Lyle, you old son of a bitch, what's been keeping you?"), and he once told Sam Gilmore's sister that he'd speak to a ladies' group in Thibodaux if she'd take him to visit Miss Ludovine Garic—not mentioning that Miss Ludovine resided in the graveyard. He was always a great admirer of Grace King: he dedicated his book *Fabulous New Orleans* to her, and served as pallbearer and eulogist at her funeral. It was at one of Miss King's Friday afternoon salons that he met Cammie Henry, the mistress of Melrose Plantation, near Natchitoches, who was in the process of turning her place into a retreat for writers and artists. By 1926 Saxon was spending many weekends and the odd month at Melrose, a 250-mile journey each way. He said he found it easier to write there, but one suspects the real draw was the leisure and his friendship with "Miss Cammie," who soon became "Aunt Cammie."

Saxon was an early and avid preservationist. He lived in the Quarter from his first days in New Orleans, when he roamed its streets with his fellow journalist Flo Field and his boyhood friend George Favrot, despite the warnings of friends that those streets were not just seedy but dangerous. (They were right: Saxon claimed that he was once bound and tortured by three burglars who didn't believe he had no valuables.) Soon Alberta Kinsey and a few other urban pioneers joined him. After renting a couple of places on Royal Street he was finally able to buy one, and moved his collection of period furniture there in 1920. From his position at the *Times-Picayune* he preached that the only way to save the "hundreds of splendid houses" in the Quarter was "to buy them, to restore them as best you can—to change them in no important detail of construction—and, finally, to live in them." (His friends Natalie Scott and John McClure did just that in 1921.)

Basso described Saxon as "sort of the Ward McAllister of the New Orleans intellectual circles," and he certainly did resemble that social arbiter of Gilded Age New York in the pleasure he took in introducing people to one another (Sherwood Anderson and Edmund Wilson to Grace King, for example) and in organizing parties and entertainments. He was astonishingly kind and generous to his friends—among his papers at Tulane are thank-you notes from Jack McClure and Oliver La Farge for loans ($40 and $50, respectively) in the mid-1920s—but it wasn't just money. When Spratling needed an introduction for a portfolio of his French Quarter sketches, Saxon wrote it; when Natalie Scott's brother died, he wrote a moving condolence letter that she saved all her days; and he used his position at the *Times-Picayune* to review (always favorably) his friends' books and gallery exhibits and to publicize their activities.

Saxon's biographer describes him as "a clean, elegant figure, [with] classic good looks." He was tall and slim, with black hair and eyes "not just blue," a friend recalled, "but *pale* blue, the kind you don't forget." Elizabeth Anderson said that he was "charming and gallant" with "exquisite manners," and "looked aristocratically remote even in a seersucker suit that dared not rumple when worn by him." Perhaps not surprisingly, another friend sniffed that "Lyle always has some woman or other swooning away in his background."

Sketch of Saxon and (perhaps) Roark Bradford, by Caroline Durieux

For the most part they swooned in vain, but there were exceptions. One was Olive Lyons, a glamorous poet and socialite ten years older than he, and married, whose relationship with Saxon—only possibly a romance, although he did keep her photograph by his bed—caused gossip among their friends and perhaps contributed to his decision to leave for New York.

Saxon's plan to get away from New Orleans didn't really work. His Christopher Street apartment became a shelter for friends from down home, who called it "the Southern Protective Association." (Faulkner and Spratling were among the many who enjoyed its hospitality.) Moreover, soon after he got to New York the *Century Magazine* sent him back to Louisiana to write about the devastating floods of 1927. His articles were reworked for *Father Mississippi,* a book so successful that he wrote three more in the next three years: *Fabulous New Orleans, Old Louisiana,* and *Lafitte the Pirate.* Like it or not,

Saxon had found his calling as, in one reviewer's words, "essentially a biographer, a biographer of places as well as of people." These works of more-or-less nonfiction—he used fictitious personas, not labeled as such, to present accurate information about his subjects and misleading information about himself—were what his manservant Joe Gilmore called "eatin' books." They sold briskly and made him a celebrity (in New Orleans at least), which led to even more demands on his time for speeches and public appearances. For the next several years he settled into a pattern of half a year or so in New York and the other half in New Orleans or, for long stretches, at Melrose, where he devoted hours to letter-writing, drinking, carousing, and training chickens to light on his arm—just about anything, in fact, except finishing his novel. In 1935 he was appointed state director of the Federal Writers' Project, where he did an outstanding job, negotiating the tricky politics, supervising scores of field workers, and producing two of the best WPA guidebooks and a folklore compilation from the leftovers. He also showed that his preservation impulse wasn't limited to architecture by campaigning to get New Orleanians to mask for Mardi Gras. "Mr. New Orleans," as people had begun to call him, viewed his local celebrity with mixed feelings, observing wryly when asked for his autograph by one tourist too many, "I started out to be a writer and ended up as a souvenir."

Finally, in 1937, fourteen years after he started it, Saxon finished *Children of Strangers*, set among the mixed-race Creoles who lived near Melrose. He was a novelist at last. That year he bought his final property in the Quarter, a Madison Street house with a lovely courtyard where he enjoyed having Joe Gilmore serve him drinks, but in 1944, finances strained yet again, he had to sell it. He and Joe moved to a suite in the St. Charles Hotel and he began to work on a rambling memoir disguised as a tribute to Gilmore, his devoted true friend whom he called "Black Saxon." (Another friend completed *The Friends of Joe Gilmore* after Saxon's death.)

Saxon had never been healthy, and a lifetime of bad habits didn't help. His friends rallied around—had masses said for him at the cathedral, brought a holy relic to his hospital room, put rabbis and Christian Science practitioners to work, and even tried gris-gris—but, in 1946, Saxon died in Baptist Hospital. He was fifty-five years old. Even though he'd once written that New Orleans was "the woman to whom I offer my love," his body was returned to Baton Rouge for burial next to his mother and grandmother.

Harold Levy, 32

"Il Maestro" Harold Levy came from a wealthy and cultivated Jewish family. His father, who owned the Crescent Paper Box factory, was a sophisticated art collector who bought and sold internationally and served in the 1920s as an agent for Joseph Duveen, the hugely influential art dealer who once famously remarked that "Europe has a great deal of art, and America has a great deal of money." Harold's mother was the daughter of a German immigrant who had prospered as a cotton broker, and the Levys lived with her parents in their Garden District house until Harold's teenage years.

After Harold went to Harvard (Class of 1915), he returned to manage the family's factory and lived with his parents, who had moved to their own place near Audubon Park. He had always been musical, however, and after Le Petit Theatre was founded in 1919 he jumped at the opportunity to become its musical director. He stayed with the box factory—after his father died in 1925, he was its president—but he and a friend moved into a third-floor apartment in the upper Pontalba building to be closer to the theater, where (a book about American community theater observed) he could be found "most any afternoon." His place had a large double parlor and a grand

IL MAESTRO LEVY
DE LE PETIT OPERA

A few years later

piano, and Ronald Hargarve, who lived downstairs, decorated it in "Oriental" style with beaverboard arches and cardboard tube columns—all painted strawberry pink. Arabic verse was stenciled on the walls, the windows were draped with green and blue fabric, and concealed blue lights imitated moonlight. Soon, Cicero Odiorne recalled, "it was a party every night at Harold's." One evening, people "lolled about on Harold's divans . . . which were soft as whipped cream . . . smoking cigarettes in long holders and talking in sophisticated monosyllables" while "Jenny Pitot played La Cathedrale Engloutie in the simulated moonlight." Another night Julius Friend brought a roulette wheel, and someone once lost $70 in a craps game in the bedroom (it wasn't Natalie Scott: she talked to the dice like a pro). Levy liked to play the piano while people sang, and he was known for his puns and limericks.

Le Petit Opera
Louisianais
Presents
THE FRENCH OPERA OF
Mignon
By Ambroise Thomas

(The Old French Opera House)

The Tulane Theatre
April 11, 1928, 8:15 p. m.
Under the direction of
Maestro Ernesto Gargano

The Old French Opera House on a program for Le Petit Opéra.

The caption for Spratling's sketch alludes to the short-lived Petit Opéra Louisianais, which Levy served as a board member, and in 1927 his Orchestre du Petit Theatre du Vieux Carré made its debut at Flo Field's play *A La Creole* (it's unclear how long the orchestra stayed in existence), but for the most part, Levy was a sort of Zelig figure, popping up in the background of everyone else's story. He was at Harvard with Edward Nagle, Virginia Parker's future husband. In Paris to study conducting, he showed up at Cicero Odiorne's Montparnasse studio. When Ronald Hargrave was working on Majorca, Levy corresponded with him and gave the *Times-Picayune* a Spanish newspaper's glowing review of Hargrave's work. He drank with Keith Temple and Oliver La Farge at La Farge's "Wigwam." He discussed poetry with William Faulkner over inexpensive French Quarter lunches, and he took along his Harvard friend John Dos Passos, when Dos Passos came for a visit. In later years, several Famous Creoles recalled lunches at Levy's apartment where someone read aloud from a smuggled copy of *Ulysses*.

Levy's moment of literary immortality came when Faulkner's sonnet "The Faun" was published in the *Double Dealer* and dedicated "To H. L." because Levy had helped Faulkner finish the poem.

Levy had a pleasant if uneventful life. What he wrote for his Harvard twentieth anniversary in 1935 had been true for a good many years already: "I am president of the Crescent Paper Box Factory, Inc. Otherwise, I am fisherman, bachelor, bon vivant, and director of musical productions at Le Petit Theatre du Vieux Carré."

Levy continued to work with the box factory and with Le Petit Theatre (he was on the board for nearly twenty-five years). Rather late in life, he married an old friend, a New Orleans woman, daughter of a local lawyer, who had been living in the lower Pontalba building. The couple moved to larger accommodations on St. Ann Street between Bourbon and Royal, where they lived until Harold's death in 1981. From his father he inherited artistic taste and a good many fine pieces of art—although he acquired Ronald Hargrave's portrait of Sherwood Anderson for his living room on his own.

One more Zelig moment: In 1959, while John Howard Griffin was changing his skin color for his book *Black Like Me,* he stayed in the old slave quarters behind the Levys' house.

Caroline Wogan Durieux, 30

CARRIE WOGAN WAS A REAL CREOLE, not just a Famous one. Although she got her surname from an Irish great-grandfather, she grew up surrounded by French-speaking cousins and aunts, as the daughter of a well-off sugar refinery superintendent. When she was four years old she decided to be an artist, and she was already an able watercolorist when she went to Newcomb College to study with Ellsworth Woodward. Although she sometimes chafed under Woodward's old-fashioned tutelage—once, when she was told to copy one of his paintings, she even copied his signature by way of protest—her student work was shown in the 1917 annual show of the Art Association of New Orleans at the Delgado Museum. The Art Association gave her a scholarship, which, added to the money intended for her debut, took her to the Pennsylvania Academy of the Fine Arts. At PAFA she was part of a New Orleans colony that included Virginia Parker (Nagle), Fanny Craig (Ventadour), and Weeks Hall (future New Orleanian Dan Whitney was there about the same time). She was also introduced to Modernism there, and made a good many connections who would prove useful later in her career.

She returned to New Orleans in 1920, taught briefly at Newcomb, and married Pierre Durieux, a childhood neighbor, whose business took the cou-

CAROLINE WOGAN DURIEUX

ple first to Cuba, then, in 1926, to Mexico. She spent most of the 1920s in Latin America, but she wrote some poetry for the *Double Dealer,* as did her younger brother, Daniel, and she often came back to New Orleans to visit her family and naturally hung out with the Arts and Crafts Club crowd, which included Charles Bein, whom she'd known since her teenage years. She showed her paintings and drawings at the Club in 1922, she and Dan Whitney had a joint show there in 1926, and she showed some pencil sketches and floral paintings in a group show the next year.

Durieux went on to become the best-known painter among the Famous Creoles—the only one, in fact, with a real national reputation. But that was in the future.

In the late 1920s, she parked her son with her mother in New Orleans during the school year and concentrated on expressing what one critic called "her private brand of happy sophistication" in her art. Living in "Mexico City for work and Taxco for play," she fell in with a group of Mexican revolutionary artists including Diego Rivera, who painted her portrait in 1929. She came to share their left-wing politics (Anna Wogan called her "my red sister"), which added a new edge to her work—nothing militant, just stiletto jabs at the smug and self-important, but Rivera wrote, "Not since the 18th century perhaps, have such subtle social chronicles been so ably put on canvas"; an article in *Art Digest* called her work "politely cruel, charmingly venomous"; and a writer for the *Chicago Daily News* put her in "the royal line of the satirists—Hogarth, Daumier, Lautrec, George Grosz. . . ." In 1936, when Durieux had a solo show at the Arts and Crafts Club of what the *Times-Picayune* called her "social satires and symbolic stylizations," the *Item-Tribune* announced that "New Orleans' first great painter has arrived."

Portrait by Diego Rivera

The next year she and her husband moved back to New Orleans, where she taught at the Arts and Crafts Club and worked for a time on the Federal

La Classe de Dessin (1934)

Writers' Project before taking a faculty position at Newcomb College. From 1939 until 1943 she was also state director of the Federal Arts Project. Her work continued to be popular with both the public and the critics. She had done her first lithograph in 1931, and her work in that medium was particularly esteemed. In 1943 she accepted a position at Louisiana State University, which she held until her retirement in 1964. During her time in Baton Rouge, she experimented with innovative printmaking techniques, notably one that employed radioactive ink, and her string of honors and awards and prestigious shows continued until her death in 1989.

Genevieve Pitot, 25

GENEVIEVE PITOT WAS THE OTHER genuine Creole, with Caroline Durieux, among the Famous Creoles. A Pitot ancestor had been the city's second mayor, and after her father died she grew up on Esplanade Avenue in a French-speaking household that included her mother, three sisters, a brother, her mother's parents, two unmarried aunts, a bachelor uncle, and a bachelor cousin. From an early age (two, she said) she showed talent at the piano; as a child she played ragtime for family dances and studied locally. At seventeen she amused the visiting French piano virtuoso Alfred Cortot by playing Chopin with jazzy licks. Cortot urged her to study with him in Paris, and when the World War ended in 1919, Pitot did that, staying for three years. While in Paris, she adopted the French pronunciation of "Pitot" (the final consonant was pronounced in Louisiana.)

Back in New Orleans, trying to make a living as a concert pianist, she contributed some Parisian glamor to the French Quarter crowd. Lyle Saxon

GENEVIEVE PITOT
PIANISSIMO APASSIONATA

Portrait by Pops Whitesell

Another sketch by Spratling

reported in the *Times-Picayune* that at one concert she wore one of designer Jean Patou's "most daring creations," and decades later Cicero Odiorne recalled "Jenny, in white silk, stretched out on the divan, under the light," at Ronald Hargrave's place. Everyone else remembered her Dance of the Seven Veils at Les Folies du Vieux Carré (her respectable family was not amused). Looking back, Marc Antony said that she was "a fun girl of the twenties" and "crazy as could be," and she acknowledged that the scene was "kind of mad, with the parties."

After little more than a year, she decided that New Orleans couldn't support her concert career, so she went on the road. (Rehearsing for a concert in Birmingham, she was accidentally trapped for three hours in a trick chair left on the stage by Harry Houdini.) In 1924 she moved to New York, where she hung around dance auditions to pick up work from dancers who needed an accompanist and modeled nude for a photographer (she didn't tell her family). In 1925 she talked her way into the office of the president of the Aeolian Company and got a job cutting player-piano rolls of songs with titles like "Chrysanthemums" and "Alpine Storm." "I was put into what was called the 'salon music' department," she told an interviewer in 1978. "They were cheap waltzes, cheap music." One reviewer agreed, saying that "Amoureuse" was "a terribly conventional waltz tune, though Miss Genevieve Pitot does her very excellent best to disguise this." Still, it paid the bills, and she made at least fifty-five rolls between 1925 and 1929.

At some point in these years, she gave birth to a son she named Opus One, who died in infancy. During the pregnancy, she recalled, she was thinking about putting the baby up for adoption when William Faulkner and Keith Temple, who were in New York, came to see her and urged her to keep the child, saying that they would raise it for her. Fifty years later, she was still laughing about that offer.

Pitot continued to pursue a concert career in the late 1920s, returning occasionally to play in New Orleans. A performance of *Rhapsody in Blue* (she had met George Gershwin at New York parties) was not a success, since the day was unbearably hot and the audience couldn't hear the piano, but a later recital (including a Franck piece performed with a string quartet assembled by Harold Levy) went better. Her many New York performances included a program of modern French music at Carnegie Hall in 1928. Meanwhile, she was still playing for dancers, and she hit the big time when she met the avant-garde choreographer Michio Ito at another New York party and began to accompany his performances. The Pitot-Ito combo performed in New York and Boston.

Although Pitot would have a few more well-received solo recitals and a 1934 series of radio broadcasts, her future lay in her work with ballet and, especially, modern dance. In the 1930s she played for classes taught by Martha Graham, Agnes de Mille, and other major choreographers, and composed dance music for important figures in modern dance such as José Limón, Doris Humphrey, Charles Weidman, and Hanya Holm. But her most lasting association was with Helen Tamiris, whom she met at a Greenwich Village restaurant, where most evenings she played classical music from 7:00 until 10:00 and "everything else" until 2:00 or later. Pitot began playing for Tamiris's company, and soon was composing for many of her dances, including her *Walt Whitman Suite*. In 1936 the two women joined the WPA's Federal Dance Project, and collaborated on four productions, of which the most notable was *How Long, Brethren?*, a "dance-drama" set to music from a collection called *Negro Songs of Protest*, arranged by Pitot. The twenty-voice Federal Theater Negro Chorus sang Pitot's semi-operatic arrangements while a troupe of white and mostly Jewish girls mimed cotton-picking and, at the end, set off into "a red dawn." (Dance historian Ellen Graff notes that the black singers were off-stage and uncredited in the original program, and remarks that one song "pointedly observe[d] that 'White folk he ain't Jesus, he jes' a man grabbin' biscuit out of poor darkie's hand,' [but] the irony that white dancers were grabbin' the spotlight from poor darkies' faces apparently never was noticed." In fact, the audience at Harlem's Lafayette Theater probably noticed it when the production went there after its downtown run.)

Sometime in the 1930s, Pitot married a New Yorker named Joe Sullivan. During World War II, while Joe was winning a Bronze Star in France, she toured state fairs playing for the fan dancer Sally Rand. After the war she moved to Broadway, where in 1947 she arranged the dance music—and wrote much of it—for the hit musical *High Button Shoes*. In the next eighteen years she did dance arrangements or composed for nineteen musicals, including *Kiss Me Kate, Kismet, L'il Abner, Can-Can,* and *Call Me Madam.* She also worked off-Broadway, and one project for the 1958 Jacob's Pillow Dance Festival must have brought back memories of her days as a Famous Creole: she wrote the music for another "dance-drama" based on Sherwood Anderson's *Winesburg, Ohio.*

But her husband died in 1961, and after "*Hair* killed the Broadway musical," as she put it scornfully, work became more scarce, so she returned to New Orleans in the 1970s. She gave two concerts at Tulane, was interviewed by the newspapers, had visits from player-piano enthusiasts, and seemed to be on her way to a happy retirement when she was mugged and seriously injured. As a nondriver, wearing a brace, using a cane, and running short of money, she depended on the kindness of friends. Fortunately, she had many of them. She died in New Orleans in 1980.

Albert Bledsoe Dinwiddie, 55

IF A. B. DINWIDDIE LOOKS A LITTLE out of his element among the "artful and crafty" Famous Creoles, it's because few could have been less Bohemian than this son of a Presbyterian clergyman, married to the daughter of another. Through an unfortunate accident he was born in Kentucky, but Dinwiddie was a Virginian who bore the name of his grandfather, the Confederacy's assistant secretary of war. He was educated at Mr. Jefferson's university, where he received his B.A., his M.A., and, at twenty-one, his Ph.D., with a dissertation on indirect discourse in Thucydides. He taught for a while at a Presbyterian college in Tennessee, then went to Göttingen to study higher mathematics. In 1906 Tulane hired him and four years later he was full professor of mathematics, chairman of his department, and dean of the College of Arts and Sciences. In 1918, he was named president of the university.

So what is this establishment figure, a man of extreme respectability and sobriety (a posthumous profile said that "his rapid-fire wit was reserved for his intimates"), doing in such unconventional company?

It probably helped that he was Bill Spratling's boss—Spratling always liked to cultivate rich and powerful patrons—and even if Dinwiddie wasn't

ALBERT BLEDSOE DINWIDDIE
B. A., M. A., Ph. D., L. L. D.

really part of the French Quarter circle, he certainly helped to make it possible. Without the Tulane that he largely shaped, it would have been a different, and diminished, scene. Dinwiddie was largely responsible for turning Tulane into a serious university. He pushed through a major endowment drive in 1920 that supported everything from faculty recruitment and new departments to new buildings and a big-time athletic program. His service as a trustee of the Carnegie Foundation for the Advancement of Teaching and on innumerable other boards and commissions was making Tulane's name known nationally, while at the same time he kept a close eye on local minutiae. He forced out an ineffectual chairman of the Department of Middle American Research to make room for the ambitious young Frans Blom, for example, and he helped to engineer N. C. Curtis's return to Tulane's architecture department, which he'd left for the University of Illinois. True, as dean and president, he stifled William Woodward's efforts to introduce a fine arts curriculum for Tulane's male students, but even that wound up contributing to the establishment of the Arts and Crafts Club's art school, which an *Item-Tribune* cartoon announced as "The Only Art School in the South Where *Men* As Well As Women Can Get *Good Art* Training."

During Dinwiddie's presidency, Tulane's endowment increased from $3 million to $10 million and its student body doubled. When he died in 1935, *Time* magazine commented, rightly, that "he built up [Tulane] from a small sectional institution into one of the major universities of the South."

Samuel Louis Gilmore Jr., 27

FAMOUS CREOLES SHOWS THE LANKY Gilmore (he was six feet, one and a half inches tall) in a typically languid pose. It was one of the book's inside jokes that Spratling's drawing and its caption refer to the flower-bearing shoe-fetishist who is one of Venus's attendants in Aubrey Beardsley's *Under the Hill*. When Gilmore made *New Orleans Magazine*'s list of eligible bachelors, the magazine warned: "Flirts with the muses only." Gilmore—"Louis" in his literary work, but "Sam" to his friends—had inherited wealth (his mother was a plantation heiress and his father was a prominent lawyer, a member of the Pickwick Club, New Orleans city attorney and, at the time of his death in 1910, a congressman), so he never had to work and, according to his nephew, except for wartime service in the Army Corps of Engineers, never did.

But that judgment is too harsh. He labored hard and ceaselessly at his writing. As early as 1912, working for a congressman in Washington before beginning college at Columbia University, he wrote his mother excitedly about the poems he was writing. A few years later, he was publishing them in *Poetry* and the *Little Review,* in some very

Passport picture, 1916

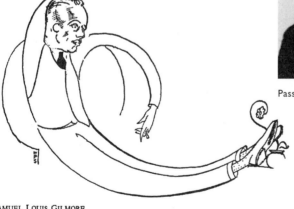

SAMUEL LOUIS GILMORE
LE REPOS DE FLORIZEL

good company indeed. After the inauguration of the *Double Dealer,* he was all over it, serving in various capacities including associate editor, and contributing poetry, short plays, stories, book reviews, and money (he was listed for a while as one of the magazine's "patrons"). Frances Jean Bowen observed in her history of the magazine that "there was no doubt of his pleasure in and consecration to the literary arts." Gilmore seemed well on the way to becoming an established poet. The *New York Times* noted of a 1923 issue of the *Little Review* that "the contributors include the indefatigable Baroness von Freytag-Loringhoven, Louis Gilmore, and Guillaume Apollinaire"; one of his poems won a $25 prize from the *Fugitive,* organ of the Nashville group of that name; and another was chosen for *Best Poems of 1923–27.*

But when one of Gilmore's admirers, some years later, referred to his "Mauve Decade style" as "an acerb mixture of Ronald Firbank and the pre-prison Oscar Wilde," he put his finger on why Gilmore's work is not to everyone's taste. Ezra Pound complained about Gilmore's poem "Improvisation," which repeated the phrase "My thoughts are": Pound's thought was that "a little art might be expected in finding a variant on that particular phrasing." And Bowen, who observes that Gilmore's verse was "always clever, always mocking, uniformly brittle," adds that "a dose of sixty or so poems at a sitting leaves the reader with a throat-burn from too much pepper." A sample, from the January 1923 *Double Dealer*:

> *To A Fly*
> O importunate
> O fly
> You too
> Shall appear in my verses
> The amber
> Of the mausoleum
> Is the measure
> Of its condescension.

Gilmore's plays could also be a little precious. *Bagatelle,* a one-acter set in "an Arab's tent on the edge of the desert," appeared in the *Double Dealer.* It opens with Shabiya "The Gazelle" playing a lute, and pausing to ask a passer-by, "In Allah's name, wilt thou not rest in the shade?" In 1928 the play was staged by the Lake Charles Little Theatre (a decision perhaps influenced by the fact that Gilmore was on its board of directors), which immediately afterward imposed a ban on "untried work."

On the storied Lake Pontchartrain excursion, Gilmore made a pass at William Spratling—"I'm sorry but I just like boys and that's all there is to it," he explained when Spratling demurred. Subsequently he served as the model for Mark Frost, author of short and obscure poems and inveterate bummer of cigarettes, in Faulkner's *Mosquitoes.* Gilmore seems to have exuded an air of ineffectuality and dilettantism, reinforced by episodes like the time he and Faulkner took a small sailboat out and found that "between them the best they could do was go around in circles." His older sister, Martha—a formidable clubwoman, preservationist, and civic activist—once noted that the Gilmore line was in danger of dying out, since neither Sam nor her cousin Arthur had ever married, but that "nothing much will be lost by this failure," since her grandfather and father were "the only dividend this family has produced."

In later years Gilmore became almost a recluse. Bowen interviewed him in 1952 and reported: "Fastidious to the point of effeminacy in personal appearance and in house furnishings, he maintains a charming bachelor quarters in a small house behind his sister's establishment. . . . Caviar, wine and Bach are the chief accompaniments." He grew increasingly conservative, writing in 1972 to William Odiorne, his friend from the *Double Dealer* days, that he would probably vote for George Wallace, "that unsinkable cock sparrow," for president. He kept writing poetry and trying to publish it, but with decreasing success. In 1959, the Pelican Press in New Orleans published *Vine Leaves and Flowers of Evil,* a slim volume of his verse and his translations of Baudelaire, dedicated to Natalie Scott and two other friends. (He sent a signed copy to William Buckley.) He placed five poems with the *Texas Quarterly* about the time that magazine reprinted *Sherwood Anderson and Other Famous Creoles.* The old Fugitive poet Donald Davidson wrote that "I find myself, as of old, very fond of your poems," and recommended a book of them to the Vanderbilt University Press. But the press turned it down. By 1972, five months before he died, Gilmore had turned to a vanity press, getting a quote for an edition of 750 copies. The last of the impressive collection of rejections in his papers at Tulane is a letter from the Wesleyan University Press postmarked two weeks after his death.

Grace King, 74

SPRATLING BASED HIS SKETCH of Grace King on a portrait by the well-known painter Wayman Adams that hung in the Delgado Museum, spiced with what Spratling fancied was a touch of Beardsleian decadence. As in the original portrait, King is flanked by her two maiden sisters, who managed her household and made her literary career possible.

The oldest of the Famous Creoles, daughter of a New Orleans lawyer and sugar planter, King had been a teenager during Reconstruction, a difficult time for her family that left her with bitter memories. She used those memories explicitly in her 1913 novel, *The Pleasant Ways of St. Médard,* but in fact they had led to her entire literary career. As she told Lyle Saxon in 1926, she began to write from "a sort of patriotism—a feeling of loyalty to the South"; all of her generation, she said, "were anxious to defend the South we loved when it was represented so badly in literature"—and in time she became a leading champion of the Old South and its ways.

She wrote her first short story in 1885, after discussing the fiction of

GRACE KING, PORTRAIT BY WAYMAN ADAMS ✛
AUBREY BEARDSLEY ✛ WILLIAM SPRATLING

Portrait in Delgado Museum, the original for Spratling's sketch.

George Washington Cable with the editor of *Century* magazine, who was visiting New Orleans. Although she was not a Creole herself, King had gone to French schools as a girl (she dropped little French phrases into her conversation and pronounced even words like *amateur* in the French way), and she objected to Cable's treatment of Creoles and his sympathy for blacks. When the editor challenged her to do better, she began writing the next day. Soon her work was appearing regularly in his magazine and others, and eventually she published thirteen books, about evenly divided between fiction and history. (Sometimes the distinction was not all that clear. She once had an argument with her friend and mentor, the historian Charles Gayarré, about whether stories of white cruelty to blacks should be suppressed. She thought they should be.)

For years, King's famous Friday afternoon salons drew local and visiting writers, and her literary friends included Mark Twain, whose cigars she smoked at his home in Connecticut, and Julia Ward Howe (of all people). In 1891, on one of her several European trips, she lectured on Sidney Lanier at Newnham College, Cambridge. By the 1920s she was loaded with honors, decorated by the French government, and D. Litt. (Tulane).

In short, she sounds like an unlikely chum for the Bohemian crowd. But they admired and respected her. She was, in fact, as Sherwood Anderson observed, "a sincere craftsman." Moreover, although she lived a mile or so uptown, she lent her considerable influence to the younger people's cause of preserving and restoring the old buildings of the French Quarter, and she had been doing that before most of them were born. As early as 1884, at

the New Orleans World Industrial Cotton Centennial Exposition (where Julia Ward Howe was in charge of the Woman's Department), Miss King produced a display that celebrated the Vieux Carré's architecture, and, later, most of her stories, novels, and histories portrayed, at least by implication, the Quarter's lost elegance. As she wrote in the foreword to an early guidebook, "We wander through old streets, and pause before the age-stricken houses; and, strange to say, the magic past lights them up." Perhaps her greatest contribution came in 1924 when she took her place at the head of the campaign to reclaim the French Quarter for respectable womanhood by accepting the presidency of Le Petit Salon (see page 53). This "bright new constellation . . . in the social sky," as she described it, soon acquired its clubhouse adjoining Le Petit Theatre, and its weekly meetings brought its members face-to-face with the squalor and the charm of the neighborhood.

When Miss King died in New Orleans, in the first days of 1932, her friend Lyle Saxon eulogized her as "our greatest writer and our greatest woman." A few months after her death, a new play she had written about Jean Lafitte was produced at the old Beauregard house in the French Quarter and her autobiography was published. The *New York Times* observed that "'genteel' [is] the adjective, above all others, that should be applied to the *Memories of a Southern Woman of Letters*." Quite possibly that was the author's intention.

Weeks Hall, 32

A TOURIST ONCE REMARKED, "Of all the Southern mansions I have visited, Weeks Hall is the most beautiful." She was not the first to confuse the master of Shadows-on-the-Teche with the house that was his obsession and his legacy. The inscription on Spratling's caricature, "Weeks Hall by Moonlight," is a little joke along the same line.

In 1919, the young Hall's widowed aunt—his "substitute mother," to whom he was always close—helped him to buy a stately 1834 plantation house in New Iberia built by his great-grandfather, a sugar planter. A high school dropout, Hall had studied on a scholarship at the Pennsylvania Academy of the Fine Arts and served in a navy camouflage unit on the Gulf Coast during World War I. In 1922, after a trip to Europe on a PAFA traveling scholarship, Hall moved into the grand, but dilapidated, house—home at one time, he said, to six Italian families—and he lived in The Shadows for the rest of his life. He engaged preservationist and architect Richard Koch to oversee the carefully limited modernization of the building, while he undertook the restoration of the gardens himself. In 1923 D. W. Griffith filmed *The White Rose* at The Shadows; it was the first of many movies shot there and

BARON TECHE

Griffith the first of many famous visitors (others included Cecil B. DeMille, Emily Post, and Walt Disney).

"Baron Teche" was active in the French Quarter scene, from a distance. He was one of the fifteen "male workers in the graphic arts" who founded the New Orleans Art League, and he came in regularly to teach at the Arts and Crafts Club, served on its board and the selection committee for the Benjamin Prize, and won the prize himself in 1926. He won another prize at an annual membership exhibition for an oil of a magnolia blossom (a favorite subject). When he came to an Arts and Crafts Club Bal des Artistes with a yellow and pink mustache and wig, the *States* reporter wrote that "I heard someone say he represented a nightmare but that is just an opinion."

Hall also brought the French Quarter to New Iberia. When Spratling and Natalie Scott came to work on their book about Louisiana plantations, Sam Gilmore's sister, Martha, came with them, and recalled that the place "was very run down, but Weeks had wonderful things in it and he loved it

Painting that won the Benjamin Prize.

Hall (left) and friends painting at Shadows-on-the-Teche

very, very much." The four sat by the lily pond in the moonlight and told stories ("Weeks had a wonderful repertoire"). When Sherwood Anderson came to New Orleans, Hall sent his aunt around with a rather peremptory summons to The Shadows, which Anderson obeyed. Lyle Saxon and Charles Bein also visited the place, Alberta Kinsey painted it, and Hall entertained Fanny Craig there (he had met her in Paris). His housekeeper reported that Hall was heartbroken when Fanny called from Paris in 1923 to say that she had married Jacques Ventadour, and blamed that disappointment for Hall's heavy drinking and lack of interest in other women. Hall's homosexuality is a more obvious explanation for the latter, but he did keep Fanny's photograph and the wedding announcement until his death.

The high point of Hall's artistic career was probably a 1928 one-man show at the Arts and Crafts Club. One critic observed that it offered "nearly every method of expression known to present day painters," giving the effect of "a variety performance consisting of a classic ballet, a popular song, black-face comedy, an operatic number, and a clog dance, with all numbers applauded from different sections and for different reasons." The critic himself applauded "the half-dozen pieces of merit." In 1925 Sherwood Anderson wrote that, although Hall had "a better painter's mind and feeling than almost anyone I know," he was "so frightened and twisted by life that he can't do anything really healthy." Elizabeth Anderson concurred: She found Hall "a strange and tragic person," a "slight man with . . . a curious soft quality that looked, somehow, unformed. From beneath black bangs, his narrow cat's eyes stared out at a world he could not fathom." She developed "a kind of horror" of The Shadows, feeling that "there was something terribly wrong in that reliquary of the past and it was something that was neither visible nor audible." Edmund Wilson had the same reaction. When he visited The Shadows, Hall put his pet macaw on the mantel and pulled its tail from time to time to make it squawk as he told stories that Wilson found less funny than he did. Seen through a haze of absinthe, Hall's features seemed to be "decomposing" and his smile, "apparently genial and friendly," was "actually arrogant and slightly offensive." All in all, Wilson thought there was "something rather sinister about the whole place."

As time went on, Hall became even stranger. Sometimes he dealt with importunate tourists by impersonating a (nonexistent) idiot twin brother. Other times, he just rushed at them in his underwear, shaking his cane and shouting, "Get out of here, you goddamn silly women!" He collected cardboard advertising figures, which he put in his windows and in guests' beds. He telephoned his friends at all hours—and strangers, too. When H. L. Mencken refused to take a 1:00 a.m. call, Hall sent him a telegram telling him that unless he came to visit and eat gumbo, "you are a coward and you have no stomach." He was drinking even more heavily and smoking nearly five packs a day.

Hall called himself "the Last of the Nigger-Lovers," and his friend Jonathan Williams reported that the only local people he cared for were his two black manservants, Clement and Raymond, with whom he had a close and probably intimate relationship. He was also fond of the great jazz cornetist Bunk Johnson, who worked for a while in the gardens at The Shadows; when Johnson died, Hall conspired with the local priest to have him secretly buried in the Hall family plot. Novelist Henry Miller reported that some of Hall's "imperative impulses" were so "spectacular and weird" that even Miller found them "impossible to describe in print"; an evening with him was "like a private séance with Dr. Caligari." When Sherwood Anderson brought his new wife to visit in the 1930s, she told her diary that Hall was "the weirdest person I ever saw."

Although his work was shown in the 1930s and 1940s at the Delgado, PAFA, and the Corcoran, he moved away from painting, particularly after an automobile accident in 1935 crushed his right wrist. He took up photography and worked with color transparencies, which he manipulated in various ways. But more and more of his attention was directed toward ensuring that Shadows-on-the-Teche would be preserved.

Hall considered himself "a trustee of something fine which chance has put in my hands to preserve," and he took his duties very seriously, appealing unsuccessfully to the National Park Service to take the place over, inviting influential people to visit, even appearing on Dave Garroway's television program to appeal for help. Finally, in 1958, the National Trust for Historic Preservation accepted the property, after Hall had built an endowment to maintain it. (He stopped drinking and cut back on expensive dinners, and the only long-distance telephone calls he made were anxious ones to the Trust.) Hall got the news on his deathbed.

He was buried on the grounds of The Shadows. In 2004, *Possessed by the Past*, a play based on his life, premiered at Lander University in South Carolina.

William Spratling, 25

WHEN BILL SPRATLING CAME TO New Orleans in 1922 to take a job in Tulane's architecture school, he quickly made himself at home. The Orleans Alley apartment he rented from Natalie Scott ("in spite of discreet insinuations from older members of the faculty" that living in the Quarter wasn't quite the thing) came with his very social landlady's services as cicerone. Spratling and the decade-older woman became fast friends, and in a matter of weeks he was mentioned in her newspaper column as a newcomer whose "apartment has already taken its place as one of the chosen nuclei of the Quarter." Less than three years later the *Item-Tribune Magazine* described Spratling as "prominent in the art life of the 'old quarter.'" His place was "a rendezvous for a small group of friends . . . occupied in artistic and scientific pursuits," young Freddie Oechsner wrote, obviously pleased to be one of the group, and Oliver La Farge recalled that writers who visited New Orleans also turned up there, "as everyone did."

Unlike his future housemate Bill Faulkner, Spratling was perfectly at ease with art lovers and patrons who were merely onlookers; Natalie Scott observed that gatherings at his place included not just "those who know how to take art and intellectuality pleasantly," but also "some of the social

Detail from *Famous Creoles*

Portrait by Pops Whitesell

world who find such atmosphere congenial." "A party of the unique kind which only the French Quarter at its best can produce" included Lyle Saxon, the Sherwood Andersons, some other Famous Creoles, and a Scandinavian sculptor, but also some socially prominent Orleanians who could be described as hangers-on. The article that reported that also gushed about Spratling's décor, "a pleasant harmony of things chosen with discriminating taste."

Spratling's father ran a hospital for epileptics in upstate New York and he was born there, but his parents died when he was young and he was passed around among his father's Southern relatives, where he picked up the accent that one friend said was pretty much identical to William Faulkner's Mississippi drawl. The nearest thing he had to a home was the family farm near Auburn, Alabama; he went to high school there and then to the local college (what later became Auburn University), where his drawing ability was such that he found himself teaching in the architecture department while still an undergraduate. Although he left Auburn in 1921 without a degree, Tulane hired him to teach graphics, freehand and cast drawing, architectural history, and a life class (including lectures on anatomy with "all the major bones and muscles named and illustrated on the blackboard").

Elizabeth Anderson once described him in a seersucker suit, "slight and dark as a Mexican, with his jutting jaw and eyes that squinted half defiantly at the world." Despite his habitually dour expression (there seem to be no photographs of him smiling), he had a wicked and sometimes ribald sense of humor. He liked to shock people and laughed, often, with "a slow, quiet, chuckling ripple." Cicero Odiorne wrote that his friend was "an artist to his fingertips," especially with "human material," an artist whose greatest talent lay in "directing the activity of others," but Mrs. Anderson recalled that he "was always arranging people's lives with the very best of intentions, though not always the best of results." He could be stubborn about it, too. His neighbor Joyce Stagg had a boarding arrangement with him that ended when he insisted that she eat raw eggplant for breakfast. He was a chain-smoker who liked his cocktails prepared with great ceremony, and he became such a fixture on the French Quarter party circuit that even his absence made news: one society note about a "studio party" reported that "everyone there regretted sincerely and wholeheartedly that Bill Spratling didn't show up."

It helped that he had good connections. Natalie Scott not only introduced him to society, but also enlisted him in the activities of Le Petit Theatre. Caroline Durieux took him to museums and shows and talked with him about art. N. C. Curtis, who had come to Tulane from Auburn a decade earlier, probably helped Spratling get the Tulane job and certainly became his mentor, collaborating with him on publications like *The Wrought Iron Work of Old New Orleans* (1925), and introducing him to the Arts and Crafts Club, where he was soon showing his drawings and teaching evening courses. Almost every week Spratling took his Tulane sketching classes on the streetcar to the French Quarter and turned them loose to draw buildings, tombs, and boats on the levee. They had lunch at Arnaud's for 50 cents and sometimes ended up at Spratling's studio. He always needed money, so he took on some evening classes for draftsmen and wrote his first book, *Pencil Drawing,* to aid in their education. He did drafting work for Moise Goldstein's firm, while Natalie Scott found him some work at the *States* and often used his pencil portraits with her articles. He published *Picturesque New Orleans,* a portfolio of French Quarter sketches. (Lyle Saxon wrote an introduction and recommended it in his column as a Christmas present.)

Spratling's financial straits notwithstanding, Saxon noticed that he had a way "of disappearing overseas and of returning a few months later, laden with the spoils of Europe in his sketchbook." He got to Europe most summers; a show at the Arts and Crafts Club of some drawings and pastels from

Detail from a picture of the Tulane faculty: President Dinwiddie center; Spratling at left.

his 1924 trip was "the talk of the town," and Meigs Frost, in the *States,* called Spratling "a master of his craft." (The show also included "a glaring nude," which a reviewer speculated was put there "out of sheer bravado, perhaps," observing that it showed "a good knowledge of anatomy.") When Faulkner arrived in the spring of 1925, Spratling rented him a spare room, and the two Bills lived briefly on Orleans Alley before they headed off to Europe together for the summer. Spratling painted for a while on Majorca with Ronald Hargrave and Conrad Albrizio before rejoining Faulkner in Paris. The two checked out *la vie bohème* with Cicero Odiorne and Harold Levy, and Spratling picked up a copy of *Ulysses,* which he smuggled through U.S. customs and proudly showed to his students in the fall.

Back in New Orleans, Spratling and Faulkner moved around the corner to another of Natalie Scott's properties, where Spratling converted a fourth-floor attic to an apartment-studio (Spratling "likes high art," *New Orleans Life* joked). He was even busier than before, publishing in architectural journals, showing and teaching at the Arts and Crafts Club, lecturing at the Delgado Museum, designing postcards of French Quarter scenes for tourists and Christmas cards for his friends, illustrating the Tulane yearbook, and sketching seventy-five plantation houses for a book he was doing with Natalie Scott. (*Old Plantation Houses in Louisiana* finally appeared in 1927.) Every morning he rode the streetcar with Oliver La Farge and Frans Blom to Tulane. But there was still time for play. Informal gatherings almost every evening were punctuated by events like Sherwood Anderson's Lake Pontchartrain cruise and the annual Arts and Crafts Club ball. (The day after one ball, Spratling's students observed that he came to class with socks of two different colors.) Spratling was often in the company of Esther DuPuy—one of a couple of women linked to him romantically, at least by gossip.

It looked as if Spratling was comfortably settled in New Orleans, but in 1926 he took his summer vacation in Mexico instead of Europe. His archeologist friend Blom had connections that put Spratling right in the middle of Mexico's artistic life, and he was enthralled. Later that year, when he and Faulkner put together *Famous Creoles,* his love affair with New Orleans was cooling.

In the next couple of years, the Famous Creoles began to disperse and Spratling's fascination with Mexico intensified. In 1927 he published an article on the country in *Architectural Forum*—the first of many publications—and he went back to visit that summer. He showed his Mexican work at the Arts and Crafts Club, and arranged for his Mexican artist friends to talk and show their work there. An article in 1928, based on some time he'd spent among the mixed-race Creoles near Melrose Plantation, would prove to be his last non-Mexican writing. About the time it appeared he abruptly and somewhat mysteriously quit his job at Tulane, and that summer he went to Mexico for the third time. The next spring he found a house in Taxco, a quaint colonial village on the road from Mexico City to Acapulco, and he moved to Mexico for good.

That proved to be a good move. In time, he would become one of the world's finest designers of silver jewelry and silverware, and in consequence he would also become a pilot, yachtsman, adventurer, horticulturalist, entrepreneur, friend of the rich and famous, and connoisseur of pre-Columbian art. He revitalized a moribund Mexican silver-working tradition and transformed his new hometown of Taxco. He also invented the margarita (or so he said).

He kept up his New Orleans ties. In fact, Natalie Scott soon joined him in Taxco, and eventually Elizabeth Anderson did, too. Caroline Durieux kept a house there for a time, and other Famous Creoles came to visit, some more than once. He returned to New Orleans a few times, but on his last visit, in 1956, he said that so many of his old friends were gone that walking the streets made him "feel a little sad. I feel like Rip Van Winkle." He died in an automobile accident in 1967, and was buried with many honors in Taxco.

William Faulkner, 29

IN 1926 BILL FAULKNER WAS NOT YET *William Faulkner,* Nobel laureate and eminence. He was just "a strange young man who had yet to publish anything of great importance" (as his friend Spratling described him). Keith Temple remembered him as "the sort of person you wouldn't have looked at twice" and "the silent member of every gathering," someone who "said very little and drank very much." Otherwise, there wasn't much to distinguish him from the dozen other "odd fish" Jimmy Feibleman saw hanging around the *Double Dealer* offices, except maybe his arrogance. Once, Feibleman recalled, when "a number of would-be writers were sitting around smoking, drinking whiskey and talking," the conversation turned to *Hamlet* and this "little man . . . with a small moustache and a slightly receding chin" who'd been sitting on the floor, silently nursing his bottle, piped up: "I could write a play like *Hamlet* if I wanted to." Then he fell silent again.

Detail from *Famous Creoles*

Feibleman was not impressed. He found Faulkner "an amiable, though dull, fellow." It probably didn't help that his too-large tweed jacket and the filthy raincoat he also used as a dressing gown "always looked as if he had slept in them," as one friend recalled. Others remembered his nicotine-stained fingers, his usual need for a haircut, and his frequent practice of going barefoot. Feibleman thought that women made Faulkner awkward, which may explain why Genevieve Pitot found him "not very communicative"—"he sat in a corner and he drank"—and Flo Field said that when she met him, "he backed away from the introduction."

Faulkner could indeed be remote and taciturn, especially with strangers. Albert Goldstein, an editor of the *Double Dealer*, thought he was "very, very moody" and "a very shy person when he was sober, which was only about half the time." But with close friends he could be downright frolicsome. He and Anderson, for example, spent hours amusing themselves and others (though perhaps not as much) by spinning tall tales about their swamp-dwelling creature, Al Jackson.

Faulkner had known Anderson's wife, Elizabeth, in New York, and looked her up when he arrived in New Orleans, early in 1925. Her husband happened to be at home, and the two writers hit it off almost immediately—Anderson, almost alone in discerning the young man's unusual promise, was happy to share his literary advice and opinions; Faulkner provided the respectful audience that Anderson craved. The two spent hours walking around the city. The Andersons also introduced Faulkner to Spratling, who lived just around the corner; Faulkner moved in with him, and the two Bills became regulars at the Andersons' Saturday-night dinners. Through Spratling and the Andersons, Faulkner became part of what he called "my New Orleans gang," subsequently the Famous Creoles.

Elizabeth Anderson recalled that Faulkner "loved to put things over on people and sometimes his audience never would realize they had been duped," and Spratling agreed that his housemate "was always a leg puller." But Faulkner could be less than amusing when he misled others about his background and experiences. He'd begun the practice back in Mississippi, trying to be something more than an Ole Miss dropout and failed postmaster by embroidering his wartime service with the RAF (which the Armistice actually ended before he'd left ground school), and adding a "u" to "Falkner" to give himself a more patrician veneer (his nickname in Oxford became "Count No-'Count"). In New Orleans—"the city," he said, "where imagination takes precedence over fact," and one where people hadn't known him all his life—he really cranked it up. Sometimes he took episodes from other people's lives (a couple from Spratling's, for instance) and claimed them for his own. Sometimes he pretended to be a tough guy, a former rum-runner or deckhand on a fishing schooner. But his most persistent role was that of the ex-RAF officer who drank heavily to ease the pain of his war wounds, a man with a cane, a limp, a clipped British accent, and a silver plate in his skull. Only the cane was real—and the "wounds" didn't keep Faulkner from entering his apartment by scaling the iron balconies to it, as he often did—but most people believed the story. The *Double Dealer* introduced its new contributor as someone who had "made a brilliant record" and been "severely wounded" as a wartime flyer. Novelist Anita Loos, visiting the Andersons, heard people say, "You can't expect much of Bill because he has that plate in his head and he isn't very smart," and Sherwood put the crippled aviator in a short story.

Faulkner also sometimes affected the role of the Mississippi planter-aristocrat, languidly drawling and pointedly courteous. Ham Basso, impressed by Faulkner's "beautiful manners [and] his soft speech" (as well as "his controlled intensity and his astonishing capacity for hard drink"), called him "the little Confederate." True, a lady whose book club he refused to address found him "not very sociable and rude as hell," but he could be courtly when he felt like it. Jimmy Feibleman was struck that Faulkner always addressed Roark Bradford's wife as "Ma'am," although he knew her well; he always called Elizabeth Anderson "Miss Elizabeth"; and John McClure's wife found him a "nice, pleasant Southern boy." But Faulkner didn't let it go at that: in planter mode he was also known to refer to his illegitimate children back in Oxford, to share the amusing sayings of the Negroes on his family's "place," and to drink moonshine he said was made on the plantation.

Most people who knew Faulkner had something to say about his drinking. Under his chair in Spratling's sketch are the liquor bottles that he usually had at hand: Sherwood Anderson recalled an overcoat with additional pockets sewn in to carry them. Spratling acknowledged that "Faulkner, of course, drank constantly"—Flo Field once saw him bring beignets home from the French Market and eat them for breakfast with a glass of corn liquor—and although Spratling added that "I don't think I ever saw him really drunk—perhaps a little vague, but never sloppy," that must be set against Feibleman's encounter with an unshaven Faulkner, his white linen suit filthy and his face cut, after a binge that had apparently included some fights.

In New Orleans, Faulkner certainly had his share of fun and games—

loop-the-loops in a stunt plane with Ham Basso, various high jinks *chez* Spratling, trading Al Jackson anecdotes with Anderson—as well as all that hard drinking, sometimes far past the point of fun and games. He also fell in hopeless, unrequited love with a free-spirited young woman who apparently never even read the sonnets he wrote for her. But despite all the tomfoolery and fruitless courtship, he was reading voraciously, discussing what he'd read, absorbing material and influences. Marc Antony recalled this "somewhat strange, totally independent young man [roaming] around the streets, talking and listening." And unlike many other literary young men, Faulkner was writing incessantly. Every morning, Spratling said, when he woke up "Bill would already be out on the balcony with a drink, usually alcohol and water, banging away at his typewriter." Anderson noticed as well: "I used to hear his typewriter rattling away as I went through the passageway. I heard it in the morning, in the afternoon and often late at night. He was always at it, pounding away."

He had come to New Orleans as an aspiring poet, but under Anderson's influence he was becoming a writer of fiction. He began writing sketches— short stories, really—about various New Orleans characters for the *Double Dealer* and even sold some to the *Times-Picayune* under the general title "Mirrors of Chartres Street." He also polished off his first novel, *Soldiers' Pay,* and sent it to Anderson's publisher, Liveright (the story—probably apocryphal—is that Anderson agreed to recommend it if he didn't have to read it). In July 1925 he and Spratling went to Europe. Faulkner found England too expensive to enjoy (he went there to see an RAF surgeon about his wounds, he told a friend), but he loved Paris. There, he took long walks with Spratling's old friend from the Quarter, photographer Cicero Odiorne. He went to Shakespeare and Company (and probably bought the copy of Joyce's banned *Ulysses* that was in his library until his death). He went to concerts and museums and the Moulin Rouge. He grew a beard.

Back in New Orleans, after *Soldiers' Pay* was published he spent less time with the *Double Dealer* crowd and more with Roark Bradford, Lyle Saxon, and other men who were actually writing books, not just talking about them. In general, he had less patience than Spratling did with the wealthy patrons and dilettantes who hung out in the Quarter. At an Arts and Crafts Club ball that Spratling had helped to organize, for instance, Faulkner—the only one not in costume—just sat on the floor and drank from a bottle in a paper bag. Later he wrote his mother, "More funny folks, all breaking their necks trying to have a good time." In his second novel, *Mosquitoes,* he revealed his

Faulkner in Paris, photographed by
William Odiorne.

distaste for the hangers-on he regarded as parasites. (Ironically, he used his
advance for that novel to take a couple of friends who would resent it when
they saw it—Lillian Marcus and her brother Julian Friend, an editor of the
Double Dealer—to supper at Galatoire's.)

Faulkner moved back to Mississippi at the end of 1926. He had lived in
New Orleans for less than sixteen months altogether, but in that short time
he had written two novels (*Mosquitoes* would be published the next spring)
and he had the makings of more in his head. He settled in to write, and published eight in eight years, including most of his best, and best-known, starting with *The Sound and the Fury* (1929) and continuing to *Absalom, Absalom!*
(1936). What the writer Flannery O'Connor would call "the Dixie Limited"
was out of the station and thundering down the track.

Faulkner never lived in New Orleans again, and he seldom even visited.
A decade or so after he left, he wrote a friend there that "I don't come back
much because I had more fun there than I ever had and ever will have again
anywhere now."

Elizabeth Prall Anderson, 42

IN 1922 ELIZABETH PRALL WAS MANAGING the Doubleday bookstore in New York when she met Sherwood Anderson, whose second marriage was falling apart. Before long, the couple were living together in Reno, waiting for Anderson's divorce. The day after it was granted, in April 1924, Elizabeth became the third Mrs. Anderson, and soon the couple moved to New Orleans. Sherwood had wanted to live there since an earlier visit, and Lillian Marcus had already found them a three-room furnished apartment in the upper Pontalba building, with a view of Jackson Square and the cathedral. Elizabeth wrote that she "went about the place, exclaiming over the impossibly high ceilings and fine wrought iron work." But soon an even better place became available when Lyle Saxon decided to sublet an apartment on the third and fourth floors of the same building. The rent was steep—$110 a month—but it came with an even better view and some of Saxon's furniture that Sherwood pronounced "magnificent." After the floors were sanded and

ELIZABETH ANDERSON

Sketch by Spratling, 1925

Elizabeth and Sherwood, photographed by Imogen Cunningham.

The view from the Andersons' apartment, painted by Spratling

the ironwork repainted, 540B St. Peter Street was one of the most elegant addresses in what was still a rather shabby neighborhood, and Elizabeth Anderson was its chatelaine.

She also put up $300 and became a partner with Lucille and Marc Antony in the Leonardi Studios, a decorating shop in the next block. She and Sherwood needed the money, she said, but she may also just have wanted something interesting to do. In any case, she reported later that "the shop was run along languid, leisurely lines . . . and we never did make any money," but it provided yet another gathering place for their friends.

In his memoirs, Spratling wrote that Sherwood was "the story-teller-oracle," but "his wonderful wife Elizabeth was the quiet priestess of the temple." Faulkner had known Elizabeth in New York, and renewed the acquaintance when he got to New Orleans in 1924. She put him up at her place for a while, but then suggested that he take a room around the corner with Spratling, who was already an intimate of the Andersons. The two Bills and the Andersons became very close neighbors, seeing each other almost every day. Elizabeth took a somewhat maternal interest in the younger men: Faulkner wrote his mother at one point that Elizabeth had taken over the management of his funds, and she lent him her copy of *The Golden Bough* when she found that he hadn't read it. She also had a maternal interest—she was obliged to—in Sherwood's teenaged son (by his first wife), who had hitchhiked to New Orleans. There was some tension between Elizabeth and her stepson— "a rather wild boy," she said, "gangling and awkward and dead sure that he was full grown and ready to join our friends as an equal"—but after a few months he shipped out as a mess boy on a freighter.

In fact, she had a maternal interest in her husband. She tried to make him sit at his desk for three hours every morning. She urged him to go on lecture tours to promote his work. She admired him greatly, but critic Irving Howe observed that she also "felt a need to make his unpolished genius acceptable to the more genteel reader. She persuaded him to tone down his resplendent clothes, she made him keep regular hours, she had him take her to a New Orleans country club and be photographed with Dorothy Dix—and for a while he obeyed." In retrospect, however, the problem is obvious: "Elizabeth Prall was a fine woman, but hardly the sort who could remain married very long to Sherwood Anderson."

In April 1926 the Andersons had paid cash for a grand old place on Governor Nicholls Street, but by the time *Famous Creoles* appeared they had rented it and moved to the mountains of southwest Virginia. Sherwood had decided it was time to move on from New Orleans. Within a couple of years he decided that it was also time to move on from Elizabeth. While she was visiting her parents in California, he sent her a brutal letter asking her not to return. She destroyed her wedding ring and his letters, and until the end of her life she refused to communicate with various scholars seeking information about him. She managed a bookstore in Palo Alto until 1935, when Natalie Scott sent an invitation to visit Taxco, the Mexican town where she and Spratling had settled. Elizabeth went and, as Scott had no doubt intended, she liked it so much that she stayed.

She had a full and rewarding life in Mexico. To provide employment for local women, she set up Estudio Taxco, which made dresses for sale to the town's many tourists, and she designed the fabrics for it herself. She learned Spanish and translated the poetry of a seventeenth-century Mexican nun. With the help of a coauthor, she wrote a score-settling memoir of her life with Sherwood Anderson. In short, she finally became "artful and crafty" in her own right.

She and Spratling became even closer friends than they had been in New Orleans. Looking back on his funeral, after his untimely death in 1967, she wrote: "It was strange, I thought. I miss Bill Spratling so very much more than I ever missed Sherwood Anderson." Nine years later, she died in Taxco herself.

NOTES

THESE NOTES AND THE ILLUSTRATION credits that follow use the following abbreviations:

CCC   Carvel Collins Collection of William Faulkner Research Materials, Harry Ransom Humanities Research Center, University of Texas at Austin.

CHRC   Cammie G. Henry Research Center, Watson Memorial Library, Northwestern State University, Natchitoches, Louisiana.

THNOC   The Historic New Orleans Collection.

LaRC   Louisiana Research Collection, Howard-Tilton Memorial Library, Tulane University.

JBP   Joseph Blotner Papers, Louis Daniel Brodsky Collection of William Faulkner Materials, Special Collections and Archives, Kent Library, Southeast Missouri State University, Cape Girardeau, Missouri.

Many of the notes refer to newspaper clippings from the files of these and other archives, often unsourced or undated, and even more often lacking page numbers. Since these were too rich a resource to ignore, I have gone ahead and used them, citing what information I have, hoping that scholars will understand and betting that other readers won't care. I have also often cited secondary sources, even when I have examined the primary sources they draw on, believing that most normal readers will find it more useful to be referred to, say, Joel Williamson's *Faulkner and Southern History* than to the interviews archived in Joseph Blotner's papers that Williamson used extensively. Either reference should establish that I didn't just make something up, and it's certainly easier to find and to read Williamson's book than to forage in the Blotner papers in Cape Girardeau (although both experiences are remarkably pleasant).

The vast trove of documents archived online at ancestry.com proved invaluable: manuscript census returns for addresses, occupations, ages, and family connections; draft registrations for more on occupations and addresses; ships' passenger lists for comings and goings; passport applications for addresses and even a few photographs; and much more. For those materials I have simply cited ancestry.com as the source, sometimes crediting the genealogical research of Dale Volberg Reed, who can really make those documents tell stories. Anyone willing to subscribe to that service can probably replicate the process by which Dale or I came to some conclusion. (Full disclosure, as they say in the media: I found ancestry.com to be so useful that I bought a modest amount of stock in the company.)

PREFACE

vii **Noggle's historiographical essay:** Burl Noggle, *The Fleming Lectures, 1937–1990* (Louisiana State Univ. Press, 1992).

INTRODUCTION: TWO BILLS AND A BOOK

This chapter is based on Joseph Blotner, *Faulkner: A Biography,* vol. 1 (Random House, 1974), unless otherwise indicated.

1 **"Sort of a private joke":** William Spratling, *File on Spratling: An Autobiography* (Little, Brown, 1967), 28.

2 **Quotations from Natalie Scott:** John W. Scott, "William Spratling and the New Orleans Renaissance," *Louisiana History* 45, no. 3 (summer 2004): 313–14 (at 314n, 1928 should obviously be 1926).
  Dog Latin epigraph: Email to author from Professor E. Christian Kopff, University of Colorado, 25 August 2010.

3 **"I don't think it's very funny":** Spratling, *File, on Spratling,* 29.
  Had truly hurt Anderson: William Faulkner, "Sherwood Anderson: An Appreciation," in Ray Lewis White, *The Achievement of Sherwood Anderson: Essays in Criticism* (Univ. of North Carolina Press, 1966), 196.
  Asked Spratling for another: A second-printing copy of *Famous Creoles* in the Louis Daniel Brodsky Collection of William Faulkner Materials at South-

east Missouri State University contains a note from Spratling to Anderson saying that the only two copies he has left are equally battered, and not to give this one away.

3 **Upwards of \$2,000:** Bookfinder.com, 11 August 2011.

"A mirror of our scene": Spratling, *File on Spratling*, 29.

4 **"Internationally famous locally":** Edward Dreyer, "Some Friends of Lyle Saxon," epilogue to Lyle Saxon, *The Friends of Joe Gilmore* (Hastings House, 1948), 163.

5 **Neither of the major museums:** Confirmed by Kevin Grogan and David Houston at the Morris and Ogden museums of Southern art, respectively. Some of Spratling's work is in the Historic New Orleans Collection, the Louisiana State Museum, and the Special Collections of the Tulane University Library.

Native New Orleanians held themselves apart: Chance Harvey, *The Life and Selected Letters of Lyle Saxon* (Pelican, 2003), 86.

A social circle: On the concept of *social circle*, see Charles Kadushin, *The American Intellectual Elite* (Transaction Publishers, 2005), esp. xiii, 9–12. Kadushin develops a concept introduced by Georg Simmel, in *Conflict and the Web of Group Affiliations* (1922; reprint, Free Press, 1955).

"Grand Old Man": Spratling, *File on Spratling*, 22.

"Royal Personage": Hamilton Basso, "William Faulkner, Man and Writer," *Saturday Review,* 28 July 1962, 11.

6 **Extensive literature on Bohemia:** Particularly useful examples include Elizabeth Wilson, *Bohemians: The Glamorous Outcasts* (I. B. Tauris, 2000); Joanna Richardson, *The Bohemians: La Vie de Bohème in Paris, 1830–1914* (Macmillan, 1969); D. J. Taylor, *Bright Young People: The Rise and Fall of a Generation, 1918–1940* (Chatto and Windus, 2007); D. J. Taylor, "The Beautiful and the Damned," *The Guardian,* 29 September 2007; Virginia Nicholson, *Among the Bohemians: Experiments in Living, 1900–1939* (Viking Press, 2002); Sisley Huddleston, *Bohemian Literary and Social Life in Paris: Salons, Cafés, Studios* (Harrap, 1928); Arthur Ransome, *Bohemia in London* (1907; reprint, Amazon Publishing, 2002).

The World of the Famous Creoles

LIFE IN THE QUARTER

13 **"Creole version of the Left Bank":** Hamilton Basso, "William Faulkner, Man and Writer," *Saturday Review,* 28 July 1962, 11.

14 **Shasta Daisies Society:** James W. Thomas, *Lyle Saxon: A Critical Biography* (Summa Publications, 1991), 40.

"Boyish and boisterous": Inez Hollander Lake, *The Road from Pompey's Head:*

The Life and Work of Hamilton Basso (Louisiana State Univ. Press, 1999), 14.

14 **Quotations from Spratling:** William Spratling, *File on Spratling: An Autobiography* (Little, Brown, 1967).

Bearded men: Letter from William Wisdom to Carvel Collins, 19 July 1963, Flo Field folder, CCC 6.8.

15 **Faucets as anatomical features:** Interview with Caroline Durieux, Baton Rouge, 26 March 1963, CCC 4.34.

"Death-defying platform": Field to Spratling, 1 October 1962, Flora Field collection, Newcomb Archives, Newcomb College Center for Research on Women.

16 **Escape from the stifling heat:** Genevieve Pitot's recollection, in W. Kenneth Holditch, "William Spratling, William Faulkner, and Other Famous Creoles," *Mississippi Quarterly* 51, no. 3 (summer 1998): 423–34.

Faulkner tried to persuade Mrs. Field: Joseph Blotner, *Faulkner: A Biography,* vol. 1 (Random House, 1974), 495.

"Fine game of tag": Hamilton Basso, "William Faulkner, Man and Writer," *Saturday Review,* 28 July 1962, 12.

Quotation from La Farge: Oliver La Farge, *Raw Material* (Houghton Mifflin, 1945), 117–18, 131.

17 **Classic Bohemia of Paris:** Joanna Richardson, *The Bohemians: La Vie de Bohème in Paris, 1830–1914* (Macmillan, 1969).

Patronized bordellos: See, e.g., Edmund Wilson, *The Twenties: From Notebooks and Diaries of the Period* (Macmillan, 1975), 186.

Vice in the Quarter and nearby: Anthony Stanonis, "An Old House in the Quarter: Vice in the Vieux Carré of the 1930s," Department of History, Loyola University of New Orleans, 1996–1997, www.loyno.edu/~history/journal/1996-7/Stanonis.html.

Carmers' experience: Interview with Carl and Betty Carmer, 23 August 1965, JBP 2479/008.

Anderson and Aunt Rose: W. Kenneth Holditch, "Rising Star," *Gambit Weekly,* 22 September 1997, www.weeklywire.com/ww/09-22-97/gambit_covs.html.

Tom Anderson's tavern: Interview with Joyce McClure, New Orleans, 20 March [1960?], CCC 9.14; interview with Harold Dempsey, New Orleans, 2 February 1963, CCC 4.28.

"The lowest joint in New Orleans": Interview with Carmers.

Flo Field quotations: Letter to Sydney Field, 4 April 1931, in Field collection, Newcomb College Center for Research on Women.

18 **"Dazzling collection":** Basso quoted in Frances Jean Bowen, "The New Orleans Double Dealer: 1921–May 1926, A Critical History" (Ph.D. diss., Vanderbilt University, 1954).

18 **Odiorne remembered:** Interviews with W. C. Odiorne, Hollywood, California, 15–16 February 1963, CCC 11.1.

"New Orleans debutantes": Elizabeth Anderson and Gerald R. Kelly, *Miss Elizabeth: A Memoir* (Little, Brown, 1969), 89.

Anderson quotation: Letter to Jerome Blum, [2 February 1922], in Charles E. Modlin, ed., *Sherwood Anderson: Selected Letters* (Univ. of Tennessee Press, 1984), 30–31.

"Drank a lot and talked a lot": Interview with Mrs. Ernest Samuel (Adaline Katz), Bay St. Louis, Mississippi, 29 March 1963, CCC 15.27.

Temple quotation: Stella Pitts, "The Quarter in the Twenties," *Dixie*, 26 November 1972, 44

Fischer quotation: Blotner, *Faulkner*, vol. 1, 496.

"Well lubricated" parties: Kate Rose, "Unsung Composer Genevieve Pitot," *Figaro*, 10 November 1978.

19 **"We could do our friends proud":** Spratling, *File on Spratling*, 27.

Temple and Pitot quotes: W. Kenneth Holditch, "William Faulkner and Other Famous Creoles," in Joseph R. Urgo, ed., *Faulkner and His Contemporaries* (Univ. Press of Mississippi, 2004).

"Prohibition was a personal affront": Anderson and Kelly, *Miss Elizabeth*, 90.

"New Orleans did not seem to have heard of it": James K. Feibleman, *The Way of a Man: An Autobiography* (Horizon Press, 1969), 217.

Inviting cops for drinks: Interview with Marc and Lucille Antony, New Orleans, 1 and 3 February 1965, JBP 2479/007.

Any of several bayou routes: Calvert Stith, "New Orleans: Non-Guide-Book Style," *New Orleanian*, 6 September 1930, 37.

Faulkner's fantastic yarns: Blotner, *Faulkner*, vol. 1, 427.

Elizebeth Werlein's count of bars: Anthony Stanonis, "'A Woman of Boundless Energy': Elizebeth Werlein and Her Times," *Louisiana History* 46, no. 1 (winter 2005): 16.

Liquor in teacups: John W. Scott, "William Spratling and the New Orleans Renaissance," *Louisiana History* 45, no. 3 (summer 2004): 317.

"Speakeasies flourished": Anderson and Kelly, *Miss Elizabeth*, 80–81.

Store like Joe Cascio's: Blotner, *Faulkner*, vol. 1, 427. (Blotner has it as Cassio, but it is Cascio in *Soards' 1923 New Orleans Directory*).

20 **Defrocked priest-bootlegger:** Interview with Anita Loos, 18 January 1966, JBP 2479/003.

Spratling bought ten large jugs: Anderson and Kelly, *Miss Elizabeth*, 90.

Harold Levy's druggist friend: Interview with Harold Levy, New Orleans, winter 1963, CCC 8.40.

Going "fishing": Blotner, *Faulkner*, vol. 1, 427.

20 "Needle beer": Thomas, *Lyle Saxon*, 40.
    Juniper essence from Solari's: Holditch, "William Spratling, William Faulkner, and Other Famous Creoles."
    Rolling the cans for aeration: Spratling, *File on Spratling*, 28.
    Favorite drink was absinthe: Scott, "William Spratling and the New Orleans Renaissance," 317.

21 **Swiss man who made it himself:** Blotner, *Faulkner*, vol. 1, 524.
    "Great pitchers for all our parties": Spratling, *File on Spratling*, 28.
    Quotations from Elizabeth Anderson: Anderson and Kelly, *Miss Elizabeth*, 83–90.
    "Was it good?": Pitts, "The Quarter in the Twenties," 44.
    "Georgia Boy" Boyd: Carvel Emerson Collins, introduction to William Faulkner, *New Orleans Sketches* (Univ. Press of Mississippi, 1958), xxvi.
    Black Baptist evangelist in Algiers: "Rev. James G. M'Pherson," *New York Times*, 10 April 1936, 24.
    Mother Catherine: Natalie Scott to Sidonie Scott, 29 April 1930, box 3, folder 18, Natalie Vivian Scott collection, M123, LaRC.
    Baron Hanno von Schucking; parties most nights: Blotner, *Faulkner*, vol. 1, 523–24.
    Double Dealer **crowd gathered:** Inez Hollander Lake, "Paris in My Own Backyard: Hamilton Basso," in *Literary New Orleans in the Modern World*, ed. Richard S. Kennedy, 42 (Louisiana State Univ. Press, 1998).

22 **"A bottle or so of absinthe":** La Farge, *Raw Material*, 114.
    Spratling quotations: Spratling, *File on Spratling*, 17.
    Andersons' Saturday dinner parties: Basso, "William Faulkner, Man and Writer," 11.
    Tujague's or Tortorici's: Interview with Louis Andrews Fischer, 2 February 1965, JBP 2479/007.
    Details of excursion: From Walter B. Rideout, *Sherwood Anderson: A Writer in America*, vol. 1 (Univ. of Wisconsin Press, 2006), 572–73; Blotner, *Faulkner*, vol. 1, 417–19; Anderson and Kelly, *Miss Elizabeth*, 118–21; except as noted below.
    The Antonys' recollections: Interview with Marc and Lucille Antony, New Orleans, winter 1963, CCC 1.13.
    Marc Antony said Saxon was there: Chance Harvey, *The Life and Selected Letters of Lyle Saxon* (Pelican, 2003), 291n.
    Spratling's autobiography: Spratling, *File on Spratling*, 29.

23 **Everyone kicked in:** Interview with Samuel Louis Gilmore, New Orleans, 3 February 1965, JBP 2479/003; interview with Marc Antony, New Orleans, 1 and 3 February 1965, JBP 2479/004.
    "Truly negligible book": Basso, "William Faulkner, Man and Writer," 12.

24 **Some critics have disagreed:** e.g., M. Thomas Inge, "The Dixie Limited: Writ-

ers on Faulkner and His Influence," *Faulkner Journal of Japan* 1 (May 1999), wwwsoc.nii.ac.jp/wfsj/journal/No1/IngeRevd.htm.

24 **"Trashily smart":** Daniel J. Singal, *William Faulkner: The Making of a Modernist* (Univ. of North Carolina Press, 1997), 81.

Mrs. Maurier was Lillian Marcus: Anderson and Kelly, *Miss Elizabeth,* 120.

"Unctuous Mrs. Maurier": "Books: Mosquitoes," *Time,* 4 July 1927.

Mrs. Maurier was Elizabeth Anderson: Cleanth Brooks, *William Faulkner: Toward Yoknapatawpha and Beyond* (Louisiana State Univ. Press, 1990), 378.

Mrs. Maurier was Elizebeth Werlein: Joseph Blotner, *Faulkner: A Biography* (Univ. Press of Mississippi, 2005), 183.

"Right amount of acid": Interviews with Odiorne, CCC 11.2.

Marcus fumed about portrayal: Holditch, "William Faulkner, and Other Famous Creoles."

Bal des Quat'z Arts: See, e.g., Felix Youssoupoff, *Lost Splendor* (Jonathan Cape, 1953), chapter 15, and Jacques Guiton, *A Life in Three Lands: Memoirs of an Architect* (Branden Books, 1991), 66.

Account of the Folies du Vieux Carré: Taken (except as noted below) from interview with Friend and Goldstein, M1151, LaRC; "Scenes Attending Ball of Folies du Vieux Carre," *States,* 7 January 1923; and Lyle Saxon, "Moorish Wedding Starts First Annual Artists' Ball," *Times-Picayune,* 1 January 1923, 1–2.

25 **Albrizio's costume and policeman's uniform:** Bowen, "The New Orleans Double Dealer."

Genevieve Pitot: The "dance of Salome" reported in the *States* is almost certainly the one Pitot did, mentioned in Holditch, "William Faulkner and Other Famous Creoles."

Pitot danced barefoot: Bowen, "The New Orleans Double Dealer."

26 **Newspaper story announcing event:** "Bal des Artistes to Be Brilliant," unsourced and undated (but 1925) clipping in Dan Whitney folder, THNOC. The description of the ball that follows is taken from this story and from "Bohemia Skates Off Humdrum Air at Artists' Ball: Dancers' Costumes Vie With Decorations for Grotesque Honors," clipping from *Times-Picayune,* 19 April 1925, in Dan Whitney folder, THNOC.

Faulkner didn't enjoy it: Scott, "William Spratling and the New Orleans Renaissance," 301.

"Another night of fun and frolic": Announcement of "Artist Ball," MSS 247, Arts and Crafts Club collection, THNOC.

Socially prominent party-goers: E.g., "The Arts and Crafts Ball," unsourced clipping, MSS 247, Arts and Crafts Club collection, box 7, folder 423, THNOC.

Ticket prices: Vertical Files, "Arts. Societies. Arts and Crafts Club. Undated and 1922–28," folder 1, LaRC.

Proceeds for upkeep of building: "Spain is Theme of Artist Ball," undated (but 1927) clipping from *Item*, MSS 247, Arts and Crafts Club collection, box 7, folder 423, THNOC.

26 **"Gorgeous hidden panorama"**: "Ball of Arts and Crafts Club Will Rival Any This Side of Paris, Say Leading Spirits of Quarter," *Times-Picayune*, 20 November 1927, 22.

Typical headlines: "Secrecy Shrouds Preparations for Arts, Crafts Ball," *Morning Tribune*, 20 November 1927; "Arts and Crafts Ball Next Month to be Gay Soiree," *Item-Tribune*, 20 November 1927; "Ball of Arts and Crafts Club Will Rival Any This Side of Paris."

"Lavish and daring schemes of color": "Plans Under Way for Artists' Ball," unsourced and undated clipping, MSS 247, Arts and Crafts Club collection, box 7, folder 423, THNOC.

27 **Drawing "to illustrate the spirit"**: "Arts and Crafts Ball Next Month to be Gay Soiree."

"Modernistic mode"; "zippy" chorus line: Unsourced clipping, 1927, MSS 247, Arts and Crafts Club collection, box 7, folder 423, THNOC.

"Mysticism and beauty": "Secrecy Shrouds Preparations."

"Out-of-town celebrity": "Arts and Crafts Ball Next Month to be Gay Soiree."

Chicago Arts Ball: "Secrecy Shrouds Preparations."

Lady Godiva tryouts: Meigs O. Frost, "Three Ladies Offer For Godiva-ing, But—," *States*, 4 December 1927, 1–2.

Painting of Godivas: "W.G.W.," "Arts and Crafts Club Ball Bad for the Eyes," clipping from *States*, 11 December 1927, MSS 247, Arts and Crafts Club collection, box 7, folder 423, THNOC.

"Like the Beaux Arts ball": "Ball of Arts and Crafts Club Will Rival Any This Side of Paris."

"Pseudo Bachannalian revels": George N. Coad, "New Orleans Tries to Revive Culture," *New York Times*, 25 December 1927, E2.

Anderson hinted at its nature: Sherwood Anderson, *Dark Laughter* (Boni and Liveright, 1925; reprint, Liveright, 1960), 181–82.

28 **"Almost naked parties"**: Evelyn Waugh, *Vile Bodies* (Eyre Methuen, 1978), 123.

"Any really successful party": Virginia Nicholson, *Among the Bohemians: Experiments in Living, 1900–1939* (Viking Press, 2002), 264.

Costumes "very scanty": Interview with Elise Friend and Albert Goldstein, M1151, LaRC.

"Abbreviated costumes"; "red-hot jazz band": "Arts and Crafts Club Ball Bad for the Eyes."

"Best, dampest": "Arts Ball Is Riot of Costumes, Color, Jubilant Good Fellowship," unsourced clipping, 12 December 1927, MSS 247, Arts and Crafts Club collection, box 7, folder 423, THNOC.

28 **Costumes at one ball:** "Arts Ball Is Riot of Costumes," "Arts and Crafts Club Ball Bad for the Eyes."

Newspaper accounts of another: Clipping from *States,* 1 May 1927, in Weeks Hall folder, THNOC; "The Arts and Crafts Ball [112]," unsourced and undated (but 1927) clipping, MSS 247, Arts and Crafts Club collection, box 7, folder 423, THNOC; and unsourced and undated (but 1927) clipping in MSS 247, Arts and Crafts Club collection, box 11, folder 441, THNOC. This was the April 1927 ball, and the description following is from these clippings unless otherwise noted.

Whitney's decorations: "Bohemia Skates Off Humdrum Air at Artists' Ball."

29 **Murals of an octopus:** "Arts Ball Is Riot of Costumes"; "Arts and Crafts Club Ball Bad for the Eyes."

"Haven of angels and devils": "Arts and Crafts Club Members Prepare for Ball," undated (but 1927) clipping from *Times-Picayune,* MSS 247, Arts and Crafts Club collection, box 7, folder 423, THNOC.

Philistine from the *States*: Clipping from *States,* 1 May 1927, in Weeks Hall folder, THNOC.

Planning committee: "Spain is Theme of Artist Ball."

Parody of *A La Creole*: Scott, "William Spratling and the New Orleans Renaissance," 318 (Scott dates this incorrectly as 1928).

Balls in 1930 and 1931: Meigs O. Frost, "Arts Ball to Be Brilliant Affair," unsourced and undated (but 1930) clipping, MSS 247, Arts and Crafts Club collection, box 7, folder 423, THNOC; "Ball of Artists Will Take Stars for Inspiration," *Times-Picayune,* 13 April 1930; Barry J. Holloway, "Artist Colony of New Orleans Turns to Crime," *Berkeley Daily Gazette,* 11 April 1931, 2.

"Imitation Greenwich Village parties": Feibleman, *Way of a Man,* 165.

MAKING A SCENE

31 **Tulane School of Architecture:** Bernard Lemann, Malcolm Heard Jr., and John P. Klingman, eds., *Talk About Architecture: A Century of Architectural Education at Tulane* (Tulane University School of Architecture, 1993).

Department of Middle American Research: Daniel S. Berman, "The Middle American Research Institute: Seventy Years of Middle American Research at Tulane" (Master's thesis, Tulane University, 1995), 12.

33 **Lecture on Mexico in 1925:** John W. Scott, "William Spratling and the New Orleans Renaissance," *Louisiana History* 45, no. 3 (summer 2004): 310n.

Bein and others in Orizaba: Unsourced clipping, "October 1930," in Dan Whitney folder, THNOC.

Blom's shows at Arts and Crafts Club: See, e.g., clippings from *Times-*

Picayune, 12 November 1930, and *Item-Tribune,* 5 November 1930, in MSS 247, Arts and Crafts Club collection, THNOC.

33 **"Standing joke" about Mayan architecture:** Lemann et al., eds., *Talk About Architecture,* 84.

"One of the hottest competitive newspaper towns": "The Press: Contemptuous Item," *Time,* 18 December 1939.

34 **Bradford's $15 a week:** Interview with Mary Rose Bradford, Houston, Texas, 2 March 1963, CCC 2.26.

Architecture column for Spratling: John W. Scott, *Natalie Scott: A Magnificent Life* (Pelican, 2008), 246.

Dan Whitney illustration for Saxon: Lyle Saxon, "The Toil of Worship," *Times-Picayune,* 27 April 1924.

Faulkner sketches in *Times-Picayune*: Carvel Emerson Collins, ed., *New Orleans Sketches* (Univ. Press of Mississippi, 2002).

What must have been a record: Lyle Saxon, "What's Doing," *Times-Picayune,* 25 October 1925, 2.

Typical story: Frederick Oechsner, "Summer's End Brings Artists Home to Plan Many Exhibitions," *Morning Tribune,* 18 September 1926.

"If New Orleans has any pride": Meigs Frost, "Splendid Exhibits at Orleans Arts and Crafts," *States,* 18 November 1924.

35 **Scott was an investor in the *Double Dealer*:** Scott, *Natalie Scott,* 475n.

Scott plugged *Famous Creoles*: [Natalie Scott], "Peggy Passe Partout," *States,* 19 December 1926, 7.

Oechsner promoted *A la Creole*: "Le Petit Theatre Eager for Flo Field's Play," *Item-Tribune,* 13 February 1927.

Performing in Mrs. Goldberg's house: History at www.lepetittheatre.com/about.asp, accessed in summer 2009 (now removed).

Membership figures and dues (here and below): *Your Little Theatre: A Resume* (1934–1935), in Vertical Files, "Entertainment. Theatre. Le Petit Theatre du Vieux Carre," LaRC.

Saxon's suggestion: Lyle Saxon, "Pontalba Artist Colony Plan Gets Wide Approval," *Item,* 26 January 1919, section 1, page 12.

36 **Flophouse:** Scott, "William Spratling and the New Orleans Renaissance," 289n.

$17.50 a month: *Your Little Theatre.*

Mrs. Nixon first president; Loving Cup: Letter from Emma Douglass Genre to Bernard Lemann, 4 March 1966, in Vertical Files, "Entertainment. Theatre. Le Petit Theatre du Vieux Carre," LaRC.

"Fairy godmothers": History at www.lepetittheatre.com/about.asp.

Koch designed new building: History at www.lepetittheatre.com/about.asp.

36 **Performance history, cast, and crew data:** Online at www.stageclick.com/venue/3.aspx.

Pseudo-Slavic item: "The Little Stone House," in George Calderon, *Eight One-Act Plays* (BiblioBazaar, 2009), 31. (Calderon was an English playwright and translator of Chekhov.)

37 **Dunsany at dedication:** Genre to Lemann, in Vertical Files, "Entertainment. Theatre. Le Petit Theatre du Vieux Carre," LaRC.

38 **"Only Little Theatre . . . which can present French plays":** Silas Bent, "Greenwich Village on Royal Street," *New York Times Book Review and Magazine*, 23 July 1922, 4.

A la Creole: Based on Hermann B. Deutsch, "Hail 'A la Creole!' a Perfect Whimsical Play of Quarter; and Flo Field Doing It All," *Item*, 15 March 1927, unless otherwise indicated.

Oechsner promoted *A la Creole*: Oechsner, "Le Petit Theatre Eager for Flo Field's Play."

Cast and credits: Program for "A La Creole," March 1927, THNOC.

"Little Creole spinster": Flo Field, letter to the editor, *Time*, 2 August 1943.

39 **Deutsch's one-acter:** The play was *Conscience*, presented 19 March 1924; see www.stageclick.com/show/15198.aspx.

"Tear-spattered curtain speech": "Triumph Scored by Flo Field," *Times-Picayune*, 15 March 1927, 5.

"Greatest single cultural force": George N. Coad, "New Orleans Tries to Revive Culture," *New York Times*, 25 December 1927, E2.

"Manifestation of the guild spirit": Herschel Brickell, "The Literary Landscape," *North American Review* 235, no. 5 (May 1933): 474.

After-theater party at Quartier Club: Scott, *Natalie Scott*, 239.

Material on the *Double Dealer*: From Frances Jean Bowen, "The New Orleans Double Dealer: 1921–May 1926, A Critical History" (Ph.D. diss., Vanderbilt University, 1954), and "Julius Weis Friend's History of the *Double Dealer*," *Mississippi Quarterly* 31 (fall 1978): 587–604, unless otherwise indicated.

40 **"We were disillusioned":** Jim Amoss, "William Faulkner and Other Famous Creoles," *Lagniappe* (*States-Item* magazine), 6–12 March 1976, 3.

Paul Godchaux Jr.: Godchaux soon dropped off the magazine's masthead and he is barely mentioned, if at all, in accounts of the magazine's history. He was associate editor of issue number 1, however, and business manager for issue number 2, and he and two of his relatives were listed as "guarantors" in an early issue.

"Sons of several rich men": Charles E. Modlin, ed., *Sherwood Anderson: Selected Letters* (Univ. of Tennessee Press, 1984), 30.

Feed catalogs for farmers: Amoss, "William Faulkner and Other Famous Creoles," 3.

40 *New Orleans Illustrated News* **announced:** Scott, *Natalie Scott,* 475n.

42 **Mencken "didn't know what he was talking about":** Albert Goldstein, "Discoveries of The Double Dealer," *Dixie* (*Times-Picayune* magazine), 21 January 1951, 6.

Double Dealer **"has the right air":** Albert Goldstein, "The Creative Spirit," in *The Past as Prelude: New Orleans 1718–1968,* ed. Hodding Carter, 180 (Tulane University, 1968).

Anderson one of those who met each month: Elizabeth Anderson and Gerald R. Kelly, *Miss Elizabeth: A Memoir* (Little, Brown, 1969), 82–83.

43 **"2nd rate stuff by 1st rate writers":** Quoted in Thomas Bonner Jr., "The *Double Dealer* and the Little-Magazine Tradition in New Orleans," in *Literary New Orleans in the Modern World,* ed. Richard S. Kennedy, 23–35 (Louisiana State Univ. Press, 1998).

"Itinerant literary men": James K. Feibleman, *The Way of a Man: An Autobiography* (Horizon Press, 1969), 37, 268.

44 **Circulation reached about three thousand:** Amoss, "William Faulkner and Other Famous Creoles," 3. Amoss's article is based on an interview with Albert Goldstein. Bowen puts the figure at fifteen thousand to eighteen thousand, but that seems very unlikely.

45 **"Bowed out mainly because its work was done":** Goldstein, "Discoveries of The Double Dealer."

Material on the Arts and Crafts Club: From Laura Clark Brown, "New Orleans Modernism: The Arts and Crafts Club in the Vieux Carré, 1919–1939," *Louisiana History* 41, no. 3 (summer 2000): 317–43, and Louise C. Hoffman, *Josephine Crawford: An Artist's Vision* (Historic New Orleans Collection, 2009), unless otherwise indicated.

Meeting in Alberta Kinsey's studio: Clipping from *New Orleans Life,* June 1926, in William C. Odiorne folder, THNOC. See also Judith Bonner, "All the Artful and Crafty Ones," *Historic New Orleans Collection Quarterly* 11, no. 1 (winter 1993): 4–6, and Ethel Hutson, "The First New Orleans Artists' Guild, and Its Successors," typescript in Vertical Files, "Arts. Societies. Artists' Guild," LaRC.

Sarah Henderson's support for Club: "Scope and Content Note," MSS 247, Arts and Crafts Club collection, THNOC.

Henderson's travel and household information: From passenger lists, passport applications, and census records on ancestry.com.

46 **Newcomb and Tulane architecture school representation:** Judith H. Bonner, "An Artistic Legacy: The New Orleans Arts and Crafts Club," *Louisiana Cultural Vistas* (spring 2007): 13.

47 **"Indefatigable worker":** Vera Morel, "The Story of An Art School—And How

It Grew," unsourced and undated (but ca. 1926) clipping in MSS 247, Arts and Crafts Club collection, box 7, folder 412, THNOC

47 **Famous Creoles' presence:** Arts and Crafts Club bulletins, June 1922–June 1923, June 1923–June 1924, and June 1924–June 1925, and *New Orleans Art School Year Book, 1926–1927,* in Vertical Files, "Arts. Societies. Arts and Crafts Club. Undated and 1922–28," LaRC.

48 **Art School enrollment and Club dues:** Frederick Oechsner, "Arts and Crafts Club, Proven Factor in Local Art, Invites New Members," *Morning Tribune,* 29 December 1926.

Description of activities: From Morel, "The Story of An Art School—And How It Grew."

50 **1924–1925 activities:** Arts and Crafts Club bulletin, June 1924–June 1925, in Vertical Files, "Arts. Societies. Arts and Crafts Club. Undated and 1922–28," LaRC.

Joint meeting with Poetry Society: Unsourced and undated (but 1928) clipping, MSS 247, Arts and Crafts Club collection, box 11, folder 441, THNOC.

Mexican handicrafts: "Scope and Content Note," MSS 247, Arts and Crafts Club collection, THNOC.

Spratling's shows and visits from his friends: Scott, "William Spratling and the New Orleans Renaissance," 311–12.

51 **Frans Blom at Club:** Clippings from *Times-Picayune,* 12 November 1930 and 16 February 1936, and *Item-Tribune,* 5 November 1930, in MSS 247, Arts and Crafts Club collection, box 11, folder 441, THNOC.

Mexico became popular: See Jean Moore Bragg and Susan Saward, *Painting the Town: The Woodward Brothers Come to New Orleans* (Jean Bragg Gallery, 2004), 261–64.

El Tereno, Majorca: Biography of Hargrave by Sean Hemingway (dated 2006), www.askart.com/askart/artist.aspx?artist=5023147. See also Abel G. Warshawsky, *Memories of an American Impressionist* (Kent Univ. Press, 1980), 223.

Ocean Springs Art Colony: Vera Mobel [Morel], "Modern Painting Conservatively Done," *Morning Tribune,* 22 September 1926; Frederick Oechsner, "Arts and Crafts Club Show Sunday," *Morning Tribune,* 18 September 1926; and "Promises of Balls, Exhibitions in Fall Tide Orleans Art Colony Through Dull Summer Season," unsourced clipping, in Marion [sic] Draper folder, THNOC.

Natchitoches Art Colony: E.g., Mary Belle McKellar, "The First Art Colony of the South," *Dallas Morning News,* 25 April 1926. Melrose Scrapbook 78, CHRC, is entirely devoted to clippings and ephemera dealing with the colony.

51   **Melrose Plantation:** Correspondence with Mary Linn Wernet, CHRC, August 2010.

53   **Quartier Club activities and members:** Mimeographed announcement, dated 10 November 1923, in Vertical Files, "Organizations. Quartier Club," LaRC.

Hugh Walpole in Lyceum series: Scott, *Natalie Scott,* 248.

Raid on dining room: Anthony Stanonis, "'A Woman of Boundless Energy': Elizabeth Werlein and Her Times," *Louisiana History* 46, no. 1 (winter 2005): 16.

"A circle of distinguished ladies": Grace King, *Memories of a Southern Woman of Letters* (Macmillan, 1932), 386.

Le Petit Salon charter, officers, and activities: 1927 *Bulletin,* in Vertical Files, "Organizations. Le Petit Salon," LaRC.

King on "French Salons": "Football Again to Give Color to Week-End Social Activities," *Times-Picayune,* 25 October 1924, 10.

54   **New clubhouse and later activities:** [Genevieve Munson Trimble], *Le Petit Salon: A History of Its Fifty Years, 1924–1974* (Le Petit Salon, 1974).

Program covers: Vertical Files, "Music. Opera. Petit Opera Louisianais," LaRC.

Musical director: Harold George Scott, *Lelia: The Compleat Ballerina* (Pelican, 1975), 55.

"Response has not indicated certain success": Coad, "New Orleans Tries to Revive Culture."

THE DIFFERENCE DIXIE MADE

56   **"The Fact is New Orleans":** Guy Manners, *Atmosphere* (Robert True, 1922), quoted in Cathy Chance Harvey, "Lyle Saxon: A Portrait in Letters" (Ph.D. diss., Tulane University, 1980).

57   **Literary community no more than fifty:** Oliver La Farge, *Raw Material* (Houghton Mifflin, 1945), 125.

"Beguiled by the superficial trappings": Harold Sinclair, *The Port of New Orleans* (Doubleday, Doran, 1942), 280.

"Local-color damnation": Lewis P. Simpson, "New Orleans as a Literary Center," in *Literary New Orleans, Essays and Meditations,* ed. Richard S. Kennedy, 82 (Louisiana State Univ. Press, 1992).

58   **Faulkner's sketches "hackwork":** Cleanth Brooks, "A Note on Faulkner's Early Attempts at the Short Story," *Studies in Short Fiction* 10 (1973): 381, 383.

"Bohemia is only a stage": Arthur Ransome, *Bohemia in London* (1907; reprint, Amazon Publishing, 2002), 266.

58 **"Angular, retired maiden schoolteachers"**: Sinclair, *Port of New Orleans,* 279–80.

"Little known outside Louisiana": George E. Jordan, "The Laura Simon Nelson Collection, 1840s–1970s," in William H. Gerdts, George E. Jordan, and Judith H. Bonner, *Complementary Visions of Louisiana Art* (Historic New Orleans Collection, 1996).

59 **Virginia Parker as "newcomer"**: Howard DeVree, "A Round-Up for Summer," *New York Times,* 26 June 1938, 129.

"No work of international significance": Laura Clark Brown, "New Orleans Modernism: The Arts and Crafts Club in the Vieux Carré, 1919–1939," *Louisiana History* 41, no. 3 (summer 2000): 341.

"No great shakes": Sinclair, *Port of New Orleans,* 279.

"Attacks on the virtue of Negro artists": Douglas Goldring, quoted in Virginia Nicholson, *Among the Bohemians: Experiments in Living, 1900–1939* (Viking Press, 2002), 49.

60 **"Open to men, women and children"**: Vera Morel, "The Story of An Art School—And How It Grew," unsourced and undated (but ca. 1926) clipping in MSS 247, Arts and Crafts Club collection, box 7, folder 412, THNOC

Little Arts and Crafts Club: Federal Writers' Project, *New Orleans City Guide* (Houghton Mifflin, 1938), 101.

Negro unit of Louisiana Writers' Project: Joan Redding, "The Dillard Project: The Black Unit of the Louisiana Writers' Project," *Louisiana History* 32, no. 1 (winter 1991): 47–62.

Margaret Walker and Richard Kirk: Kay Bonetti, "An Interview with Margaret Walker Alexander," *Missouri Review* 15, no. 1 (1992): 11.

Richmond Barthé: Federal Writers' Project, *New Orleans City Guide,* 102.

Letter from Jean Toomer: Interview with Albert Goldstein and Elise (Mrs. Julius) Friend, M1151, LaRC.

Hurston's research on hoodoo: Robert E. Hemenway, *Zora Neale Hurston: A Literary Biography* (Univ. of Illinois Press, 1980), 123.

61 **"Didn't have a phonograph"**: La Farge, *Raw Material,* 114.

"Slatternly washerwoman": William Spratling, *File on Spratling: An Autobiography* (Little, Brown, 1967), 16, 27.

Joyce Stagg's cook, Cecile: Interviews with W. C. Odiorne, Hollywood, California, 15–16 February 1963, CCC 11.1.

Andersons' cook: Elizabeth Anderson and Gerald R. Kelly, *Miss Elizabeth: A Memoir* (Boston: Little, Brown, 1969), 85, 104–5.

Levy's "dinner club": Interviews with Odiorne, CCC 11.1.

62 **"Nubian Louis"**: Lyle Saxon to Natalie Scott, [June 1926], in Natalie Vivian Scott collection, M123, LaRC.

62 **Lucille Antony's "negro studies":** "A Tour Through the Studios of the Vieux Carre Artists," *Item-Tribune Magazine*, 4 January 1925, 3.

63 **Sketches of Afro-Creoles:** William Spratling, "Five Studies of Cane River Characters from the Sketch-Book of William Spratling," *Scribner's Magazine* 83 (January–June 1928): 410–18.

Alberta Kinsey: Catherine B. Dillon, "Alberta Kinsey's New Orleans Show," *Chicago Evening Post Art World*, 11 December 1928, clipping in Alberta Kinsey folder, Art and Artist files, Smithsonian American Art Museum/National Portrait Gallery Library.

64 **Charles Bein:** Marguerite Williams in *Chicago Daily News*, quoted in clipping from *Morning Tribune*, 18 September 1926, Marion [*sic*] Draper folder, THNOC.

Symposium at the University of Mississippi: Doreen Fowler and Ann J. Abadie, eds., *Faulkner and Race* (Univ. Press of Mississippi, 2007). See also Charles D. Peavy, *Go Slow Now: Faulkner and the Race Question* (Univ. of Oregon Press, 1971).

Sherwood Anderson quotation: Walter B. Rideout, *Sherwood Anderson: A Writer in America*, vol. 1 (Univ. of Wisconsin Press, 2006), 541. See also page 449, as well as Charles E. Modlin, ed., *Sherwood Anderson: Selected Letters* (Univ. of Tennessee Press, 1984), 30–31, 53, 63; Sherwood Anderson, *Sherwood Anderson's Notebook* (Boni and Liveright, 1926; reprint, Paul P. Appel, 1970), 64, 223; William A. Sutton, ed., *Letters to Bab: Sherwood Anderson to Marietta D. Finley, 1916–33* (Univ. of Illinois Press, 1985), 183–84; Welford Dunaway Taylor and Charles E. Modlin, eds., *Southern Odyssey: Selected Writings by Sherwood Anderson* (Univ. of Georgia Press, 1997), 11, 26ff.

Typology of stereotypes: Sterling A. Brown, "Negro Character as Seen by White Authors," *Callaloo*, no. 14/15 (February–May 1982): 79.

Saxon's racial views: Lawrence N. Powell, introduction to Federal Writers' Project, *New Orleans City Guide 1938*, reprint ed. (Garrett County Press, 2009).

65 **Flo Field stories:** Three stories in *The Delineator* (1918–1921), in Flora Field collection, Newcomb Archives, Newcomb College Center for Research on Women.

Scott's cookbook: Natalie Scott, *Mirations and Miracles of Mandy* (Robert H. True, 1929).

"Childlike, irresponsible, hopeless": Sybil Kein, *Creole: The History and Legacy of Louisiana's Free People of Color* (Louisiana State Univ. Press, 2000), 137.

Dix's Mirandy stories: Harnett T. Kane, *Dear Dorothy Dix* (Doubleday, 1952), 117.

"Funny 'nigger'": Roark Bradford, in foreword to *Ol' Man Adam an' His Chillun* (Harper and Brothers, 1928).

65 **Basso's short story:** Inez Hollander Lake, *The Road from Pompey's Head: The Life and Work of Hamilton Basso* (Louisiana State Univ. Press, 1999), 24–25. **"The trick is to write nigger stories":** Anderson, *Sherwood Anderson's Notebook,* 107.

Serious novels: Lewis P. Simpson, "Roark Whitney Wickliffe Bradford (1896–1948)," in *Southern Writers: A Biographical Dictionary,* ed. Robert Bain, Joseph M. Flora, and Louis D. Rubin, 44–45 (Louisiana State Univ. Press, 1979).

"Unpleasantly realistic": "Books: Black Bunyan," *Time,* 31 August 1931.

"Good Roark Bradford Southern-Negro story": Letter to Bradford from David Stick, editor of *American Legion Magazine,* in Roark Bradford collection, M20, Tulane University.

66 **"To think other than as they did":** La Farge, *Raw Material,* 119.

Odiorne-Gilmore correspondence: Odiorne to Gilmore, 10 July 1972, and Odiorne to Martha Gilmore Robinson, 2 July 1973, in Samuel Louis Gilmore Jr. collection, M695, LaRC.

Du Bois Literary Prize: "The Du Bois Literary Prize," *The Crisis* 38 (August 1931): 278.

Ventadour on black list: See a list of those "associated with SCEF [Southern Conference Education Fund] and/or Carl Braden personally" (being on the SCEF mailing list was sufficient) in *Report of the Florida Legislative Investigation Committee to the 1961 Session of the Legislature,* 18, found in the files of the Mississippi State Sovereignty Commission, at mdah.state.ms.us/arrec/digital_archives/sovcom/.

Michael Gold and Lyle Saxon: Chance Harvey, *The Life and Selected Letters of Lyle Saxon* (Pelican, 2003), 90.

67 **"We were nearly ignorant of politics":** "Julius Weis Friend's History of the *Double Dealer,*" *Mississippi Quarterly* 31 (fall 1978), 587–604.

THREE POPULATIONS

68 **"The milieu enabled them":** Oliver La Farge, *Raw Material* (Houghton Mifflin, 1945), 126.

New Orleanians "don't care what you do": W. Kenneth Holditch, "William Spratling, William Faulkner, and Other Famous Creoles," *Mississippi Quarterly* 51, no. 3 (summer 1998): 423.

"Popular Bachelors of New Orleans": "Popular Bachelors of New Orleans," *New Orleans Life* 2, no. 6 (February 1927): 13, and no. 7 (March 1927): 17.

69 **Esther DuPuy:** John W. Scott, "William Spratling and the New Orleans Renaissance," *Louisiana History* 45, no. 3 (summer 2004): 317.

Harold Levy found it hard to credit: Blotner's note inserted in his interview with William Spratling, Taxco, Mexico, 28–30 January 1965, JBP 2479/004.

69 **"Good-fairy of Frenchtown"**: Letter to Maude Chambers, in Chance Harvey, *The Life and Selected Letters of Lyle Saxon* (Pelican, 2003), 243. ("Fairy" meaning "effeminate male homosexual" was first recorded in 1895, according to the *Online Etymology Dictionary*, www.etymonline.com/index.php?term=fairy.)

"Peculiar virility": Lyle Saxon, "Art Association Exhibition Disappoints Through Absence of Many Louisiana Painters," unsourced clipping, 28 February 1928, Weeks Hall folder, THNOC.

"Miasmas rising from the Teche": Edward Dreyer, "Some Friends of Lyle Saxon," epilogue to Lyle Saxon, *The Friends of Joe Gilmore* (Hastings House, 1948), 154–55.

"Uptown marriage": Holditch, "William Spratling, William Faulkner, and Other Famous Creoles."

"Criss-crossed with perverts": Quoted in Will Fellows, *A Passion to Preserve: Gay Men as Keepers of Culture* (Univ. of Wisconsin Press, 2004), 228.

70 **Gay involvement in preservation**: Fellows, *Passion to Preserve*, 25–35. Fellows devotes a chapter specifically to New Orleans (217–29).

"Most of the intellectuals": Howard Mumford Jones, ed., *Letters of Sherwood Anderson* (Little, Brown, 1953), 310.

Jewish population and percentage of white population: *American Jewish Yearbook, 1927–28* (Jewish Publication Society of America, 1927), 245, and table 19 in Campbell Gibson and Kay Jung, *Historical Census Statistics on Population Totals by Race, 1790 to 1990, and by Hispanic Origin, 1970 to 1990, for Large Cities and Other Urban Places in the United States,* Working Paper No. 76, Population Division, U.S. Census Bureau, February 2005.

Officers of the Arts and Crafts Club: Arts and Crafts Club bulletin, June 1924–June 1925, Vertical Files, "Arts. Societies. Arts and Crafts Club. Undated and 1922–28," folder 1, LaRC.

Committee of the Quartier Club: Mimeographed announcement, dated 10 November 1923, in Vertical Files, "Organizations. Quartier Club," LaRC.

Founders of Le Petit Theatre: History at www.lepetittheatre.com/about.asp, accessed in summer 2009 (now removed).

71 **"Several older Jewish families"**: Jones, ed., *Letters of Sherwood Anderson,* 310.

72 **Mardi Gras krewes excluded Jews**: Robert Tallant, *Mardi Gras . . . As It Was* (Pelican, 1989), 179–81.

Member of the Godchaux family: Justin Vogt, "The Krewes and the Jews," *Tablet,* 16 February 2010.

Solomon Wexler: Louis Marshall Warfield, *Builders of Our Nation: Men of Nineteen-Fourteen* (American Publishers' Association, 1915), 813; "Solomon Wexler, Banker, Dies At 53," *New York Times,* 23 April 1921, 10.

72 **Trillin quotation:** Calvin Trillin, "U. S. Journal: New Orleans—Mardi Gras," *New Yorker,* 9 March 1968, 143.

73 **Historical material on Sicilian immigrants:** From A. V. Margavio and Jerome J. Salomone, *Bread and Respect: The Italians of Louisiana* (Pelican, 2002), unless otherwise indicated.
Cow in top-floor apartment: [Sydney S. Field], "Biographical Notes on Flo Field," in Flora Field collection, Newcomb Archives, Newcomb College Center for Research on Women.

74 **Life "conducted at open windows":** La Farge, *Raw Material,* 118.
Bohemian neighborhoods originally Italian: Herbert Gold, quoted in John Geluardi, "The Fight for the Bohemian Soul of North Beach's Caffe Trieste," *SF Weekly,* 10 December 2008.
"Distrust and neutralize all written laws": Luigi Barzini, *From Caesar to the Mafia* (Bantam, 1972), 75.
"Il Siciliano" (pseud.), "What Makes a Sicilian?": online at ilsiciliano.net/page32_what_makes_a_sicilian.php.

75 **"Silver Dollar Sam" Carollo:** Carl Sifakis, *The Mafia Encyclopedia,* 2nd ed. (Facts on File, 1999); "occupation" and address from *Soards' New Orleans Directory, 1921* (Soards Directory Company, 1921).
Juniper essence: Reported by Genevieve Pitot, in Holditch, "William Spratling, William Faulkner, and Other Famous Creoles."

76 **Sidney Mttron Hirsch:** Joseph M. Flora, Lucinda Hardwick MacKethan, and Todd W. Taylor, eds., *Companion to Southern Literature* (Louisiana State Univ. Press, 2002), 284.
Jewish populations: *American Jewish Yearbook, 1927–28,* 244–45. Estimates for 1917–1918 are eight thousand for New Orleans, three thousand for Nashville, nineteen hundred for Charleston.

UPTOWN, DOWNTOWN

77 **"Underneath the brilliance":** Interviews with W. C. Odiorne, Hollywood, California, 15–16 February 1963, CCC 11.1.
"When one of us achieved anything": Oliver La Farge, *Raw Material* (Houghton Mifflin, 1945), 125–26.
"Mutual friendliness and good will": Hamilton Basso, "William Faulkner, Man and Writer," *Saturday Review,* 28 July 1962, 11.
Grace King: Grace King, *Memories of a Southern Woman of Letters* (Macmillan, 1932), 397.

78 **"Lady fictioneers":** *Double Dealer* editorial quoted by Albert Goldstein, "The Creative Spirit," in *The Past as Prelude: New Orleans 1718–1968,* ed. Hodding Carter, 178 (Tulane University, 1968).

78 **Review of *Creole Families of New Orleans*:** *Double Dealer* 1 (May 1921): 211.
Avant-garde students: Jean Moore Bragg and Susan Saward, *Painting the Town: The Woodward Brothers Come to New Orleans* (Jean Bragg Gallery, 2004), 217.
Henderson grumbled: Louise C. Hoffman, *Josephine Crawford: An Artist's Vision* (Historic New Orleans Collection, 2009), 51.

79 **"The French Quarter is now falling into decay":** Lyle Saxon, "Pontalba Artist Colony Plan Gets Wide Approval," *Item,* 26 January 1919, section 1, page 12.
Businessman William Schultz: Anthony Stanonis, *Creating the Big Easy: New Orleans and the Emergence of Modern Tourism* (Univ. of Georgia Press, 2006), 141–42.
Association of Commerce supporting private efforts: Stanonis, *Creating the Big Easy,* 153.

80 **Proposal for Pontalba artists' studios:** Doris Kent, "New Orleans' Plan to Form Art Center About Jackson Square and Pontalba Buildings," *Times-Picayune,* 16 February 1919, Magazine section, 1.
Woodward brothers' early attention to French Quarter: Bragg and Saward, *Painting the Town,* 136–37, 148, 160, 224.
Elizabeth Werlein's book: Anthony Stanonis, "'A Woman of Boundless Energy': Elizabeth Werlein and Her Times," *Louisiana History* 46, no. 1 (winter 2005): 15.
Artists in Quarter at end of nineteenth century: *Knute Heldner and the Art Colony in Old New Orleans* (Jean Bragg Gallery, 2000), 6–7.
Daughters of 1776–1812: Helen Pitkin Schertz, "Is the Vieux Carré a Permanent Asset?" *New Orleans Life* 2, no. 9 (June 1927), 8.
William Ratcliffe Irby: Will Fellows, *A Passion to Preserve: Gay Men as Keepers of Culture* (Univ. of Wisconsin Press, 2004), 217–18.

81 **"Den of thieves"; Kinsey-Saxon exchange:** "Close-Ups," *New Orleanian,* 20 September 1930, 20.

82 **Odiorne's observations:** Interviews with W. C. Odiorne, Hollywood, California, 15–16 February 1963, CCC 11.1; letter to Carvel Collins, 15 March 1963, W. C. Odiorne folder (2 of 2), CCC 11.2 (Odiorne's ellipsis).
"Literati Rub Elbows": "Arts Ball Is Riot of Costumes, Color, Jubilant Good Fellowship," unsourced clipping, 12 December 1927, MSS 247, Arts and Crafts Club collection, box 7, folder 423, THNOC.
"Bond salesmen of real life": "W. G. W.," "Arts and Crafts Club Ball Bad for the Eyes," clipping from *States,* 11 December 1927, MSS 247, Arts and Crafts Club collection, box 7, folder 423, THNOC.
Junior League pony ballet: "Arts Ball Is Riot of Costumes."
Chelsea Arts Club ball: Virginia Nicholson, *Among the Bohemians: Experiments in Living, 1900–1939* (Viking Press, 2002), 145.

83 **"One of the most interesting events"**: Undated (but 1927) clipping from *States,* MSS 247, Arts and Crafts Club collection, box 7, folder 423, THNOC.
Chaired invitation committee: Undated (but 1927) clipping from *States,* MSS 247, Arts and Crafts Club collection, box 7, folder 423, THNOC.
Danced at 1925 ball: "Bal des Artistes to Be Brilliant," unsourced and un-dated (but 1925) clipping in Dan Whitney folder, THNOC.
Junior League Review: Program for 1925, in Vertical Files,"Organizations. Junior League of New Orleans. Junior League Review," LaRC.

84 **"I had a social standing"**: Lynn Simross, "Memories of a Bohemian in Paris, 1924," *Los Angeles Times,* 14 April 1977, F1.
La Farge observations: La Farge, *Raw Material,* 115.
Green Shutter Tea Room: Lyle Saxon, "What's Doing," *Times-Picayune,* 25 October 1925, 2.
"Orleanians who have taken up the study of art": Clipping from *Item,* 6 February 1921, in Ellsworth Woodward folder, THNOC.
"Someone always seems to be rushing off": Unsourced and undated (but 1927) clipping, MSS 247, Arts and Crafts Club collection, box 7, folder 418, THNOC.
Information on Johnstons: From the 1920 census, on ancestry.com.
Saxon comment: Saxon, "What's Doing."

85 **"You can give such wonderful parties!"**: Unsourced clipping, 7 November 1924, in MSS 247, Arts and Crafts Club collection, THNOC.
"Rent an ordinary furnished room": Calvert Stith, "New Orleans: Non-Guide-Book Style," *New Orleanian,* 6 September 1930, 37.
"Dilletante gang downtown": "Uptown—Downtown—Back of Town," *New Orleanian,* 15 December 1930, 17.
Faulkner showed up barefoot: W. Kenneth Holditch, "Rising Star," *Gambit Weekly,* 22 September 1997.
Edna St. Vincent Millay: Alan Brown, *Literary Levees of New Orleans* (Star-rhill Press, 1998), 23.
Party at the Baroness Pontalba Tea Room: "Uptown—Downtown—Back of Town."

THE END OF AN INTERLUDE

86 **"Women are putting their bridge-winnings"**: Helen Pitkin Schertz, "Is the Vieux Carré a Permanent Asset?" *New Orleans Life* 2, no. 9 (June 1927), 10.
"In the days of its decay": Hamilton Basso, "New Orleans Letter," *Transition,* no. 15 (February 1929), 149–50.
"Italian vendor of garlic": Beatrice Cosgrove, "Historic Heart of New Orleans Saved," *New York Times,* 21 February 1926, SM10.
"Tattered clothes fluttered": Martha Gilmore Robinson, quoted in "Vieux

Carré Commission History," www.nola.gov/RESIDENTS/Vieux-Carre-Commission/History-and-News.

87 **What happened has happened elsewhere:** Elizabeth Wilson, *Bohemians: The Glamorous Outcasts* (I. B. Tauris, 2000), 41–49. On London and Paris respectively, see also Virginia Nicholson, *Among the Bohemians: Experiments in Living, 1900–1939* (Viking Press, 2002), 29; Sisley Huddleston, *Bohemian Literary and Social Life in Paris: Salons, Cafés, Studios* (George G. Harrap, 1928), 32–34.

Attic room in the Pontalba building: Walter B. Rideout, *Sherwood Anderson: A Writer in America,* vol. 1 (Univ. of Wisconsin Press, 2006), 460.

Saxon's sixteen-room house: Chance Harvey, *The Life and Selected Letters of Lyle Saxon* (Pelican, 2003), 61.

"A quart of milk and fifteen cents worth of red beans and rice": James K. Feibleman, *The Way of a Man: An Autobiography* (Horizon Press, 1969), 271–72.

88 **"Polyglot bottom of the melting pot":** Cosgrove, "Historic Heart of New Orleans Saved."

Saxon foresaw domino effect: Lyle Saxon, "Pontalba Artist Colony Plan Gets Wide Approval," *Item,* 26 January 1919, section 1, page 12.

What amounted to a walking tour: T. P. Thompson, "The Renaissance of the Vieux Carré," *Double Dealer* 3, no. 14 (February 1922): 85–89.

Italian family and their chickens: Interview with Mrs. Ernest Samuel (Adaline Katz), Bay St. Louis, Mississippi, 29 March 1963, CCC 15.27.

89 **Visit by Weeks Hall's aunt:** Ray Lewis White, ed., *Sherwood Anderson's Memoirs: A Critical Edition* (Univ. of North Carolina Press, 1969), 460–62.

Immigrants "slowly giving place": Cosgrove, "Historic Heart of New Orleans Saved."

"The usual teashops": Silas Bent, "Greenwich Village on Royal Street," *New York Times Book Review and Magazine,* 23 July 1922, 4.

Green Shutter Tea Room: Interview with Carl Carmer, 23 August 1965, JBP 2479/008.

The Quarter's Book Shop: Interview with Harold Dempsey, New Orleans, 2 February 1963, CCC 4.28.

90 **"Studios and more studios":** Undated and unsourced clipping in Spratling folder, THNOC.

"Rather proud of the fact": Schertz, "Is the Vieux Carré a Permanent Asset?" 8.

Paul Morphy Book Shop: Thompson, "Renaissance of the Vieux Carré," 87–88.

"Picked up its skirts": Calvert Stith, "New Orleans: Non-Guide-Book Style," *New Orleanian,* 6 September 1930, 37.

"Smartest new shops": "Doings in the Vieux Carré," *New Orleans Life,* November 1925, 27. THNOC holds eleven issues, from May 1925 until August 1927, plus one issue of the *Orleanian* ("formerly *New Orleans Life*") from July 1928. The magazine appears to have begun publication in 1924.

91 **"No tears need be shed"**: George N. Coad, "New Orleans Tries to Revive Culture," *New York Times*, 25 December 1927, E2.

"French Quarter . . . has become a fad"; "the most ardent of the poseurs": Bent, "Greenwich Village on Royal Street," 4.

Shimmying and slumming: Interview with Mrs. Ernest Samuel (Adaline Katz), Bay St. Louis, Mississippi, 29 March 1963, CCC 15.27.

92 **"Attic poets"**: Interviews with W. C. Odiorne, Hollywood, California, 15–16 February 1963, CCC 11.1.

"The whole quarter is filling up": Harvey, *The Life and Selected Letters of Lyle Saxon*, 228.

Carmer's mocking piece: Carl Carmer, "Salon," *New Orleanian*, 27 September 1930, 15.

Basso quotations: Hamilton Basso, "New Orleans Letter," *Transition*, no. 15 (February 1929), 149–50. The hapless poetizer was a recent Washington and Lee graduate named John Dandridge Stanard, whose *Just Thoughts: A Book of Verse* was published by The Quarter's Book Shop in 1928. Stanard's copy of *Famous Creoles*, inscribed to him by Spratling, is now in the Brodsky Collection at Southeast Missouri State University.

"Sharp distinction": Oliver La Farge, *Raw Material* (Houghton Mifflin, 1945), 126.

"Cultural antics of the boys and girls": Coad, "New Orleans Tries to Revive Culture."

93 **New Orleans Art League**: Meigs O. Frost, "New Art Body Makes Bow with Fine Exhibit," clipping from *States*, 4 December 1927, Weeks Hall folder, THNOC; see also Vertical Files, "Arts. Societies. New Orleans Art League," LaRC.

Spratling complaint about buses: Taylor D. Littleton, *The Color of Silver: William Spratling, His Life and Art* (Louisiana State Univ. Press, 2000), 82.

"A curio for wintering visitors": Josef Von Klinger, "Vieux Carre Soliloquy," *New Orleanian*, 13 September 1930, 30.

Saxon's walking tour: Lyle Saxon, "French Quarter without a Guide," *Times-Picayune*, 2 March 1924.

"Mad house": Anthony Stanonis, "'Always in Costume and Mask': Lyle Saxon and New Orleans Tourism," *Louisiana History* 42, no. 1 (winter 2001): 57.

"The vogue of the French Quarter": "Close-Ups," *New Orleanian*, 20 September 1930, 20–21.

"Won't be the same place in ten years": Basso, "New Orleans Letter," 149–50.

"I'm going to tell you": Sherwood Anderson, "New Orleans: A Prose Poem in the Expressionist Manner," *Vanity Fair* 26 (August 1926), 97.

93 **"Too many country boys and girls":** Bradford to Lyle Saxon, in Harvey, *The Life and Selected Letters of Lyle Saxon,* 208.
"The old Quarter ain't what she used to be": Stanonis, "Always in Costume and Mask," 57.
"Unmistakable smell of paint": "Doings in the Vieux Carré," 27.

94 **Vann Woodward quotations:** Letter to Glenn W. Rainey, 22 July [1930], C. Vann Woodward papers, MS 1436, Manuscripts and Archives, Yale University Library. (I thank Michael O'Brien for this gem.)
Mrs. Schertz's report: Schertz, "Is the Vieux Carré a Permanent Asset?"
Natalie Scott's property: John W. Scott, *Natalie Scott: A Magnificent Life* (Pelican, 2008), 257.
Knoblock book: K. T. Knoblock, *There's Been Murder Done* (Harper and Brothers, 1931), xiii–xiv. Knoblock was married to Adaline Katz.
Odiorne's and Kinsey's opinions: Odiorne to Carvel Collins, 15 March 1963, in W. C. Odiorne folder (2 of 2), CCC 11.2.
"A tourist camp": Von Klinger, "Vieux Carre Soliloquy," 30.

95 **"Let us stroll into the Vieux Carré":** "The Man in the Iron Mask," *High Hatter,* June 1936, 11, from "the scrapbook of Mrs. Daniel Whitney," THNOC.

96 **"Decent people driven out":** "The Man in the Iron Mask," 20.
"Came then the dawn": Draft introduction to "The Knight Takes the Queen," in Flora Field collection, Newcomb Archives, Newcomb College Center for Research on Women.
"Little, fragile, prolific Alberta Kinsey": "The Man in the Iron Mask," 20.
WPA's guide to Louisiana: Louisiana Writers' Project, *Louisiana: A Guide to the State* (Hastings House, 1941), 169.

The Annotated *Sherwood Anderson and Other Famous Creoles*

99 **Irby's suicide:** Gaspar J. "Buddy" Stall, *Buddy Stall's French Quarter Montage* (Pelican, 2006), 51.

101 **Olive Lyons:** From Chance Harvey, *The Life and Selected Letters of Lyle Saxon* (Pelican, 2003), 97, except as below.
Edmund Wilson's admiring sketch: Edmund Wilson, *The Twenties: From Notebooks and Diaries of the Period* (Macmillan, 1975), 185.

FLO FIELD

Sketch based on abstract and CD of 7 January 1962 interview and on [Sydney S. Field], "Biographical Notes on Flo Field," in Flora Field collection, Newcomb Archives, Newcomb College Center for Research on Women, unless otherwise indicated.

104 **Day job with city:** Hermann Deutsch, "World Affairs of No Concern Compared to a Lady of Grace," unsourced and undated (but 1971) clipping in Field collection, Newcomb Archives.

Mother as newspaperwoman: Martha R. Field, *Louisiana Voyages: The Travel Writings of Catharine Cole,* ed. Joan B. McLaughlin and Jack McLaughlin (Univ. Press of Mississippi, 2006).

"Little Flo"; watching mother write; debut; mother's sickroom; darky stories: Frederick Oechsner, "Le Petit Theatre Eager for Flo Field's Play" *Item-Tribune,* 13 February 1927.

105 **Article in *Leslie's Weekly*:** Anna Cosulich, "Southern Women Who Have Made Their Mark in Journalism," *Leslie's Weekly,* 12 February 1903.

Marriage failed: Her marriage certificate and some letters from her husband are in the Field collection, Newcomb Archives.

Intimated father was O. Henry: W. Kenneth Holditch, "William Spratling, William Faulkner, and Other Famous Creoles," *Mississippi Quarterly* 51, no. 3 (summer 1998). Her son, Sydney, was born in 1910.

Ironwork: "Ironwork of Old New Orleans," *Times-Picayune,* 12 March 1916, Magazine section, 3.

Fifteen-dollar weekly salary, Morphy House, 35-cent suppers, sitting on gallery: Deutsch, "World Affairs of No Concern."

Darky stories: Oechsner, "Le Petit Theatre Eager for Flo Field's Play."

Philharmonic Society: "Flo Field," *New Orleanian,* 1 January 1931, 23.

"Swing[ing] down Royal Street"; "years younger than I": Unpublished reminiscences in Field collection, Newcomb Archives.

106 *A la Creole:* See pages 38–39.

"Negro waif musicians": "Sidewalk Troupe Off for North," *Times-Picayune,* 27 December 1928, 17, and "Sleepy City Challenged!" undated and unsourced clipping in Field collection, folder 6B, Newcomb Archives.

Made the national news: E.g., "Negro Waif Musicians Are Taken to Pennsy," Associated Press story in *Port Arthur News,* 27 December 1927.

Honorary member of Orleans Club: "Women Given Recognition for Community Service," *Times-Picayune,* 27 February 1927.

Booking at New York's Palace: "Dusky Sidewalk Shufflers to Make Stage Debut in East," *Times-Picayune,* 6 January 1929, 14.

Philadelphia try-out: "Flo Field," *New Orleanian.*

Louisiana community theaters: e.g., "Flo Field Takes Part in Own Play," *Times-Picayune,* 7 November 1931, 18.

Pasadena, of all places: Flo Field, letter to the editor, *Time,* 2 August 1943.

Limited edition: Flo Field, *A la Creole* (Natchez Graphics, 1953).

Visit to Spratling: "Mrs. Field Back from Mexican Trip," *Times-Picayune,* 5 February 1931.

106 **"Folding money":** Spratling to Field, 16 October 1961, Field collection, folder 4B, Newcomb Archives.

Typewriter near bed: Bettye Anding, "Flo Field Recalls Yesterday but Today Intrigues Her," *States-Item,* 11 June 1969, 34.

Continued to write: Flo Field, "Golfers Putt Where Men Fought Duels," *New York Times,* 8 June 1930, 83, and correspondence and manuscripts from 1950s (including rejection slip from *True*) in Field collection, Newcomb Archives.

Taste of her style as a guide: The material in the booklet was published simultaneously as an article, "Rue Royale," in *New Orleanian,* 15 November 1930.

Cable's house in Garden District: Federal Writers' Project, *New Orleans City Guide* (Houghton Mifflin, 1938), 117; "The Man in the Iron Mask," *High Hatter,* June 1936, from "the scrapbook of Mrs. Daniel Whitney," THNOC, indicates that she had moved before 1936.

Speaking to community groups: E.g., "Flo Field Talks to Big 10 Alumni," *Times-Picayune,* 4 July 1933, 5.

Clay Shaw: See letters to Sydney from 1920s onward in Field collection, folder 4, Newcomb Archives.

107 **Luncheon in her honor:** Clipping from *Item,* 7 May 1950, in Field collection, Newcomb Archives.

Official historian, pharmacy museum: "N.O. Writer's Services Set," unsourced and undated (but circa September 1972) clipping from Field collection, Newcomb Archives.

Sydney's career: Letters to Flo Field from Charles Hanson Towne, editor of *Harper's Bazaar,* 19 September 1927, and from The Editors, *Ladies' Home Journal,* 3 April 1928, in Field collection, Newcomb Archives; biographical note on dust jacket of S. S. Field, *The American Drink Book* (Farrar, Straus, and Young, 1953).

Dividing her time: See correspondence from 1950s and "Jeers Greeted City's First Girl Reporter, Then Praise," unsourced clipping, 12 April 1950, in Field collection, Newcomb Archives.

Died at 96: "N.O. Writer's Services Set."

Birthday party: Tommy Griffin, "Lagniappe," *States-Item,* 24 May 1972.

"Never had any sense": Anding, "Flo Field Recalls Yesterday."

SHERWOOD ANDERSON

Sketch based on Walter B. Rideout, *Sherwood Anderson: A Writer in America* (Univ. of Wisconsin Press, 2006), and Walter B. Rideout, "The Most Civilized Spot in America: Sherwood Anderson in New Orleans," in *Literary New Orleans in the Modern World,* ed. Richard S. Kennedy, 1–22 (Louisiana State Univ. Press, 2006), unless otherwise indicated.

108 **"Shaggy looking man"**: Interview with Elise Friend and Albert Goldstein, M1151, LaRC.

"Long hair fell in strands": Julius Friend, quoted in Irving Howe, *Sherwood Anderson* (Methuen, 1951), 141.

109 **"Dean of American literature"**: William Spratling, *File on Spratling: An Autobiography* (Little, Brown, 1967), 29.

Stuck out his hand: Interview with Friend and Goldstein, LaRC.

"Most civilized spot": Charles E. Modlin, ed., *Sherwood Anderson: Selected Letters* (Univ. of Tennessee Press, 1984), 29.

Lunches with Saxon: Chance Harvey, *The Life and Selected Letters of Lyle Saxon* (Pelican, 2003), 75.

"Loafing on the wharfs": Modlin, ed., *Sherwood Anderson,* 31. The "Memphis newspaper man" mentioned in a letter of 2 February 1922 was almost certainly Bradford.

"As for the girls, my dear": John W. Scott, *Natalie Scott: A Magnificent Life* (Pelican, 2008), 250.

"Vamped by New Orleans": Modlin, ed., *Sherwood Anderson,* 34.

"Lion of the Latin Quarter": Marjorie Peters, "'The Most American Book,' Says Sherwood," *New Orleans Item Magazine,* 7 December 1924, 2.

"We walked and talked": William Faulkner, "Sherwood Anderson: An Appreciation," in *The Achievement of Sherwood Anderson: Essays in Criticism,* ed. Ray Lewis White, 194 (Univ. of North Carolina Press, 1966).

"I noticed he was a cripple": Sherwood Anderson, *Southern Odyssey: Selected Writings by Sherwood Anderson,* ed. Welford Dunaway Taylor and Charles E. Modlin (Univ. of Georgia Press, 1997), 16.

Things he imagined became so real: Peters, "The Most American Book," 2.

110 **"Could be a struggling, poor writer"**: Elizabeth Anderson and Gerald R. Kelly, *Miss Elizabeth: A Memoir* (Boston: Little, Brown, 1969), 113.

Father came from a Southern family: Modlin, ed., *Sherwood Anderson,* 36, 40.

"I try being a black man": Sherwood Anderson, *Sherwood Anderson's Notebook* (Boni and Liveright, 1926; reprint, Paul P. Appel, 1970), 64, 132.

"Nigger craze": Anderson, *Southern Odyssey,* 26, 27.

"Muscles in the sunlight": Marjorie Peters, "Modernist Beguiled by Old New Orleans," *Times-Picayune,* 19 April 1925, section 1-B, 1–2.

"Bright blue racetrack shirt": Faulkner, "Sherwood Anderson: An Appreciation," 195.

"A corduroy shirt, a loud green one": James K. Feibleman, *Way of a Man: An Autobiography* (Horizon Press, 1969), 159.

"Looks of approval": Anderson, *Sherwood Anderson's Notebook,* 64.

Invited by Grace King: Robert Bush, *Grace King: A Southern Destiny* (Louisiana State Univ. Press, 1983), 300.

110 **"God, what a man!":** Lyle Saxon to Sherwood and Elizabeth Anderson, 12 September 1926, Sherwood Anderson papers, Newberry Library, Chicago, Illinois.

Opening Arts and Crafts Club season: Unsourced and undated clipping in Dan Whitney folder, THNOC.

Benjamin Prize committee: Clipping from *Chicago Evening Post Art World,* 20 April 1926, in Weeks Hall folder, Art and Artist files, Smithsonian American Art Museum/National Portrait Gallery Library.

Good-naturedly agreed to interviews: Lyle Saxon, "Authors Agree That Hard Work Is Half Battle," *Times-Picayune,* 14 March 1926, section 1-B, 1. See also, e.g., Peters, "The Most American Book," and Peters, "Modernist Beguiled by Old New Orleans," section 1-B, 1–2.

"What he had, he shared": Hamilton Basso, "William Faulkner, Man and Writer," *Saturday Review,* 28 July 1962, 11.

"A heart as big as his frame": Interviews with W. C. Odiorne, Hollywood, California, 15–16 February 1963, CCC 11.1.

"Warm, generous, merry": Faulkner, "Sherwood Anderson: An Appreciation," 198.

111 **"Enjoyed hugely his position":** Anderson and Kelly, *Miss Elizabeth,* 88.

"Faulkner and Sherwood enjoyed each other," Basso and Oechsner at his feet: Spratling, *File on Spratling,* 17, 22.

Feibleman's judgment: Feibleman, *Way of a Man,* 159, 270.

"The one writer here of promise": Modlin, ed., *Sherwood Anderson,* 69–70.

Anderson learned Faulkner had lied; scholars suggest other explanations: Joseph Blotner, *Faulkner: A Biography,* vol. 1 (Random House, 1974), 497–99.

Faulkner thought Anderson was hurt: Faulkner, "Sherwood Anderson: An Appreciation," 199.

"A good prospect": Howard Mumford Jones, ed., *Letters of Sherwood Anderson* (Little, Brown, 1953), 155.

Anderson's tutorial method: Faulkner, "Sherwood Anderson: An Appreciation," 197.

"Ideal place for an American writer": Anderson, *Southern Odyssey,* 40.

"Planning to spend the rest of our lives": Jones, ed., *Letters of Sherwood Anderson,* 152.

"He has work that must be done": Peters, "The Most American Book," 2.

"My little hidden hole": William A. Sutton, ed., *Letters to Bab: Sherwood Anderson to Marietta D. Finley, 1916–33* (Univ. of Illinois Press, 1985), 220.

"Lion-tamers and social folk": Pieter Stuyvesant, "Parnassus Under the Levee," *New Orleanian,* 25 October 1930, 19.

112 **"Heat and mosquitoes":** Anderson, *Southern Odyssey,* 26.

112 **Couldn't understand Spratling's plans:** Ray Lewis White, ed., *Sherwood Anderson's Memoirs: A Critical Edition* (Univ. of North Carolina Press, 1969), 493.
"Women flocked around him adoringly": Anderson and Kelly, *Miss Elizabeth,* 103.
Divorce on grounds of desertion: William A. Sutton, "Elizabeth Prall Anderson (1884–1976)," *Winesburg Eagle* 1, no. 2 (April 1976): 7.
Vacationing with Antonys: Jones, ed., *Letters of Sherwood Anderson,* 372.
New Orleans in half-ton truck: Feibleman, *Way of a Man,* 164, 274.

NATHANIEL CORTLANDT CURTIS

Sketch based on entry in John A. Mahé II and Rosanne McCaffrey, eds., *Encyclopaedia of New Orleans Artists* (Historic New Orleans Collection, 1987), unless otherwise indicated.

113 **Yearbook drawings:** Bernard Lemann, Malcolm Heard Jr., and John P. Klingman, eds., *Talk About Architecture: A Century of Architectural Education at Tulane* (Tulane University School of Architecture, 1993).
Scholarly articles: N. C. Curtis, "The Creole Architecture of Old New Orleans: With Illustrations of Wrought and Cast Iron from the Collection of Photographs at Newcomb College," *Architectural Record* 43 (1918): 435–46, and N. C. Curtis, "Some Thoughts on the Architectural Beauties of Old New Orleans; Their Proper Preservation," *Building Review* (13 January 1917): 5–6.
Drawings of St. Louis Hotel: N. C. Curtis, "The Dome of the Old St. Louis Hotel," *Architectural Record* 39 (1916): 355–58.
114 **Early exhibitions:** Clippings in N. C. Curtis file, THNOC.
Auburn president's daughter: Nathaniel C. Curtis Jr. in Lemann et al., eds., *Talk About Architecture,* 91.
Time in Illinois: Abbye A. Gorin, "The Design Architect: Nathaniel Curtis, FAIA (1917–1997)," chapter 3 of *The Rivergate,* electronic book (Howard-Tilton Memorial Library, Tulane University, 2000), available at www.tulane.edu/~rivgate/.
"Spick and span": N. C. Curtis, "Blend of New Trends in Architecture with Tradition of South," *Times-Picayune,* July 26, 1936. (Urbana is not named, but is plainly the town discussed.)
"Hard to imagine anyone's desire to go to Urbana": R. B. McKenna, "The Art Season," undated clipping from the *Orleanian,* MSS 247, Arts and Crafts Club collection, box 7, folder 417, THNOC.
Arts and Crafts Club activities: Clippings in N. C. Curtis file, THNOC, and in N. C. Curtis collection, M5, LaRC.
AIA activities: Letters in Curtis collection, box 1, LaRC.

114 **Books:** N. C. Curtis and W. P. Spratling, *The Wrought Iron Work of Old New Orleans* (American Institute of Architects, n.d.), and N. C. Curtis, *New Orleans: Its Old Houses, Shops and Public Buildings* (Lippincott, 1933).
On his buildings and avocations: Letter from his son, Nathaniel Curtis Jr., to THNOC, 16 September 1986, in N. C. Curtis file, THNOC.
University of North Carolina thesis: "The Relation of Mathematics to Music and Poetry," undergraduate thesis, University of North Carolina, Chapel Hill, 1920.
On work in Chapel Hill: *Daily Tar Heel* (University of North Carolina), 11 April 1931.

115 **Library building at Tulane:** Gorin, "The Design Architect."

FRANS BLOM

Sketch based on Robert L. Brunhouse, *Frans Blom, Maya Explorer* (Univ. of New Mexico Press, 1976), and Jesper Nielsen, "Frans Blom and the Decipherment of Maya Writing," *PARI Journal* (Pre-Columbian Art Research Institute) 4, no. 2 (fall 2003): 4–9, unless otherwise indicated.

117 **Lecture at Tulane:** John W. Scott, "William Spratling and the New Orleans Renaissance," *Louisiana History* 45 (summer 2004): 310n.
"Pops" Whitesell: Jean Moore Bragg and Susan Saward, *Painting the Town: The Woodward Brothers Come to New Orleans* (Jean Bragg Gallery, 2004), 264.
Chicago World's Fair contribution: Richard D. Perry, ed., *Exploring Yucatan: A Traveler's Anthology* (Espadaña Press, 2001), 16.
Shows and movies at Arts and Crafts Club: Clippings from *Item-Tribune,* 5 November 1930; *Times-Picayune,* 12 November 1930; and *Times-Picayune,* 16 February 1936, in MSS 247, Arts and Crafts Club collection, THNOC.
Alférez exhibition: *Item,* 9 January 1934.

ELLSWORTH WOODWARD

Sketch based on Jean Moore Bragg and Susan Saward, *Painting the Town: The Woodward Brothers Come to New Orleans* (Jean Bragg Gallery, 2004), and entries in John A. Mahé II and Rosanne McCaffrey, eds., *Encyclopaedia of New Orleans Artists* (Historic New Orleans Collection, 1987), unless otherwise indicated.

120 **Teaching art history at architecture school:** Bernard Lemann, Malcolm Heard Jr., and John P. Klingman, eds., *Talk About Architecture: A Century of Architectural Education at Tulane* (Tulane University School of Architecture, 1993), 74.

120 **Rescued ironwork:** Flo Field, "Ironwork of Old New Orleans," *Times-Picayune*, 12 March 1916, Magazine section, 3.

Photographing ironwork for museum: Ellsworth Woodward, "The Story of New Orleans Iron Work," *Year Book of Tulane University School of Architecture and the H. Sophie Newcomb School of Art* (Tulane Architectural Society, 1916), 34.

Comment on Pontalba proposal: Doris Kent, "New Orleans' Plan to Form Art Center About Jackson Square and Pontalba Buildings," *Times-Picayune*, 16 February 1919, Magazine section, 1.

Natchitoches Art Colony: Email communication from Mary Linn Wernet at CHRC, August 2010.

Saxon review of Newcomb show: From *Times-Picayune*, 20 March 1923, quoted in *Knute Heldner and the Art Colony in Old New Orleans* (Jean Bragg Gallery, 2000), 66.

121 **Showed at Arts and Crafts Club:** See, e.g., Lyle Saxon, "Exhibition of Unusual Paintings Shown at Arts and Crafts Club," *Times-Picayune*, 29 February 1924, 11.

Show in Jackson: Jack Gihon, "Art in New Orleans," clipping from *Times-Picayune*, 8 April 1925, in Ellsworth Woodward folder, THNOC.

Benjamin Prize committee: "Benjamin Prize Awarded to Bein," *Item-Tribune*, 15 May 1927.

122 **Le Petit Salon honorary life member:** "Women Given Recognition for Community Service," *Times-Picayune*, 27 February 1927.

MEIGS O. FROST

Sketch based on "Meigs O. Frost, 67, Noted Author, Dies," *New York Times*, 10 June 1950, 17, and "Col. Meigs Frost Dies," *Times-Picayune*, 10 June 1950, 1–2, unless otherwise indicated.

123 **Loss of eye and shrapnel wound:** "Survived Serious Ailments," *New York Times*, 17 November 1940, 14.

Suckling pig: "Meigs O. Frost," *New Orleanian*, 27 September 1930, 27.

Free State of Jones: "The South's Strangest Army Revealed by Chief," *Item*, 20 March 1921.

Jazz cabaret: "When Romances and Glories of Social Life in Orleans Centered in Royal Street," clipping dated 19 September 1926, in N. C. Curtis collection, M5, LaRC.

Jean Lafitte: "How Lafitte Whisked Napoleon Away From Isle," *States*, 28 August 1928.

124 **Arts and Crafts Club exhibit:** "Splendid Exhibits at Orleans Arts and Crafts," *States*, 18 November 1924.

124 **Art League:** "New Art Body Makes Bow with Fine Exhibit," clipping from *States,* 4 December 1927, Weeks Hall folder, THNOC.
Lady Godiva: Clipping from *States,* 4 December 1927, MSS 247, Arts and Crafts Club collection, THNOC.
Family composition and residence: 1920 and 1930 censuses at ancestry. com.
Mrs. Frost's portrait: Lyle Saxon, "What's Doing," *Times-Picayune,* 25 October 1925.
Short story prize: "The Press: Sequela," *Time,* 20 April 1925. For references to some of Frost's stories, see the list compiled by the FictionMags mailing list at www.philsp.com/homeville/FMI/ostart.htm.
Poem: "The Bride," reprinted, e.g., in *Poverty Bay Herald* (New Zealand), 3 January 1914, 10.
Ford interview: Meigs O. Frost, "An Interview with Henry Ford: Twenty Years in the Making" (Vieux Carre Printery, 1934).
On Long machine exposé: "The Press: Contemptuous Item," *Time,* 18 December 1939.
World War II service: Franklin M. Garrett and Harold H. Martin, *Atlanta and Environs: A Chronicle of Its People and Events,* vol. 3, *Years of Change and Challenge, 1940–1976* (Univ. of Georgia Press, 1987), 78.

NATALIE SCOTT

Sketch based on John W. Scott, *Natalie Scott: A Magnificent Life* (Pelican, 2008), and "Natalie Vivian Scott," online exhibit organized by John W. Scott, www.tulane.edu/~lmiller/NVS/NVS_Home.htm, unless otherwise indicated.

126 **Junior League Review:** Program for 1925, in Vertical Files, "Organizations. Junior League of New Orleans. Junior League Review," LaRC.
"Unpaid staff member of *Double Dealer*": Albert Goldstein, "Discoveries of the Double Dealer," *Dixie* (*Times-Picayune* magazine), 21 January 1951.
"Girl who poured the 'T'": Meigs O. Frost, "Arts Ball to Be Brilliant Affair," unsourced and undated (but 1930) clipping, MSS 247, Arts and Crafts Club collection, box 7, folder 423, THNOC.
Program committee for ball: "Ball of Artists Will Take Stars for Inspiration," *Times-Picayune,* 13 April 1930.
Lake Pontchartrain excursion; Frans Blom's lecture: John W. Scott, "William Spratling and the New Orleans Renaissance," *Louisiana History* 45 (summer 2004): 300n, 310n.

127 **Praised in Saxon's column:** Lyle Saxon, "What's Doing?" *Times-Picayune*, 25 October 1925, 2.

OLIVER LA FARGE

Sketch based on D'Arcy McNickle, *Indian Man: A Life of Oliver La Farge* (Indiana Univ. Press, 1971), and Robert A. Hecht, *Oliver La Farge and the American Indian: A Biography* (Scarecrow Press, 1991), unless otherwise indicated. See also the front matter to the new edition of La Farge's *Behind the Mountains* (Sunstone Press, 2008), originally published by Houghton Mifflin, in 1956.

130 **Relations with Blom:** Robert L. Brunhouse, *Frans Blom, Maya Explorer* (Univ. of New Mexico Press, 1976), 79–84.
    "The gang on the truck were delightful": Oliver La Farge, *Raw Material* (Houghton Mifflin, 1945), 111–14.
    Eagle dance: Alan Brown, *Literary Levees of New Orleans* (Starrhill Press, 1998), 62.
    Shared with Keith Temple: Stella Pitts, "The Quarter in the Twenties," *Dixie* (*Times-Picayune* magazine), 26 November 1972, 43.
    "A place in which we could laugh and sing": La Farge, *Raw Material*, 114.
132 **Faulkner and Spratling were amused:** William Spratling, "Chronicle of a Friendship," preface to reprint edition of *Sherwood Anderson and Other Famous Creoles* (Univ. of Texas Press, 1966), 12.
    Ladies' man; gladiator costume: Interview with Harold Dempsey, New Orleans, 2 February 1963, CCC 4.28.
    Dropping glasses out dormer window: Brown, *Literary Levees of New Orleans*, 62.
    Singing "Christopher Columbo": Interview with John McClure, [New Orleans], undated, CCC 9.14.
    Early writing efforts: La Farge, *Raw Material*, 205.
    Review of *Laughing Boy*: Quoted on dust jacket of La Farge, *Raw Material*.
133 **La Farge's parents-in-law (Roscoe and Loulie Mathews):** See, e.g., *The Baha'i World: A Biennial International Record* 7 (1939), passim.

WILLIAM C. "CICERO" ODIORNE

Sketch based on a biographical note from Robert Tat Gallery, San Francisco, online at www.goantiques.com/detail,william-odiorne-doorway,616463 .html, and interviews with W. C. Odiorne, Hollywood, California, 15–16 February 1963, CCC 11.1, unless otherwise indicated.

134 **Spratling and Faulkner at Café du Dome:** Lynn Simross, "Memories of a Bohemian in Paris, 1924," *Los Angeles Times*, 14 April 1977, F1.

New Orleans friend of Spratling's: William Faulkner, *Thinking of Home: William Faulkner's Letters to His Mother and Father, 1918–1925*, ed. James Gray Watson (Norton, 1992), 200.

Gay, club-footed: Joel Williamson, *William Faulkner and Southern History* (Oxford Univ. Press USA, 1993), 205.

Studio in Pontalba: Chance Harvey, *The Life and Selected Letters of Lyle Saxon* (Pelican, 2003), 70.

Residences and occupations before New Orleans: 1900 and 1910 censuses at ancestry.com.

135 **Middle name Cunningham:** *California Death Index, 1940–1997* at ancestry .com.

Odiorne in Paris: Joseph Leo Blotner, *Faulkner: A Biography*, vol. 1 (Random House, 1974), 452, 481.

Fashion photography: Simross, "Memories of a Bohemian in Paris."

136 **"Used to roam the streets":** Odiorne to Samuel Louis Gilmore Jr., 23 November 1950, in Samuel Louis Gilmore Jr. collection, M695, LaRC.

Goldblatt's: Odiorne's World War II draft registration card, ancestry.com.

Encounter with Faulkner in California: Blotner, *Faulkner*, vol. 2, 1376.

Letters to Gilmore: Gilmore collection, LaRC.

His memoirs: Carvel Collins's transcription of much of Odiorne's manuscript is included in Collins's interview notes (CCC 11.1).

Respected Los Angeles gallery: Stephen White, *William C. Odiorne : Odiorne's Paris* (Stephen White's Gallery, 1977).

LOUISE JONAS NIXON

137 **"Mother Nixon":** Interview with Waldo Pitkin, 10 August 1977, Friends of the Cabildo Oral History Program, Louisiana Reference Collection, New Orleans Public Library.

Birthplace and date: Records at ancestry.com.

Family in Civil War: Robert N. Rosen, *The Jewish Confederates* (Univ. of South Carolina Press, 2000), 148–53.

138 **"Hebrew expression":** "Two More Senators Elected," *New York Times*, 1 February 1879, 1.

Her uncle's poem: "Confederate Note Poem," *New York Times*, 9 August 1905, 6.

Marriage date: "Louise Jonas" entry on ancestry.com.

James Oscar Nixon Sr.: Louisiana Historical Association, *Dictionary of Louisiana Biography*, www.lahistory.org/site31.php; on his parole, see the

Cumberland County, New Jersey, website: www.co.cumberland.nj.us/
content/171/217/863.aspx.

138   **Children's birthdates and residence with mother-in-law:** 1900 census at
ancestry.com.

Rosalie Nixon's book store: "The Paul Morphy Book Shop," 18 June 2010,
blog.chess.com/batgirl/paul-morphy-book-shop.

Le Petit Salon: "Women Given Recognition for Community Service," *Times-Picayune,* 27 February 1927.

Loyalty report: Online at www.footnote.com/image/3346068/James%20
Oscar%20Nixon/#3346068.

South American trip at eighty: Ship's passenger list at ancestry.com.

President until ninety: Anthony Stanonis, *Creating the Big Easy: New Orleans and the Emergence of Modern Tourism, 1918–1945* (Univ. of Georgia Press,
2006), 144.

139   **Loving cup:** List of previous winners in John Pope, "Business Council, Preservation Leader Wins TP Loving Cup," *Times-Picayune,* 29 March 2008.

Tulane degree: Beatrice Field, *Potpourri: An Assortment of Tulane's People and
Places* (1983; updated 2002), tulane.edu/alumni/upload/potpourri.pdf, 69.

Death date: Stanonis, *Creating the Big Easy,* 144.

Woman of the Year: "Clubs to Honor Six," *Times-Picayune,* 24 April 1947.

RICHARD R. KIRK

Unless otherwise indicated, information on residences, dates, and employment are from records at ancestry.com.

140   **Cane:** Clipping from *Item,* 2 June 1943, in Richard Ray Kirk collection, M882,
LaRC.

"Sardonic whimsy": Clipping from "The Literary Lantern," undated (but
1920s), Kirk collection, LaRC.

"Craftsman": Clipping from *Michigan Alumnus,* 31 March 1928, Kirk collection, LaRC.

"One good epigrammatic poet": John McClure, "Literature—and Less,"
Times-Picayune, 28 December 1924, 6.

Example of verse: Clipping from *Michigan Alumnus.*

Father died: On his passport application (archived at ancestry.com) Kirk
wrote that his English immigrant father had died when Kirk was an infant.

141   **Undergraduate career:** Clipping from *Michigan Alumnus;* "Toast to Michigan" lyricist and lyrics, available at the website of the University of Michigan
Men's Glee Club, ummgc.org/about/lyrics.

Military service and decorations: Clipping from *Item,* 2 June 1943.

141   **To Tulane in 1921:** Abstract, Kirk collection, LaRC.

Margaret Walker: Kay Bonetti, "An Interview with Margaret Walker," *Missouri Review* 15, no. 1 (1992): 11.

"Varsity Show": Internet Movie Database, www.imdb.com/title/tt0029725/soundtrack, wrongly credits Kirk as composer of the song's music.

"Half a Loaf": Clipping from *Item,* 2 June 1943.

MOISE GOLDSTEIN

Sketch based on the entry in Louisiana Historical Association, *Dictionary of Louisiana Biography,* www.lahistory.org/site24.php, and Milton G. Scheuermann Jr., "Moise Herbert Goldstein—Architect," unpublished manuscript, 2010, unless otherwise indicated.

142   **1920s work in New Orleans:** Friends of the Cabildo, *New Orleans Architecture,* vol. 7, *Jefferson City* (Pelican, 1989), and Friends of the Cabildo, *New Orleans Architecture,* vol. 8, *The University Section* (Pelican, 2000).

Curtis's role: See the letter from Nathaniel C. Curtis Jr., 16 September 1986, to Historic New Orleans Collection, in N. C. Curtis file, THNOC.

Sterns's suburban house: National Register of Historic Places registration form for Longue Vue, pdfhost.focus.nps.gov/docs/NHLS/Text/91001419.pdf.

Industrialists' lodge: Zemurray Gardens, Tangipahoa Parish Historic Places and Sites website, byermedia.com/na/la/hammond/tangi/historic/html/zemurray_gardens.html.

Pine Hills Hotel: Forrest Lamar Cooper, "A Castle on a Hill," *Mississippi Magazine,* May 2003.

Antebellum cottage and "pout house": Tammy Smith, "Secret Garden," *SunHerald.com* (Biloxi), 6 May 2010.

Art Nouveau, etc.: "Orleans Nouveau," *Regional Modernism: The New Orleans Archives,* www.regional-modernism.com/2008/01/orleans-nouveau.html.

143   **Nantucket cottage:** "Potter's Studio Becomes a Home for N.O. couple," *Times-Picayune/States-Item,* 29 January 1983.

National American Bank: Mary Louise Christovich, Roulhac Toledano, and Pat Holden, *New Orleans Architecture,* vol. 2, *The American Sector* (Pelican, 1998), 76.

Black housing project: Margaret C. Gonzalez-Perez, "A House Divided: Public Housing Policy in New Orleans," *Louisiana History* 44, no. 4 (autumn 2003): 451.

Working with Dinwiddie: Bernard Lemann, Malcolm Heard Jr., and John P. Klingman, eds., *Talk About Architecture: A Century of Architectural Education at Tulane* (Tulane University School of Architecture, 1993), 61, 64.

143 **Residence and family:** From 1930 census at ancestry.com.

Service on the Executive Committee: Arts and Crafts Club bulletin, June 1924–June 1925, in Vertical Files, "Arts. Societies. Arts and Crafts Club. Undated and 1922–28," LaRC.

Show at the Club: Jack Gihon, "Art in New Orleans," *Times-Picayune*, 8 April 1925, clipping in Dan Whitney folder, THNOC.

Senior prize essay: Jean Moore Bragg and Susan Saward, *Painting the Town: The Woodward Brothers Come to New Orleans* (Jean Bragg Gallery, 2004), 152.

Head of the Preservation Committee: Melissa Houghton, *Architects in Historic Preservation: The Formal Role of the AIA, 1890–1990* (American Institute of Architects, 1990), 12.

"Taking down the French Quarter!": Interview with Flo Field, 7 January 1962, Flora Field collection, Newcomb Archives, Newcomb College Center for Research on Women.

Prospectus: Gene Waddell, "The Only Volume in the Octagon Library: The Early Architecture of Charleston," in *Renaissance in Charleston: Art and Life in the Carolina Low Country, 1900–1940,* ed. James M. Hutchisson, Alfred Robert Kraemer, and Harlan Greene, 224, endnote 1 (Univ. of Georgia Press, 2003).

144 **Work in the Vieux Carré:** Samuel Wilson Jr., *A Guide to the Architecture of New Orleans—1699–1959* (Reinhold, 1959).

Flint-Goodridge Hospital and Dillard University: Joe M. Richardson, "Edgar B. Stern: A White New Orleans Philanthropist Helps Build a Black University," *Journal of Negro History* 82, no. 3 (summer 1997): 328–42; on the hospital, see also www.waymarking.com/waymarks/WM8NJ3.

"New American Home": Stephanie Bruno, "Thoroughly Modern in 1937," *Times-Picayune,* Inside-Out section, undated clipping in Moise Goldstein folder, THNOC.

Audubon Park zoo: Friends of the Cabildo, *New Orleans Architecture,* vol. 8, *The University Section,* 54.

Tulane association, retirement, death date: "Funeral Rites for Goldstein," *Times-Picayune,* 30 December 1972.

Sixty years' worth of art: Clipping from *Times-Picayune,* 23 April 1967, section 3, 2, in Goldstein folder, THNOC.

Tomb of his own design: Leonard Victor Huber and Mary Louise Christovich, *New Orleans Architecture,* vol. 3, *The Cemeteries* (Pelican, 1996), 53.

VIRGINIA PARKER NAGLE

Sketch based on correspondence with Lorraine Fletez-Brant, Virginia Parker Nagle's great-niece, unless otherwise indicated.

145 **"Several young girls":** Elizabeth Anderson and Gerald R. Kelly, *Miss Elizabeth: A Memoir* (Little, Brown, 1969), 118.

"Skirmishing around": Joseph Blotner, *Faulkner: A Biography,* one-volume edition (Univ. Press of Mississippi, 2005), 183.

Education and early exhibits: *Encyclopedia of New Orleans Artists, 1718–1918* (Historic New Orleans Collection, 1987); *Who Was Who in American Art* (Sound View Press, 1985); "Miss Parker Awarded Prize," *Times-Picayune,* 31 May 1922, 12; *New Orleans Topics,* December 1924, and other clippings (many unsourced) in Mary Virginia Parker folder, THNOC.

146 **Saturday life class:** Arts and Crafts Club bulletin, 1924–1925, in Vertical Files, "Arts. Societies. Arts and Crafts Club. Undated and 1922–28," LaRC; *Times-Picayune* article, 6 December 1925, in Mary Virginia Parker folder, THNOC. On the enthusiastic reception, see unsourced clipping in Weeks Hall folder, THNOC.

Joint exhibit with Spratling and Stevens: unsourced clipping from 7 November 1924 in Arts and Crafts Club scrapbook, THNOC; "Artists of City Will Show Work for Two Weeks," *Times-Picayune,* 16 November 1924; Meigs Frost, "Splendid Exhibits at Orleans Arts and Crafts," *States,* 18 November 1924.

Papers reviewed her work: See, e.g., Jack Gihon, "Exhibit of Arts Club Combines Craftsmanship and Delicacy," *Times-Picayune,* 17 November 1924; Jack Gihon, "Too Much Sameness in Exhibit Despite Outstanding Canvases," *Times-Picayune,* 24 March 1925.

Appeared in society pages: See, e.g., *Times-Picayune,* 17 October 1924, 12; *Times-Picayune,* 25 October 1924, 10.

Mother's artistic credentials: Maud May Parker, *The Missive: A Dramatic Poem* (Poet Lore, 1907), and Maud May Parker, *Louisiana: A Pageant of Yesterday and Today* (Hauser Printing, 1917).

Father killed himself: "Robt. B. Parker Found Dead," *Atlanta Constitution,* 20 December 1908, C7.

Father's occupation, residences, boarders, travels, etc.: 1900 and 1910 censuses and ships' passenger lists at ancestry.com.

Information about Edward Nagle, his mother, and the Nagles' marriage: Virginia Budny, "Gaston Lachaise's American Venus: The Genesis and Evolution of Elevation," *American Art Journal* 34 (2003–2004): 63–143, and from correspondence with Virginia Budny.

"Plenty of temperament": Samuel Slater Brown's assessment, quoted in Clive Fisher, *Hart Crane: A Life* (Yale Univ. Press, 2002), 181.

147 **Solo and group shows:** *Who Was Who in American Art* records a 1939 solo show for "Virginia Parker" at the Morton Gallery in New York; a clipping in the Virginia Parker folder, Art and Artist files, Smithsonian American Art

Museum/National Portrait Gallery Library, mentions that she contributed to a five-artist group show at Biow Associates in Washington.

FREDERICK OECHSNER

Sketch based on Oechsner's obituary in the *Times-Picayune*, 22 April 1992, unless otherwise indicated.

148 **Father's occupation, residence, and ancestry:** From 1880 and 1920 censuses at ancestry.com.
   Cable name: See invitation to October 1936 reception for Oechsner and his new wife in Frederick Cable Oechsner collection, M391, LaRC.
   "Attack of the law": Entry in "Hall of Fame," *Jambalaya* (Tulane University yearbook), 1925.
   Item and *Morning Tribune*: See the vast clipping file in the Oechsner papers, especially his column, "The Spectator," in the *Item*, ca. 1924.
   Column mentioned five Famous Creoles: *Morning Tribune*, 18 September 1926.
   Column plugging *A la Creole*: *Morning Tribune*, 13 February 1927.
149 **"Nothing to be desired":** "Triumph Scored by Flo Field," *Times-Picayune*, 15 March 1927, 5.
   Steamer, travels, languages: Tim Testerman, "Profile: Fred Oechsner," unsourced clipping (probably Florida newspaper, ca. 1977) in Oechsner papers.
   Reporting on Central America: See 1927 series for *Item-Tribune* from Guatemala in Oechsner papers.
   Positions 1927–1933, first marriage: *Current Biography: Who's News and Why, 1943* (Wilson, 1943), 564–66.
   English accent: Testerman, "Profile: Fred Oechsner."
   Time in Berlin: "F. C. Oechsner, Expert on Nazis, Dies at 89," *New York Times*, 23 April 1992, D26; see also Oechsner, "Letter from Berlin," *New Yorker*, 16 March 1940, 47.
   "Unreconstructed Southern rebel": *Current Biography*, 565.
   This Is the Enemy: Frederick Oechsner et al., *This Is the Enemy* (Little, Brown, 1942).
   Hitler's nose: "Inside Hitler," *Time*, 22 June 1942.
   OSS "black" propaganda: "Morale Operations Branch," in Paul Wolf, *OSS: The Psychology of War*, available at www.icdc.com/~paulwolf/oss/ossmo.htm.
   Second marriage: *Who's Who in America, 1962–1963* (Marquis Who's Who, 1963).
   Olga's ancestry: See the memoirs of her grandmother, Emilie Ruete, *An Arabian Princess between Two Worlds*, ed. Emeri J. van Donzel (Brill, 1993).

149 **Nuremberg and Perón:** Wire service stories—e.g., "U.P. Writer Describes Background of Trials," *Berkeley Daily Gazette,* 19 November 1945, 6, and "President Gives Interview," *Sydney Morning Herald,* 28 December 1946, 3. **Foreign Service postings:** *Who's Who,* 1963.

150 **Retirement activities:** Testerman, "Profile: Fred Oechsner."

JOSEPH WOODSON "POPS" WHITESELL

Except as noted, sketch based on Dalt Wonk, "Pops Whitesell," *Dixie* (*Times-Picayune* magazine), 29 November 1981; Virginia Taylor, "St. Peter Street Leprechaun," *Times-Picayune New Orleans States Magazine,* 29 February 1948, 6–7; and clipping of article by Anne E. Peterson in *Traces* (spring 1991), 6–13, in Pops Whitesell folder, THNOC.

152 **Junior League Review:** See the programs for 1926 and 1927 in Vertical Files, "Organizations. Junior League of New Orleans. Junior League Review," LaRC.

Portraits of Famous Creoles: These portraits are among the more than twenty-five hundred glass negatives held by the LaRC (Stella Pitts, "Tulane Gets 'Pops' Whitesell's Negatives," *Times-Picayune,* 12 February 1978, section 2, 4).

"Dreamy young men": "Meet 'Pops' Whitesell: One of America's Greatest Photographers," *Art and Physique,* series 3 (1957): 20–21, in Whitesell folder, THNOC.

153 **Frans Blom expedition:** Jean Moore Bragg and Susan Saward, *Painting the Town: The Woodward Brothers Come to New Orleans* (Jean Bragg Gallery, 2004), 264.

FANNY CRAIG VENTADOUR

Sketch based on Sara Isaac, "Age Can't Quench Woman's Fiery Spirit," *Orlando Sentinel,* 5 February 1989, and records on ancestry.com located by Dale Volberg Reed, unless otherwise indicated.

155 **Her mother's father:** "Colonel Eshleman Dies in His Eightieth Year," *Times-Picayune,* 10 July 1909.

Education, studio and early shows in New Orleans, "modern school": Typescript dated 1921, in Vertical Files, "Arts. Organizations. Artists Guild," LaRC.

New Orleans contingent at PAFA: See entry for Caroline Wogan Durieux, page 216.

156 **Study with Lhote:** From catalog description by Editions Two Cities of Ventadour's *Blue Is Recessive as in Irises: Poems.*

"Large brown woman": "The Diary of Diana," *Item,* 18 February 1923, 3–4.

Return to Paris for Salon exhibit: [Natalie Scott], "Peggy Passe Partout's Letter," *States,* 7 January 1923, 7.

Marriage to Ventadour: Morris Raphael, *Weeks Hall: The Master of the Shadows* (Harlo Press, 1981), 73.

Tango lessons: Cornelia Otis Skinner, *Our Hearts Were Young and Gay* (Dodd, Mead, 1942), 198.

League Against Imperialism: J. D. Hargreaves, "The Comintern and Anti-Colonialism: New Research Opportunities," *African Affairs* 92 (1993): 260.

Relationship with Weeks Hall: Raphael, *Weeks Hall,* 73.

Returning for three visits: Passenger lists on ancestry.com (Ventadour listed herself as a French citizen beginning in 1924).

1927 Arts and Crafts Club show: Clipping from *Morning Tribune,* 26 January 1927, in Dan Whitney folder, THNOC.

1930s show at Arts and Crafts Club: Evelyn G. Witherspoon, "Arts and Crafts Club News," *Times-Picayune,* 30 March 1934.

Death of husband: Death notice for Jacques Ventadour (d. 10 October 1936), *Times-Picayune,* 11 October 1936, 8.

1937 return and sending children home: Passenger lists on ancestry.com.

Stayed through Occupation; work in radio, journalism: Catalog description by Editions Two Cities of *Blue Is Recessive as in Irises.*

Pierre Emmanuel: Biographical sketch at www.devoir-de-francais.com/dissertation-pierre-emmanuel-155909-5559.html.

157 **Two poetry collections:** *Blue Is Recessive as in Irises: Poems* (Editions Two Cities, 1960) and *The Centre Holds* (Editions Two Cities, 1977).

ROARK BRADFORD

Sketch based on "Roark Bradford, Humorist, Is Dead," *New York Times,* 14 November 1948, 76, and Peter Stuyvesant, "Parnassus Under the Levee," *New Orleanian,* 25 October 1930, 39, unless otherwise indicated.

158 **Army discharge:** Susan L. Gordon, "Roark Bradford, 1896–1948," *Tennessee Encyclopedia of History and Culture,* www.tennesseeencyclopedia.net/entry.php?rec=124.

First marriage: "Roark Bradford and Bell Irvin Wiley: Two Writers of Lauderdale County," *River Region Monograph* (University of Tennessee, Martin, 1975). The 1910 census at ancestry.com reports that Lydia Sehorn, twenty-one, was an English teacher boarding in Halls, Tennessee.

158 **O. Henry Award:** "O. Henry Prize Winners Named at Arts Dinner," *New York Herald Tribune,* 20 January 1928.

"Bringing-Home-the-Bacon Party": Invitation in Roark Bradford collection, M20, LaRC.

Rampart Street: "Close-Ups," *New Orleanian,* 15 January 1931, 39.

159 **"Black Billy Sunday":** "Rev. James G. M'Pherson" (obituary), *New York Times,* 10 April 1936, 24.

Pontalba apartment: Susan Larson, *The Booklover's Guide to New Orleans* (Louisiana State Univ. Press, 1999).

160 *Ol' Man Adam an' His Chillun:* Roark Bradford, *Ol' Man Adam an' His Chillun* (Harper and Brothers, 1928).

Green Pastures **history:** "Roark Bradford (1896–1948)," kirjasto.sci.fi/rbradf .htm.

Divorce and remarriage: "Milestones," *Time,* 31 July 1933.

Bobbs-Merrill editor: Interview with Mary Rose Bradford, Houston, Texas, 2 March 1963, CCC 2.26.

Served only coffee: Adaline Katz Samuel, quoted in Jim Amoss, "William Faulkner and Other Famous Creoles," *Lagniappe (States-Item* magazine), 6–12 March 1976, 3.

Lousy with Charm: Manuscript in Bradford collection, M20, LaRC.

Review of play: W. M. Darling, "Roark Bradford Drama Is Lusty Tale of Quarter," *Times-Picayune,* 17 August 1927.

Bossier City: Ann Middleton, "Roark Bradford and Bossier," undated clipping from *Bossier Press-Tribune,* History Center, Bossier Parish Library, Bossier City, Louisiana.

Santa Fe: Marta Weigle and Kyle Fiore, *Santa Fe and Taos: The Writer's Era, 1916–1941* (Sunstone Press, 2008), 36, 115.

Ashes scattered: Larson, *Booklover's Guide to New Orleans.*

Serious novels: Lewis P. Simpson, "Roark Whitney Wickliffe Bradford (1896–1948)," in *Southern Writers: A Biographical Dictionary,* ed. Robert Bain, Joseph M. Flora, and Louis D. Rubin (Louisiana State Univ. Press, 1979), 44–45.

161 **National Institute of Arts and Letters:** "Twelve Elected to Arts Institute," *New York Times,* 3 January 1947, 23.

Simpson quotation: Simpson, "Roark Whitney Wickliffe Bradford," 45.

JOHN MCCLURE

Sketch based on excerpt from Jonathan Cohen, *Muna Lee: A Pan-American Life,* www.fammed.sunysb.edu/surgery/jack.html, unless otherwise indicated. Ye Olde Book Shop, 509 Royal Street, was the New Orleans representative for the Order of Bookfellows (*The Step Ladder,* September 1921, 54).

162   *The Southerner*: Announcement of first issue in "Just Ourselves," *Step Ladder* (December 1919), 31.

"Patiently unvetoed": "Julius Weis Friend's History of the *Double Dealer,*" *Mississippi Quarterly* 31 (fall 1978): 596.

"Failed, but with real honor": Review in *Times-Picayune,* 25 January 1925, 6.

Took over from Saxon: Chance Harvey, *The Life and Selected Letters of Lyle Saxon* (Pelican, 2003), 31.

163   **"Georgia Boy"**: Carvel Emerson Collins, introduction to William Faulkner, *New Orleans Sketches* (Univ. Press of Mississippi, 1958), xxvi.

Tom Anderson's: Interview with John McClure, [New Orleans], (undated), CCC 9.14; interview with Harold Dempsey, New Orleans, 2 February 1963, CCC 4.28; interview with Joyce McClure, New Orleans, 20 March [1960?], CCC 9.14.

Real-estate investment: John W. Scott, *Natalie Scott: A Magnificent Life* (Pelican, 2008), 240.

"Kindest man that ever wielded a pen": Pieter Stuyvesant, "Parnassus Under the Levee," *New Orleanian,* 25 October 1930, 32.

Anderson's reply to Toomer: Charles E. Modlin, ed., *Sherwood Anderson: Selected Letters* (Univ. of Tennessee Press, 1984), 43.

"Free of cant and jealousy": Letter to Carvel Collins, 20 January 1958, George Tichenor folder, CCC 17.33.

Eggnog on the balcony: James K. Feibleman, *The Way of a Man: An Autobiography* (Horizon Press, 1969), 224–25.

Family background: Letter from McClure to Frances Jean Bowen, 4 April 1953, in Bowen, "The New Orleans Double Dealer: 1921–May 1926, A Critical History" (Ph.D. diss., Vanderbilt University, 1954), 180ff.; see also Carolyn G. Hanneman, "McClure, John Peebles (1893–1956)," in Oklahoma Historical Society, *Encyclopedia of Oklahoma History and Culture,* digital.library.okstate .edu/encyclopedia.

"Poet historian": "Poet Historian of Arkansas Is Dead," *Ada* (Oklahoma) *Weekly News,* 29 September 1938.

Quo Vadis hobo fraternity: Howard Willard Cook, *Our Poets of Today* (New York: Moffat, Yard, 1918), 115.

164   **Mencken's praise**: Fred Hobson, "Mencken's 'Poet Born': John McClure of Oklahoma," *Menckeniana* 75 (fall 1980): 40–43.

Faint praise: Cook, *Our Poets of Today,* 114.

164 **"New Orleans' greatest literary man"**: Stuyvesant, "Parnassus Under the Levee," 32.

"Heroic helpmeet": Letter from McClure to Bowen.

Breakfast with Spratling and Faulkner: Carvel Collins, "Ben Wasson: A Personal Reminiscence," in Ben Wasson, *Count No 'Count: Flashbacks to Faulkner* (Univ. Press of Mississippi, 2006), 12–13.

In love with Albrizio: Interview with Marc and Lucille Antony, New Orleans, winter 1963, CCC 1.13.

Horses' names; never read *Mosquitoes*: Interview with John McClure, CCC 9.14.

Pallbearers: "John M'Clure Taken by Death," *Times-Picayune*, 9 February 1956.

CHARLES BEIN

Unless otherwise noted, information on travels, residences, occupations, birth and death dates, etc. are from records at ancestry.com. ("Blond six-footer," e.g., is from Bein's 1922 passport application.)

165 **"Popular Bachelors"**: "Popular Bachelors of New Orleans," *New Orleans Life* 2, no. 6 (February 1927), 13.

"Uncle Charlie": Boyd Cruise, quoted in Will Fellows, *A Passion to Preserve: Gay Men as Keepers of Culture* (Univ. of Wisconsin Press, 2004), 225.

One of the dancers: Stanley Clisby Arthur, *The Story of the Battle of New Orleans* (Louisiana Historical Society, 1915), 11.

166 **Education**: List of New Orleans Art School faculty, in Weeks Hall folder, THNOC, and Frederick Oechsner, "Charles Bein Is Awarded Benjamin Prize for 1927," *Morning Tribune*, 18 May 1927.

Studied with William Woodward: Judith H. Bonner, "William Woodward, 1859–1939: American Impressionist in New Orleans," *Arts Quarterly* 31, no.4 (October–December 2009): 9.

Teaching at Tulane: Bernard Lemann, Malcolm Heard Jr., and John P. Klingman, eds., *Talk About Architecture: A Century of Architectural Education at Tulane* (Tulane University School of Architecture, 1993), 58–65.

Began to teach at Arts and Crafts Club: Clipping from *Item*, 14 August 1921, 3, in N. C. Curtis folder, THNOC.

First director: Judith Bonner, "The New Orleans Arts and Crafts Club: An Artistic Legacy," *Arts Quarterly* 24, no. 1 (January–March 2007): 1.

"Mr. Bein in a good humor": Richard Koch, quoted in Louise C. Hoffman, *Josephine Crawford: An Artist's Vision* (Historic New Orleans Collection, 2009), 53.

166 **Classes taught:** Clipping from *Times-Picayune*, 30 September 1928, in Weeks
Hall folder, THNOC; Art and Crafts Club bulletin, June 1924–June 1925, in
Vertical Files, "Arts. Societies. Arts and Crafts Club. Undated and 1922–28,"
LaRC; clipping from *Morning Tribune*, 18 September 1926, from the scrap-
book of Mrs. Daniel Whitney, in Marion [*sic*] Draper folder, THNOC.
Shows of his Mediterranean work: Oechsner, "Charles Bein Is Awarded
Benjamin Prize for 1927."
Return visit and more recent pictures from Louisiana: Clipping from
Times-Picayune, 13 December 1925, in Charles Bien [*sic*] folder, THNOC.
Painting in Teche country; *Chicago Daily News* **quote:** Clipping from *Morn-
ing Tribune*, 18 September 1926, Draper folder, THNOC.
"Cypress Swamp": Oechsner, "Charles Bein Is Awarded Benjamin Prize for
1927."
"Baptism": Selby Noel Mayfield, "Art Club Shows Local Paintings," *Times-
Picayune*, 23 January 1928.
"Charlie Bein was a baby": Clipping from *States*, 1 May 1927, in Weeks Hall
folder, THNOC.
Trips to Mexico: Unsourced clipping, "October 1930," in Dan Whitney folder,
THNOC.

MARC ANTONY AND LUCILLE GODCHAUX ANTONY

168 **Front-page wedding story:** Marjorie Peters, "Vieux Carre Romance Just Revealed Here," *Item,* 21 October 1923, 1.
Lucille's father: Neal J. Comeaux, "The Life and Times of Leon Godchaux
The Sugar King of Louisiana," website of the Godchaux-Reserve House Historical Society, www.stjohnparish.com/grh/leon.htm.
Residential and occupational information: 1900–1930 censuses at ancestry
.com.
169 **Couple's educations:** Peters, "Vieux Carre Romance." Stephanie Cassidy, archivist at the Art Students League of New York, confirmed that Lucille studied there for three months.
Travels in 1923: Peters, "Vieux Carre Romance."
Lucille's parents' disapproval: Elizabeth Anderson and Gerald R. Kelly, *Miss
Elizabeth: A Memoir* (Little, Brown, 1969), 107.
Batik shop: Clipping from *Item,* 12 June 1921, in Marc and Lucille Antony
folder, THNOC.
Leonardi Studios in Upper Pontalba; walks with Anderson: Walter B. Ride-
out, *Sherwood Anderson: A Writer in America*, vol. 1 (Univ. of Wisconsin Press,
2006), 545–46.
Feature on artists' studios; teaching at Arts and Crafts Club: "A Tour

Through the Studios of the Vieux Carre Artists," *Item-Tribune*, 4 January 1925.

169 **Jackson exhibition:** Jack Gihon, "Art in New Orleans," *Times-Picayune*, 8 April 1925.

170 **Faulkner as tour guide:** Interview with Marc and Lucille Antony, New Orleans, winter 1963, CCC 1.13.

Lillian's distressing painting: Review of Arts and Crafts Club show, *New Orleans Topics*, December 1924, in Mary Virginia Parker folder, THNOC.

Move to Natalie Scott's building: Lyle Saxon, "What's Doing," *Times-Picayune*, 25 October 1925, 2, and John W. Scott, "William Spratling and the New Orleans Renaissance," *Louisiana History* 45 (summer 2004): 303.

171 **Taking up interior decoration:** "A Tour Through the Studios of the Vieux Carre Artists."

Decorating the Williams house and murals for the Gumbo Shop: Roulhac Toledano, *The National Trust Guide to New Orleans* (John Wiley and Sons, 1996).

"Most prominent interior design firms": Stella Pitts, "The Quarter in the Twenties," *Dixie* (*Times-Picayune* magazine), 26 November 1972, 44.

Visit to Andersons': Walter B. Rideout, *Sherwood Anderson: A Writer in America,* vol. 1 (Univ. of Wisconsin Press, 2006), 184.

Holiday with Andersons: Howard Mumford Jones, ed., *Letters of Sherwood Anderson* (Little, Brown, 1953), 372.

Show of Spratling silver: *Times-Picayune* clipping from 1958, William Spratling folder, THNOC.

Death and burial: JewishGen Online Worldwide Burial Registry, jewishgen .org/databases/cemetery/.

ELIZEBETH WERLEIN

Sketch based on Anthony Stanonis, "'A Woman of Boundless Energy': Elizebeth Werlein and Her Times," *Louisiana History* 46, no. 1 (winter 2005): 5–26, unless otherwise indicated.

172 **"Six feet tall, blonde, and cultural":** Interview with Carl Carmer, 23 August 1965, JBP 2479/008.

"Soignée [woman with] a yen for intellectuals": Loose sheet headed "Spratling 6," JBP 2479/004.

Bavarian immigrant: Genealogical research on ancestry.com by Dale Volberg Reed.

173 **Conferences as League president:** See, e.g., "Women Working for Better Laws in Many States," *Atlanta Constitution*, 10 February 1921.

173 **Quartier Club:** See pages 52–53.

Arts and Crafts Club: See, e.g., "Ball of Artists Will Take Stars for Inspiration," *Times-Picayune,* 13 April 1930 (Werlein was on the ball's program committee).

Living near Audubon Park: 1930 census at ancestry.com.

St. Ann Street house: Jeanette Raffray, "Origins of the Vieux Carré Commission, 1920–1941," *Louisiana History* 40, no. 3 (summer 1999): 295.

"Czarina" of art show: Clippings from *States,* 11 and 14 December 1932, Ellsworth Woodward folder, THNOC.

174 **"I was a nice girl":** Anthony Stanonis, *Creating the Big Easy: New Orleans and the Emergence of Modern Tourism, 1918–1945* (Univ. of Georgia Press, 2006), 142.

MARIAN DRAPER

175 **Residential histories and occupations:** 1900–1930 censuses at ancestry. com.

Ziegfeld Follies; Tulane studies: Abstract of article from *Morning Tribune,* 17 October 1926, Marion [*sic*] Draper folder, THNOC.

176 **Ocean Springs Art Colony:** Vera Mobel [Morel], "Modern Painting Conservatively Done," *Morning Tribune,* 22 September 1926.

Not the first female cheerleader: The Tulane yearbook *Jambalaya* for 1924 shows Ruth St. Martin as a cheerleader, and Draper appears only in 1925, when she is one of two female cheerleaders (with St. Martin).

Times **photograph:** *New York Times,* 1 November 1925, RPB3.

States **front-page photograph:** *States,* 27 October 1925.

Keith Temple's cartoon: *Times-Picayune,* 1 November 1925.

177 **"Hall of Fame":** *Jambalaya,* 1925.

Architecture Society: *Jambalaya,* 1927.

Did not finish her degree: Email communication from Anissa Eugene of Tulane's Office of Alumni Affairs, March 2010.

Out-of-town tryouts: Playbill for 1928 New Haven production of *Café de Danse,* Belknap Playbill and Program Collection, George A. Smathers Libraries, University of Florida (Draper is listed in the leading role).

Not in Broadway cast: *New York Times* review, 16 January 1929 (Draper had been replaced).

Appeal for information: *States-Item,* 17 February 1968.

Draper's husband: Stephen C. Manning is credited as writer of the 1945 documentary film *Hannibal Victory* (www.twainquotes.com/hannibalvictory .html), and his Treasury Department position is listed in the 1959 *Official Register of the United States* (U.S. Civil Service Commission).

177 **Marian at George Washington University:** Information provided by Ashley Locke, Assistant University Archivist at the Gelman Library, George Washington University, January 2010.

Her last years: Information provided by E. Peter Paar of Savannah, conservator for Father Robert Manning (her brother-in-law), October 2008.

CONRAD ALBRIZIO

Sketch based on a typescript and various clippings (many undated and/or unsourced) in the Conrad Albrizio folder, THNOC, unless otherwise indicated.

178 **Education:** Kathleen Orillion, *Conrad Albrizio 1894–1973* (Louisiana Arts and Science Center, Riverside Museum, Baton Rouge, 1986), and Patricia Phagan, *The American Scene and the South: Paintings and Works on Paper, 1930–1946* (Georgia Museum of Art, 1996).

Art class at Alberta Kinsey's: See clipping from *New Orleans Life*, June 1926, in William C. Odiorne folder, THNOC.

Painting in Majorca: Lyle Saxon, What's Doing," *Times-Picayune*, 25 October 1925.

179 **"Given over to that melancholy":** Selby Noel Mayfield, "Art Club Shows Local Paintings," *Times-Picayune*, 23 January 1928.

New Orleans Art League: Meigs O. Frost, "New Art Body Makes Bow with Fine Exhibit," clipping from *States*, 4 December 1927, Weeks Hall folder, THNOC.

Fresco study in Italy and France: Orillion, *Conrad Albrizio*.

State capitol murals, WPA work, "Jordan": Carolyn Bercier, "Publicly Speaking: The Civic Art of Conrad Albrizio," *Louisiana Cultural Vistas* (spring 1998): 8–19.

Union Passenger Terminal murals; marriage: Carolyn Bercier, "The Frescoes of the Union Passenger Terminal: A Tribute to Conrad Albrizio," *Louisiana Literature* 4 (spring 1987): 4–19. On murals, see also Mary Helen Crumpler, "LSU Museum of Art opens Albrizio Sketch Exhibit," *Daily Reveille* (Louisiana State University newspaper), 19 January 2006.

Rosenwald Fellowship: Phagan, *American Scene and the South*.

Stroke (and Louisiana State University career): "Former LSU Faculty Member Leaves Behind Large Body of Work," *LSU Highlights*, spring 2005.

LILLIAN FRIEND MARCUS

Sketch based on census data, ships' passenger lists, marriage and death records, etc. at ancestry.com, unless otherwise indicated.

180 **Newcomb College:** Lillian Friend papers, Newcomb College Center for Research on Women.

"Guiding hand": William Spratling, *File on Spratling: An Autobiography* (Little, Brown, 1967), 29.

Involvement with *Double Dealer*: Frances Jean Bowen, "The New Orleans Double Dealer: 1921–May 1926, A Critical History" (Ph.D. diss., Vanderbilt University, 1954).

181 **Andersons' apartment; Modernist Lecture Bureau:** Walter B. Rideout, *Sherwood Anderson: A Writer in America,* vol. 1 (Univ. of Wisconsin Press, 2006), 539.

Gilmore's opinion: Interview with Samuel Louis Gilmore, 3 February 1965, JBP 2479/003.

Spratling's opinion: Loose sheet headed "Spratling 6," JBP 2479/004.

"A bitch": Interview with "One of Dick Adams' staff, woman," New Orleans, 5 February 1965, JBP 2479/003 (Blotner noted that the woman was "related to Mrs. Julius Friend," Marcus's sister-in-law).

Elizabeth Anderson quotations: Elizabeth Anderson and Gerald R. Kelly, *Miss Elizabeth: A Memoir* (Little, Brown, 1969), 119–20.

"Nice brown little bear," "undoing, as a writer": Letters to Carvel Collins, 4 September and 1 November 1951, Lillian Friend Marcus folder, CCC 9.29.

Second marriage: Hancock County (Bay St. Louis, Mississippi) Marriage Records, www.hancockcountyhistoricalsociety.com/reference/recordmarriage.htm?id=T-227.

Social work: Transcripts sent to social work schools, Friend papers, Newcomb College Center for Research on Women.

Travels, summers, aging mother: Letters to Carvel Collins, 2 June 1952 and 19 February 1957, Marcus folder, CCC 9.29.

182 **National Council of Jewish Women:** *New Orleans Life* 1, no. 15 (January 1927), 30.

"Women Builders of New Orleans": *New Orleans Life* 2, no. 6 (February 1927), 10.

Death notice: "Deaths," *Times-Picayune,* 17 April 1974, section 1, 22 (the listing is for "Lillia [*sic*] Friend Marcus").

Opinion of Faulkner: Letters to Carvel Collins, 25 November 1951 and 19 February 1958, Marcus folder, CCC 9.29.

DANIEL WHITNEY

Sketch based on unsourced obituary in the Dan Whitney file, THNOC, unless otherwise indicated.

183 **Brought Cubism to New Orleans:** Judith Bonner, "The New Orleans Arts and Crafts Club: An Artistic Legacy," *Arts Quarterly* 45, no. 1 (January–March 2007): 16–17; see also Bonner, "Paintings from the Permanent Collection of the Historic New Orleans Collection," in William H. Gerdts, George E. Jordan, and Judith H. Bonner, *Complementary Visions of Louisiana Art: The Laura Simon Nelson Collection at the Historic New Orleans Collection* (Historic New Orleans Collection, 1996).

Studio in lower Pontalba: "A Tour Through the Studios of the Vieux Carre Artists," *Item-Tribune* magazine, 4 January 1925.

Sketches for the *Times-Picayune*: "Whitney's Career Has Been Beset by Handicaps," undated clipping from *Item-Tribune* in Whitney folder, THNOC.

Showed at YMCA: Unsourced and undated clipping from the scrapbook of Mrs. Daniel Whitney, Weeks Hall folder, THNOC.

Teaching at Arts and Crafts Club: Arts and Crafts Club bulletin, 1924–1925, in Vertical Files, "Arts. Societies. Arts and Crafts Club. Undated and 1922–28," LaRC.

One of Whitney's own works: See unsourced and undated newspaper clipping in the scrapbook of Mrs. Daniel Whitney, Daniel Whitney folder, THNOC.

Short-lived marriage: "Vieux Carré Is Startled by Paint-Box Romance," *Times-Picayune*, 18 February 1925, 1. Whitney is listed as single in the 1930 census at ancestry.com.

184 **Benjamin Prize:** Unsourced clipping, 1927(?), Marion [*sic*] Draper folder, THNOC.

Decorations for balls: "Bal des Artistes to Be Brilliant," unsourced and undated (but 1925) clipping, and clipping from *States*, 13 November 1927, both in Whitney folder, THNOC.

Show with Durieux: Clipping from *Morning Tribune*, 27 October 1926, N. C. Curtis folder, THNOC.

Group show: "Out of Town," *New York Times*, 12 February 1928, 123.

Ocean Springs Art Colony: "Promises of Balls, Exhibitions in Fall Tide Orleans Art Colony Through Dull Summer Season," and Frederick Oechsner, "Arts and Crafts Club Show Sunday," unsourced and undated (but 1926) clippings, in Draper folder, THNOC; also Vera Mobel [Morel], "Modern Painting Conservatively Done," *Morning Tribune*, 22 September 1926, Draper folder, THNOC.

"Most Beautiful Girl": Unsourced and undated clipping in Draper folder, THNOC.

Biloxi Bathing Review: Letter from Anthony Ragusin to Daniel Whitney, 30 June 1926, Whitney folder, THNOC.

Born 1894: Various sources give 1891, 1896, and 1898, but a passport application in Whitney's own hand on ancestry.com gives 1894, which is also the date from the 1900 census and from Whitney's military records.

184 **World War I record:** *Maryland Military Men, 1917–18,* on ancestry.com.
Coast Guard service: Clipping from *Times-Picayune,* 21 May 1944, in Whitney folder, THNOC.

HELEN PITKIN SCHERTZ

Sketch based on the entry in Louisiana Historical Association, *Dictionary of Louisiana Biography,* www.lahistory.org/site36.php, unless otherwise indicated.

185 **Restoration of house:** Evelyn Soule Kennedy, "The House at 1300 Moss," typescript (1971?) in Helen Pitkin Schertz File, 223–103, Evelyn Soulé Kennedy collection, Earl K. Long Library, University of New Orleans.
Dinner parties: Interview with Waldo Pitkin, 10 August 1977, Friends of the Cabildo Oral History Program, Louisiana Reference Collection, New Orleans Public Library.
"The Lady Helen": Kennedy, "The House at 1300 Moss."

186 **"Scab guide":** Interview with Flo Field, 7 January 1962, Flora Field collection, Newcomb Archives, Newcomb College Center for Research on Women.
Quartier Club: Announcement of programs for 1923, typescript in Vertical Files, "Organizations. Quartier Club," LaRC.

187 **Loving cup:** "Women Given Recognition for Community Service," *Times-Picayune,* 27 February 1927.
Information about father: *National Cyclopaedia of American Biography,* vol. 11 (James T. White and Company, 1901), 553. See also Albert Palmer Pitkin, *The Pitkin Family of America: A Genealogy of the Descendants of William Pitkin. . . .* (Lockwood and Brainard, 1887), 141.
Father's Confederate service: National Park Service, *Civil War Soldiers and Sailors System,* www.itd.nps.gov/cwss/soldiers.cfm.
Father's resignation: "Pitkin Causes the Arrest of His Secretary," *Atlanta Constitution,* 12 December 1900, 1; "Postmaster Pitkin of New Orleans Resigns," *Atlanta Constitution,* 19 December 1900, 3.
Stepmother: May W. Mount, *Some Notables of New Orleans: Biographical and Descriptive Sketches of the Artists of New Orleans and Their Work* (Privately published, 1896), 161.
Choice of the harp: "K.T.K," "Close-Ups: Great Lady," *New Orleanian,* 18 October 1930, 20–21.
Leslie's Weekly: Anna Cosulich, "Southern Women Who Have Made Their Mark in Journalism," *Leslie's Weekly,* 12 February 1903.

187 **Booth Tarkington; travels with Dorothy Dix:** Interview with Waldo Pitkin, 10 August 1977, Friends of the Cabildo Oral History Program, Louisiana Reference Collection, New Orleans Public Library.

Lunchtime oyster loaf: Harnett T. Kane, *Dear Dorothy Dix: The Story of a Compassionate Woman* (Doubleday, 1952), 64–65.

188 **Legitimate ethnography:** Newbell Niles Puckett, *Folk Beliefs of the Southern Negro* (Univ. of North Carolina Press, 1926), 192–96, 265–66.

Valuable for documenting how they spoke: Sybil Kein, *Creole: The History and Legacy of Louisiana's Free People of Color* (Louisiana State Univ. Press, 2000), 137.

Legends of Louisiana: Helen Pitkin Schertz, *Legends of Louisiana* (New Orleans Journal, 1922).

Dinner at 11:00: "K.T.K.," "Close-Ups," 20–21.

Spring Fiesta: Kennedy, "The House at 1300 Moss."

"For the ladies": *Proceedings, Ninth Annual Convention of the American Association of Insurance General Agents, April 20–21, 1934,* 19, at www.aamga.org/files/9thAnnualConventionApril20_21_1934.pdf.

"Things began to pop": Interview with Waldo Pitkin.

KEITH TEMPLE

Sketch based on Gil Webre, "Ex-Cartoonist Paints Past and Present," *Dixie* (*Times-Picayune* magazine), 19 January 1969, 8–9, unless otherwise indicated.

189 **Naturalization date:** Record of 1929 border crossing from Canada, at ancestry.com.

Law school; Arts and Crafts Club: "Temple's the Only Cartoonist-at-Law," undated clipping from *Times-Picayune,* Keith Temple notebook, THNOC.

Show of cartoons at Arts and Crafts Club: Arts and Crafts Club bulletin, June 1923–June 1924, in Vertical Files, "Arts. Societies. Arts and Crafts Club. Undated and 1922–28," LaRC.

Whitney portrait: Lyle Saxon, "What's Doing," *Times-Picayune,* 25 October 1925.

Joined Art League: Clipping from *Times-Picayune,* 16 February 1969, about exhibit of paintings at D. H. Holmes Department Store, Keith Temple notebook, THNOC.

Apartment with La Farge: Stella Pitts, "The Quarter in the Twenties," *Dixie* (*Times-Picayune* magazine), 26 November 1972, 43.

"Artificial limb maker": Passenger list at ancestry.com.

190 **Bishop of Bucktown:** Note from Anice Temple in Anice Temple/Keith Temple Scrapbook, 2004.0237, THNOC.

Twelve thousand cartoons: The LaRC has seventy-four volumes of Temple's editorial cartoons, dated from 1923 to 1966.

Marriage; "decent people": Anice Wilson Doak was listed as single and employed by the *Times-Picayune* on a 1934 passenger list at ancestry.com, but the Temples were married by June 1936, when they were among the examples of "decent people" in "The Man in the Iron Mask," *The High Hatter,* June 1936 (scrapbook of Mrs. Dan Whitney, THNOC).

191 **Served as notary:** Biographical sketch in Keith Temple notebook, THNOC.

Scores of city and river views: Photographs of many are in the Keith Temple notebook, THNOC.

Death date: Record at ancestry.com.

Canal Street department store: Clipping from *Times-Picayune,* 16 February 1969, Keith Temple notebook, THNOC.

Howard Johnson's show: Undated program for a show of fifty-one paintings of river and port at Downtown Howard Johnson's, Keith Temple notebook, THNOC.

Keith Temple Room: Clipping from *Times-Picayune,* 21 October 1973, Keith Temple notebook, THNOC.

R. EMMET KENNEDY

Sketch based on biography of Kennedy by J. B. Borel, posted on the website of the Jefferson Parish Library, www.jefferson.lib.la.us/exhibits/kennedy .htm, unless otherwise indicated. (The biography is a revised version of one that appeared in the *Gretna Chronicles,* newsletter of the Gretna Historical Society, October 1993.)

192 **Occupations:** From 1880, 1910, and 1920 censuses at ancestry.com.

Radio programs: E.g., "Radiophone Broadcast Program Tuesday Night," *Times-Picayune,* 11 April 1922, 1.

Music Teachers' National Association: Minutes of 1917 annual meeting in *Papers and Proceedings of the Music Teachers' National Association* (The Association, 1918).

193 **"Negro word for melody":** From the foreword to Kennedy, *Mellows: A Chronicle of Unknown Singers* (A. and C. Boni, 1925).

Book reviews: *New York Times Book Review,* 25 February 1934, 7 October 1934, and 8 December 1935.

RONALD HARGRAVE

Sketch based on biography of Hargrave by Sean Hemingway (2006), at www
.askart.com/AskART/artists/biography.aspx?artist=50231472006, unless
otherwise indicated.

194 **Deal for Pontalba studio:** Interviews with W. C. Odiorne, Hollywood, California, 15–16 February 1963, CCC 11.1.

Portrait acquired by Levy: Stella Pitts, "The Quarter in the Twenties," *Dixie*
(*Times-Picayune* magazine), 26 November 1972, 45, reports that he owned it
in 1972.

Passport photograph: 1915 passport application at ancestry.com.

195 *Double Dealer* **ball:** Interview with Elise Friend and Albert Goldstein, M1151,
LaRC.

Odiorne as Hargrave's apartment-mate: Interview with Harold Levy, New
Orleans, winter 1963, CCC 8.40.

Imitations of camels; perfect courtier: Interviews with W. C. Odiorne, CCC
11.1.

Docks at sundown: Letter from W. C. Odiorne to Carvel Collins, 15 March
1963, W. C. Odiorne folder (2 of 2), CCC 11.2.

Living with widowed mother: The 1930 census at ancestry.com shows Fern
Hargrave (thirty-three, divorced) and daughter Joan (seven) living with
Fern's widowed mother in Beverly Hills.

196 **"Attracted much attention":** Transcript of *Times-Picayune* article of 8 February 1922 in Vertical Files, "Arts. Societies. Arts and Crafts Club. Undated
and 1922–28," folder 1, LaRC.

Sketches of actresses and dancers: Lyle Saxon, "Exhibition of Unusual
Paintings Shown at Arts and Crafts Club," *Times-Picayune*, 29 February 1924,
11.

Hotel Roosevelt: Lyle Saxon, "Ronald Hargrave Completes New Set of Etchings," undated clipping (probably *Times-Picayune*), Ronald Hargrave folder,
THNOC.

Sazerac ad: *Times-Picayune*, Rotogravure section, 21 February 1926, 8.

Joined by Spratling in Majorca: John W. Scott, "William Spratling and the
New Orleans Renaissance," *Louisiana History* 45 (summer 2004): 302.

"Among the brigands": "Hargrave in Corsica," *New Orleanian*, 20 September
1930.

HAMILTON BASSO

Sketch based on Inez Hollander Lake, *The Road from Pompey's Head: The Life
and Work of Hamilton Basso* (Louisiana State Univ. Press, 1999), unless oth-

erwise indicated. On Basso's fiction, see also Joseph R. Millichap, *Hamilton Basso* (Twayne Publishers, 1979).

198 **Tulane honors:** *Jambalaya* (Tulane University yearbook), 1926.

199 **"Beating checks":** "Hamilton Basso," *New Orleanian,* 15 November 1930, 19.
Elizabeth Anderson recollection: Elizabeth Anderson and Gerald R. Kelly, *Miss Elizabeth: A Memoir* (Little, Brown, 1969), 88–89.
"Giddy young girl": The phrase is Elizabeth Anderson's, quoted from Anderson and Kelly, *Miss Elizabeth,* 118.
"Notable gathering of the social world": Unsourced and undated clipping, MSS 247, Arts and Crafts Club collection, box 7, folder 423, THNOC.
Relations with Faulkner; "admitted into the ball park": Hamilton Basso, "William Faulkner, Man and Writer," *Saturday Review,* 28 July 1962, 11–12.

200 **"Appalling lack of ability":** Basso, "William Faulkner, Man and Writer," 12.
Beauregard biography: Hamilton Basso, *Beauregard, the Great Creole* (Scribner's Sons, 1933).
Stayed in touch with Saxon: See, e.g., Anthony Stanonis, "'Always in Costume and Mask': Lyle Saxon and New Orleans Tourism," *Louisiana History* 42, no. 1 (winter 2001): 43n.

LOUIS ANDREWS FISCHER

Sketch based on Henri Schindler, *Mardi Gras Treasures: Float Designs of the Golden Age* (Pelican, 2001), unless otherwise indicated.

201 **Occupations, residences, and household compositions:** 1910 and 1930 censuses at ancestry.com.
Newcomb career and costuming men as women: Schindler, *Mardi Gras Treasures.*

202 **Hiawatha illustration and Saxon quote:** "Hiawatha's First Great Battle," *Times-Picayune,* 25 October 1925.
Sketch of Arts and Crafts Club: Frederick Oechsner, "Summer's End Brings Artists Home to Plan Many Exhibitions," *Morning Tribune,* 18 September 1926.
Lived in upper Pontalba apartments: Interviews with W. C. Odiorne, Hollywood, California, 15–16 February 1963, CCC 11.1.
Friendship with Spratling: Interview with Flo Field, New Orleans, 12 September 1962, CCC 6.8.

203 **Stunts at ball:** "Bal des Artistes to Be Brilliant," unsourced and undated (but 1925) clipping, in Dan Whitney folder, THNOC.

203 **"Impromptu studio party":** Unsourced clipping, 7 November(?) 1924, in MSS 247, Arts and Crafts Club collection, THNOC.
Pontalba parties: Stella Pitts, "The Quarter in the Twenties," *Dixie* (*Times-Picayune* magazine), 26 November 1972, 45.
Nietzke party: "Uptown—Downtown—Back of Town," *New Orleanian,* 15 December 1930.
Bookshop: Pitts, "The Quarter in the Twenties," 45.
Le Petit Theatre: "Art School Opens Term," unsourced and undated clipping, Louis Fischer Andrews folder, THNOC.

ALBERTA KINSEY

Sketch based on *Knute Heldner and the Art Colony in Old New Orleans* (Jean Bragg Gallery, 2000), 28–43, unless otherwise indicated.

204 **Saxon's description:** Cathy Chance Harvey, "Lyle Saxon: A Portrait in Letters" (Ph.D. diss., Tulane University, 1980), 101.
"Won't tell you how many": "Close-ups," *New Orleanian,* 20 September 1930, 20.
School teacher; summer art program: "She Paints City's Patios, Flowers," unsourced clipping, ca. 1949, MSS 247, Arts and Crafts Club collection, folder 347, THNOC.
Women's Art Club: *Who Was Who in American Art* (Sound View Press, 1985).
China painting: "A Tour Through the Studios of the Vieux Carre Artists," *Item-Tribune Magazine,* 4 January 1925, 2.

205 **New Orleans warm and name pleased her:** Vera Morel, "Alberta Kinsey's Exhibit at Arts Club Brings Out Story," *Tribune,* [14 October 1927], clipping in MSS 247, Arts and Crafts Club collection, box 11, folder 1, THNOC.
Catherine Club: Pamphlet in Vertical Files, "Organizations. Catherine Club," LaRC.
"Place I had been looking for"; paints and easel: "Close-Ups," 20.
Arithmetic lessons: Morel, "Alberta Kinsey's Exhibit at Arts Club Brings Out Story."
Saxon article on Pontalba buildings: Lyle Saxon, "Pontalba Artist Colony Plan Gets Wide Approval," *Item,* 26 January 1919, section 1, 12.
$15 a month: Interviews with W. C. Odiorne, Hollywood, California, 15–16 February 1963, CCC 11.1.
"Defenseless courtyard": "Close-ups," 20.
Reporter who visited: "A Tour Through the Studios of the Vieux Carre Artists," 2.
Flo Field's play: Draft introduction to "The Knight Takes the Queen," in

Flora Field collection, Newcomb Archives, Newcomb College Center for Research on Women.

205 **Joint show with Spratling:** Clipping from *Item,* 11 November 1923, in MSS 247, Arts and Crafts Club collection, THNOC.

Landscapes: Arts and Crafts Club bulletin, 1924–1925, Vertical Files, "Arts. Societies. Arts and Crafts Club. Undated and 1922–28," folder 1, LaRC.

206 **"Her usual sincerity":** Lyle Saxon, "What's Doing," *Times-Picayune,* 25 October 1925.

Works from summer in Europe: Morel, "Alberta Kinsey's Exhibit at Arts Club Brings Out Story"; "Orleans Artist Exhibits," *States,* [10 October 1927], clipping in MSS 247, Arts and Crafts Club collection, box 11, folder 1, THNOC.

"By-gone splendor": Selby Noel Mayfield, "Kinsey Paintings Show Past Pomp," *Times-Picayune,* 25 November 1928, 19.

"Average person who paints china": "Close-Ups," 20.

"I've just taught myself": "A Tour Through the Studios of the Vieux Carre Artists," 2.

Art Institute of Chicago and Cincinnati Art Institute: *Who Was Who in American Art.*

Left her own party: "Close-Ups," 21.

Didn't drink: "She Paints City's Patios, Flowers."

Odiorne quotations: Interviews with W. C. Odiorne, Hollywood, California, 15–16 February 1963, CCC 11.1.

Take-off on *A la Creole*: Clipping from *States,* 1 May 1927, in Weeks Hall folder, THNOC.

207 **"Friendly and kindly and close to earth":** Catherine B. Dillon, "Alberta Kinsey's New Orleans Show," *Chicago Evening Post Art World,* 11 December 1928, clipping in Alberta Kinsey folder, Art and Artist files, Smithsonian American Art Museum/National Portrait Gallery Library.

Visiting relatives: "In Memoriam," *Dayton Journal-Herald,* 17 May 1952, clipping in Alberta Kinsey folder, Art and Artist files, Smithsonian American Art Museum/National Portrait Gallery Library.

Trip to Mexico: "Close-Ups," 21.

Daniel Clark house: "She Paints City's Patios, Flowers."

Property Owners Association: Anthony Stanonis, *Creating the Big Easy: New Orleans and the Emergence of Modern Tourism, 1918–1945* (Univ. of Georgia Press, 2006), 158.

"Things I paint"; Arts and Crafts Club reopening: Frances Bryson, "Arts and Crafts Club to Reopen," unsourced and undated (but 1945) clipping in MSS 247, Arts and Crafts Club collection, THNOC.

Buried in West Milton: "In Memoriam."

LYLE SAXON

Sketch based on Chance Harvey, *The Life and Selected Letters of Lyle Saxon* (Pelican, 2003), and Anthony Stanonis, "'Always in Costume and Mask': Lyle Saxon and New Orleans Tourism," *Louisiana History* 42, no. 1 (winter 2001): 31–57, unless otherwise indicated.

209 **Cross-dressing:** Saxon's biographer Chance Harvey says that Thomas C. Atkinson of Baton Rouge told her that Saxon and his friend George Favrot were caught "in drag" and expelled, but that Atkinson offered no corroboration (email communication, December 2010).
Sold house on Royal Street: Susan Larson, *The Booklover's Guide to New Orleans* (Louisiana State Univ. Press, 1999), 98.
"This New York move is absolutely essential": Lyle Saxon to Sherwood and Elizabeth Anderson, 12 September 1926, Sherwood Anderson papers, Newberry Library, Chicago, Illinois.
"Thousands of friends"; "indolent elegance": Pieter Stuyvesant, "Parnassus Under the Levee," *New Orleanian,* 25 October 1930, 19.
"Stylish and snobbish Negro servants": Saxon's summary of Lucius Beebe's observation, in Lyle Saxon, *The Friends of Joe Gilmore* (Hastings House, 1948), 99.
"A little old ladyish": 1936 letter from Basso to Thomas Wolfe, quoted in Inez Hollander Lake, *The Road from Pompey's Head: The Life and Work of Hamilton Basso* (Louisiana State Univ. Press, 1999), 22.
"Lyle, you old son of a bitch": Joseph Blotner, *Faulkner: A Biography,* vol. 1 (Random House, 1974), 555.
Miss Ludovine Garic: Interview with Mrs. Samuel G. (Martha Gilmore) Robinson, 29 July 1972, Friends of the Cabildo Oral History Program, Louisiana Reference Collection, New Orleans Public Library.

210 **Weekends and the odd month at Melrose:** James W. Thomas, *Lyle Saxon: A Critical Biography* (Summa Publications, 1991), 51.
Roamed its streets: Unpublished reminiscences in Flora Field collection, Newcomb Archives, Newcomb College Center for Research on Women.
Bound and tortured: Will Fellows, *A Passion to Preserve: Gay Men as Keepers of Culture* (Univ. of Wisconsin Press, 2004), 221.
"Hundreds of splendid houses": Lyle Saxon, "New Orleans' Vieux Carre Now Coming into Its Own," *Times-Picayune,* 16 April 1922.
"Ward McAllister": 1936 letter from Basso to Thomas Wolfe, quoted in Lake, *Road from Pompey's Head,* 22.
Thank-you notes: Lyle Saxon collection, M4, LaRC.
Spratling's portfolio: William Spratling, *Picturesque New Orleans: Ten Sketches of the French Quarter* (Tulane Univ. Press, 1923).

210 **Condolence letter to Scott:** Natalie Vivian Scott collection, M123, LaRC.
Elizabeth Anderson quote: Elizabeth Anderson and Gerald R. Kelly, *Miss Elizabeth: A Memoir* (Little, Brown, 1969), 87, 84.
"Some woman or other swooning": Edward Dreyer, "Some Friends of Lyle Saxon," epilogue to Saxon, *The Friends of Joe Gilmore*, 147.

211 **Olive Lyons:** Thomas, *Lyle Saxon*, 50–51.
"Southern Protective Association": Thomas, *Lyle Saxon*, 81.

212 **"Essentially a biographer":** "Lafitte, the Pirate," *New Orleanian*, 1 December 1930, 20.
"Eatin' books": Patricia Brady, "Love Song to a City: The WPA Guide to New Orleans," *THNOC Quarterly* 11, no. 3 (summer 1993): 6.
Settled into a pattern: Dreyer, "Some Friends of Lyle Saxon," 146.
"Mr. New Orleans": Entry in Louisiana Historical Association, *Dictionary of Louisiana Biography*, www.lahistory.org/site36.php.
"Ended up as a souvenir": Dreyer, "Some Friends of Lyle Saxon," 164.
Children of Strangers: Lyle Saxon, *Children of Strangers* (Houghton Mifflin, 1937).
Madison Street house: Larson, *Booklover's Guide to New Orleans*, 98–99.
Masses at St. Louis Cathedral: Rosan Augusta Jordan and Frank De Caro, "In This Folk-Lore Land: Race, Class, Identity, and Folklore Studies in Louisiana," *Journal of American Folklore* 109, no. 431 (winter 1996): 47.
Returned to Baton Rouge for burial: Entry on Saxon in Louisiana Historical Association, *Dictionary of Louisiana Biography*, www.lahistory.org/site36/php.

HAROLD LEVY

213 **Occupations, residences, and ancestry:** 1910 and 1920 censuses at ancestry.com.
Agent for Joseph Duveen: Letter from Ronald Davis (Harold Levy's nephew), dated 18 October 1999, www.berthemorisot.net/home/introduction-english/provenance/attachment-1-1.
Move to upper Pontalba: 1923 passenger list at ancestry.com.
"Most any afternoon": Albert McCleery and Carl Glick, *Curtains Going Up* (Pitman, 1939), 19.
Double parlor and grand piano: Joseph Blotner, *Faulkner: A Biography*, vol. 1 (Random House, 1974), 420.

214 **Hargrave decoration; parties; crap game; puns and limericks:** Interviews with W. C. Odiorne, Hollywood, California, 15–16 February 1963, CCC 11.1–2.
Roulette wheel: Interview with Harold Levy, New Orleans, winter 1963, CCC 8.40.

214 **Le Petit Opéra:** Stella Pitts, "The Quarter in the Twenties," *Dixie* (*Times-Picayune* magazine), 26 November 1972, 45.

L'Orchestre du Petit Theatre: "Triumph Scored by Flo Field," *Times-Picayune,* 15 March 1927, 5.

Odiorne in Paris: Blotner, *Faulkner,* vol. 1, 452, 481.

Ronald Hargrave news: Lyle Saxon, "What's Doing," *Times-Picayune,* 25 October 1925.

Temple and La Farge: Pieter Stuyvesant, "Parnassus Under the Levee," *New Orleanian,* 25 October 1930, 19.

Faulkner and Dos Passos: W. Kenneth Holditch, "William Faulkner and Other Famous Creoles," in *Faulkner and His Contemporaries,* ed. Joseph R. Urgo and Ann J. Abadie, 28 (Univ. Press of Mississippi, 2004).

Lunches at Levy's apartment: Holditch, "William Faulkner and Other Famous Creoles."

215 **"The Faun" dedication:** Blotner, *Faulkner,* vol. 1, 420–21.

"Fisherman, bachelor, bon vivant": *Harvard Class of 1915: Printed for the Bicentennial* (Cambridge Printing Company, 1935), 41.

Petit Theatre board; Hargrave portrait: Pitts, "The Quarter in the Twenties," 45.

Married an old friend: The 1930 census at ancestry.com shows Gladys Goodbee, twenty, living with her mother and father (a lawyer) on Canal Street; a 1941 ship's passenger list at ancestry.com shows her still using her maiden name, but with an address in the lower Pontalba building. The JewishGen Online Worldwide Burial Registry's listing for Harold Levy (d. 1981) lists her as his wife. In 1965 Levy showed Joseph Blotner a 1923 drawing by Spratling of a group that included both him and Miss Goodbee (interview with Harold Levy, New Orleans, 5 February 1965, JBP 2479/003).

Inherited art: Letter from Ronald Davis.

Black Like Me: Susan Larson, *The Booklover's Guide to New Orleans* (Louisiana State Univ. Press, 1999), 75.

CAROLINE WOGAN DURIEUX

Sketch based on "Biographical/Historical Note," Durieux (Caroline Wogan) papers, Louisiana and Lower Mississippi Valley Collections, Louisiana State University Libraries, Baton Rouge, Louisiana, and Doug McCash, "Conflicted Caroline, Ridiculing the Road Not Taken," 28 March 2008 (available at blog.nola.com/dougmaccash/2008/03/conflicted_caroline.html), unless otherwise indicated.

216 **Irish great-grandfather; father's occupation:** Genealogical research on ancestry.com by Dale Volberg Reed.

216 **French-speaking household:** Richard B. Megraw, *Confronting Modernity: Art and Society in Louisiana* (Univ. Press of Mississippi, 2008), 133.

Chafed under Woodward: Jean Moore Bragg and Susan Saward, *Painting the Town: The Woodward Brothers Come to New Orleans* (Jean Bragg Gallery, 2004), 217.

Art Association Annual Exhibition: List of works shown, in Ellsworth Woodward folder, THNOC.

Scholarship: Megraw, *Confronting Modernity*, 133.

217 **Came back often to visit:** Passenger lists on ancestry.com.

Showed paintings and drawings in 1922: Transcript of *Times-Picayune* article of 8 February 1922 in Vertical Files, "Arts. Societies. Arts and Crafts Club. Undated and 1922–28," LaRC.

Joint show with Whitney: Clipping from *Morning Tribune*, 27 October 1926, N. C. Curtis folder, THNOC.

Pencil sketches and floral paintings: Clipping from *Morning Tribune*, 26 January 1927, Dan Whitney folder, THNOC.

Parked her son; "Mexico City for work": Elizabeth Kell, "Newcomb's Woman and Her Women," *Newcomb Alumnae News,* April 1936.

"Happy sophistication": Unsourced clipping (probably from *Mexican Life*) in William Spratling folder, THNOC.

"Subtle social chronicles"; *Chicago Daily News*: Program for "Caroline Durieux: Three Lifetimes in Printmaking" (May–June 1979), June 1 Gallery, Bethlehem, Connecticut, in Caroline Durieux folder, Art and Artist files, Smithsonian American Art Museum/National Portrait Gallery Library.

"Politely cruel": "She Is 'Politely Cruel, Charmingly Venomous,'" *Art Digest* 1 (December 1935): 14.

"Social satires": "Subtle Satires Bring Fame for Woman Painter," *Times-Picayune,* 16 February 1935.

"New Orleans' first great painter": "Caroline Wogan Durieux, Artist and Satirist, Exhibits Here," *Sunday Item-Tribune,* 23 February 1936.

218 **First lithograph in 1931:** Program for "Caroline Durieux: Three Lifetimes in Printmaking."

GENEVIEVE PITOT

Sketch based on "A Contemporary Composer Talks about Her Works," interview with Pitot by Kenneth Holditch, 18 May 1978, in the Jambalaya Program Records, 1975–1980, City Archives, New Orleans Public Library, and the entry on Pitot in Louisiana Historical Association, *Dictionary of Louisiana Biography,* www.lahistory.org/site31.php, unless otherwise indicated.

219   **Household composition:** 1910 census at ancestry.com.

220   **Jean Patou gown:** Lyle Saxon, "Rhapsody in Blue Is on Program at the Strand," *Times-Picayune,* 8 August 1926.

"Jenny, in white silk": Interviews with W. C. Odiorne, Hollywood, California, 15–16 February 1963, CCC 11.1.

Houdini story: Kate Rose, "Unsung Composer Genevieve Pitot," *Figaro,* 11 October 1978.

Modeled nude: Sharon Litwin, "Broadway Danced to Her Tune," *States-Item,* 7 June 1978, D-13.

Pitot's piano-roll titles: See Albert M. Petrak, ed., *Duo-Art Piano Roll Catalog* (Reproducing Piano Roll Foundation, n.d.), www.rprf.org/PDF/Duo-Art_Catalog.pdf.

"Amoureuse" review: William Delasaire, "Player-Piano Notes," *Musical Times,* 1 January 1926, 35–36.

Opus One: Email from W. Kenneth Holditch to author, 26 June 2010.

Faulkner and Temple offer: W. Kenneth Holditch, "William Faulkner and Other Famous Creoles," in *Faulkner and His Contemporaries,* ed. Joseph R. Urgo and Ann J. Abadie, 35 (Univ. Press of Mississippi, 2004).

221   **String quartet assembled by Harold Levy:** Elizabeth Kell, "Orleans Girl to Give Recital Oct. 12," undated clipping in Genevieve Pitot collection, M788, LaRC.

New York performances: See the many clippings in the Pitot collection, LaRC.

Carnegie Hall: "Music Schools Hold Commencement Recitals—Summer Concert Season Plans," *New York Times,* 27 May 1928, 107.

Radio broadcasts: Erik Barnouw, *A History of Broadcasting in the United States,* vol. 2, *The Golden Web, 1933 to 1953* (Oxford Univ. Press USA, 1968), 91.

Dance programs: See, among other *New York Times* articles, "Recitals by Two Dancers," 14 November 1927, 21; "The Dance: A Ballet," 15 April 1928, 117; John Martin, "The Dance: The Recital," 3 March 1929, X8; "2d Recital Staged in 'Modern' Series," 27 February 1936, 23.

Tamiris: Pauline Tish, "Remembering Helen Tamiris," *Dance Chronicle* 17 (1994): 327–60.

"How Long Brethren?": Ellen Graff, *Stepping Left: Dance and Politics in New York City, 1928–1942* (Duke Univ. Press, 1997), 94–95; Susan Manning, *Modern Dance, Negro Dance: Race in Motion* (Univ. of Minnesota Press, 2004), 101–13; and "Harlem to See Big Drama," *Chicago Defender,* 8 January 1938, 19.

Joe Sullivan: Photographs, 1961 death notice, and Bronze Star in Pitot collection, LaRC.

222   **Broadway credits:** See Pitot's entry in IBDB: Internet Broadway Database, www.ibdb.com/person.php?id=12248.

222 **Off-Broadway:** See, e.g., Louis Calta, "Livin' the Life Openin' Tonight," *New York Times,* 27 April 1957, 12.

Winesburg, Ohio: "Terrible Town," *Time,* 21 July 1958.

"*Hair* killed the Broadway musical": W. Kenneth Holditch, "William Spratling, William Faulkner, and Other Famous Creoles," *Mississippi Quarterly* 51 (summer 1998): 423–34.

Old age in New Orleans: Rose, "Unsung Composer Genevieve Pitot."

Player-piano enthusiasts: See *AMICA Bulletin* (Automatic Musical Instrument Collectors' Association) (August–September 1979).

Death in 1980: Jennifer Dunning, "Genevieve Pitot, Dance Composer," *New York Times,* 9 October 1980, B19, gives her age as seventy-one. It was seventy-nine.

ALBERT BLEDSOE DINWIDDIE

Sketch based on the well-sourced biographical sketch on the Dinwiddie Family Home Page, members.tripod.com/~ripple4u/albert.htm, and the Albert Bledsoe Dinwiddie entry in Louisiana Historical Association, *Dictionary of Louisiana Biography,* www.lahistory.org/site21.php, unless otherwise indicated.

224 **Making room for Frans Blom:** Robert L. Brunhouse, *Frans Blom, Maya Explorer* (Univ. of New Mexico Press, 1976), 64–67.

Stifled William Woodward: Jean Moore Bragg and Susan Saward, *Painting the Town: The Woodward Brothers Come to New Orleans* (Jean Bragg Gallery, 2004), 174–75.

"He built up [Tulane]": "Milestones," *Time,* 2 December 1935.

SAMUEL LOUIS GILMORE JR.

Sketch based on Frances Jean Bowen, "The New Orleans Double Dealer: 1921–May 1926, A Critical History" (Ph.D. diss., Vanderbilt University, 1954), 234ff, and entries for Gilmore and Samuel Louis Gilmore Sr., in Louisiana Historical Association, *Dictionary of Louisiana Biography,* www.lahistory.org/site24.php, unless otherwise indicated.

225 **Height:** From passport application at ancestry.com.

Aubrey Beardsley: Timothy K. Conley, "Beardsley and Faulkner," *Journal of Modern Literature* 5, no. 3 (September 1976): 345.

Eligible bachelors: "Popular Bachelors of New Orleans," *New Orleans Life* 2, no. 7 (March 1927), 17.

225　**Pickwick Club:** *Biographical and Historical Memoirs of Louisiana,* vol. 1 (Good-speed Publishing Company, 1892), 446.

　　Nephew's remark: Reported by Susan Aldridge, "Aldridge family thru Mehag and Hardy lines," ancestry.com.

　　Letter to mother: Samuel Louis Gilmore collection, M695, LaRC.

　　Publishing poems: See, e.g., "Improvisation," *The Little Review,* June 1917; "Deity," *Poetry: A Magazine of Verse,* June 1918, 132.

226　**On the way to becoming established:** "Brief Reviews," *New York Times Book Review,* 20 May 1923, 23; *The Fugitive,* December 1924; L.A.G. Strong, ed., *The Best Poems of 1923–27* (Small, Maynard, 1925 [sic]).

　　"Mauve decade style": Letter to Gilmore from Robert Jackson, 1970, Gilmore collection, LaRC.

　　Pound's complaint: Adam Piette, "Pound's 'The Garden' as Modernist Imitation: Samain, Lowell, H.D.," *Translation and Literature* 17, no. 1 (May 2008): 39.

　　Bagatelle: *Double Dealer,* February 1921; Nancy Martin Key, "A Narrative History of the Lake Charles Little Theatre, Lake Charles, Louisiana, 1927–1982" (Ph.D. diss., New York University, 1987).

227　**Pass at Spratling:** Joel Williamson, *William Faulkner and Southern History* (Oxford Univ. Press, 1993), 215, 465 n. 147.

　　Bummer of cigarettes: Interview with Marc and Lucille Antony, New Orleans, winter 1963, CCC 1.13.

　　Mark Frost; ineffectuality: Joseph Blotner, *Faulkner: A Biography,* one-volume edition (Univ. Press of Mississippi, 2005), 183, 150.

　　"Nothing much will be lost": Undated memorandum in Martha Gilmore Robinson papers, THNOC.

　　"Unsinkable cock sparrow": Odiorne to Gilmore, 10 July 1972 (Odiorne quotes Gilmore from earlier letter), Gilmore collection, LaRC.

　　Vine Leaves and Flowers of Evil: Samuel Louis Gilmore Jr., *Vine Leaves and Flowers of Evil* (Pelican, 1959). A presentation copy signed to William Buckley was for sale on Alibris.com in January 2012.

　　Texas Quarterly, **Donald Davidson; vanity press; rejection letters:** Correspondence with Exposition Press, *Texas Quarterly,* Donald Davidson, and Wesleyan University Press, as well as numerous letters of rejection, in Gilmore collection, LaRC.

GRACE KING

Sketch based on Robert Bush, *Grace King: A Southern Destiny* (Louisiana State Univ. Press, 1983), and the entry in Louisiana Historical Association,

Dictionary of Louisiana Biography, www.lahistory.org/site28.php, unless otherwise indicated.

226 **Hung in the Delgado:** Louisiana Writers' Project, *Louisiana: A Guide to the State* (Hastings House, 1941), 168.
"Loyalty to the South": Lyle Saxon, "Authors Agree That Hard Work Is Half Battle," *Times-Picayune,* 14 March 1926, section 1-B, 1.

227 **French phrases in her conversation:** Edmund Wilson, *The Twenties: From Notebooks and Diaries of the Period* (Macmillan, 1975), 188.
Argument with Gayarré; Mark Twain's cigars: Susan Larson, *The Booklover's Guide to New Orleans* (Louisiana State Univ. Press, 1999).
Julia Ward Howe at Cotton Exposition: Patricia Brady, "Literary Ladies of New Orleans in the Gilded Age," *Louisiana History* 33, no. 2 (spring 1992): 152.
"The magic past lights them up": Foreword to G. William Nott, *Vieux Carré Guide: Souvenir of Old New Orleans with Its Latin Quarter of French and Spanish Old World Romance,* quoted in Anthony Joseph Stanonis, *Creating the Big Easy: New Orleans and the Emergence of Modern Tourism, 1918–1945* (Univ. of Georgia Press, 2006), 149.

228 **Saxon's eulogy:** Chance Harvey, *The Life and Selected Letters of Lyle Saxon* (Pelican, 2005), 21.
Autobiography: Grace King, *Memories of a Southern Woman of Letters* (Macmillan, 1932).
"Genteel": "Grace King, Novelist of the 'Genteel' South," *New York Times,* 16 October 1932, BR2.

WEEKS HALL

Sketch based on Morris Raphael, *Weeks Hall: The Master of the Shadows* (Morris Raphael Books, 1981), and the entry on Hall in Louisiana Historical Association, *Dictionary of Louisiana Biography,* www.lahistory.org/site25.php, unless otherwise indicated.

231 **Tourist quoted:** Marjorie Roehl, "Eccentric Master of a Bayou Mansion," *Times-Picayune,* 14 July 1985, C-2.
"Substitute mother": Roehl, "Eccentric Master of a Bayou Mansion."
Six Italian families: Edmund Wilson, *The Twenties: From Notebooks and Diaries of the Period* (Macmillan, 1975), 189.

232 **Famous visitors:** "William Weeks Hall: The Fourth Generation," Shadows-on-the-Teche website, shadowsontheteche.wordpress.com/history/.
New Orleans Art League: Meigs O. Frost, "New Art Body Makes Bow with

Fine Exhibit," clipping from *States,* 4 December 1927, Weeks Hall folder, THNOC.

232 **Teaching at Arts and Crafts Club:** Will Fellows, *A Passion to Preserve: Gay Men as Keepers of Culture* (Univ. of Wisconsin Press, 2004), 225; article from *States* (undated, but ca. 1925), MSS 247, Arts and Crafts Club collection, folder 412, THNOC.

Served on executive board: Clipping from *Times-Picayune,* 30 September 1928, Weeks Hall folder, THNOC.

Benjamin Prize committee: "Benjamin Prize Awarded to Bein," clipping from *Item-Tribune,* 15 May 1927, Weeks Hall folder, THNOC.

Won Benjamin Prize: Clipping from *Chicago Evening Post Art World,* 20 April 1926, Weeks Hall folder, Art and Artist files, Smithsonian American Art Museum/National Portrait Gallery Library.

Magnolia blossom: R. B. McKenna, "The Art Season," *Orleanian,* clipping, MSS 247, Arts and Crafts Club collection, box 7, folder 417, THNOC.

Bal des Artistes: Clipping from *States,* 1 May 1927, Weeks Hall folder, THNOC.

Martha Gilmore's visit: Interview with Mrs. Samuel G. (Martha Gilmore) Robinson, 29 July 1972, Friends of the Cabildo Oral History Program, Louisiana Reference Collection, New Orleans Public Library.

233 **Sherwood Anderson's summons:** For a semifictionalized account of the visit from Hall's aunt, see Ray Lewis White, ed., *Sherwood Anderson's Memoirs: A Critical Edition* (Univ. of North Carolina Press, 1969), 460–62.

One-man show: Selby Noel Mayfield, "Louisiana Artist Has Club Exhibit," *Times-Picayune,* 12 February 1928, 10.

234 **"Frightened and twisted":** Letter to John Emerson and Anita Loos, 25 March 1925, in Howard Mumford Jones, ed., *Letters of Sherwood Anderson* (Little, Brown, 1953), 137.

Elizabeth Anderson's reaction: Elizabeth Anderson and Gerald R. Kelly, *Miss Elizabeth: A Memoir* (Little, Brown, 1969), 127.

Edmund Wilson's visit: Wilson, *The Twenties,* 189.

Idiot brother; telephoning at all hours; five packs a day: Henry Miller, "The Shadows," *Town and Country,* March 1942, 76.

"Goddamn silly women": Jonathan Williams, "Clarence John Laughlin," *The Jargon Society Musings for the Season,* late winter 2001, jargonbooks.com/cjlaughlin.html.

Cardboard advertising figures: Roehl, "Eccentric Master of a Bayou Mansion."

Mencken telegram: "About Weeks Hall," *New Orleanian,* 15 December 1930.

"Last of the Nigger-Lovers"; Bunk Johnson: Williams, "Clarence John Laughlin."

234 **Probably intimate relationship:** "Curt Greska" (pseudonym), in Fellows, *Passion to Preserve,* 233.

"Dr. Caligari": Henry Miller, *The Air-Conditioned Nightmare,* vol. 1 (1945–1947); reprint, New Directions, 1970), 111.

235 **"Weirdest person I ever saw":** Entry for 11 January 1935, in Hilbert H. Campbell, ed., *Selections from the Diary of Eleanor Anderson, 1933–1940,* sherwoodandersonfoundation.org/2006/07/selections_from_the_diary_of_e.php.

Show at Delgado: "Tourists Urged to Visit Museum: Splendid Art Collections on View During Gay Season," *States,* 15 February 1931, 7.

Shows at PAFA and Corcoran: See entry on Hall, W(eeks) W. [*sic*], in *Who Was Who in American Art* (Sound View Press, 1985).

"Trustee of something fine": "William Weeks Hall: The Fourth Generation," shadowsontheteche.wordpress.com/history/.

Built endowment, stopped drinking, etc.: Fellows, *Passion to Preserve,* 224.

"Possessed by the Past": See the website of the author, Raleigh Marcell, webspace.webring.com/people/er/raleighmarcell/.

WILLIAM SPRATLING

Sketch based on Taylor D. Littleton, *The Color of Silver: William Spratling, His Life and Art* (Louisiana State Univ. Press, 2000), and W. Kenneth Holditch, "William Spratling, William Faulkner, and Other Famous Creoles," *Mississippi Quarterly* 51, no. 3 (summer 1998): 423–34, unless otherwise indicated.

236 **"Discreet insinuations":** William Spratling, *File on Spratling: An Autobiography* (Little, Brown, 1967), 16–17.

"Chosen nuclei": John W. Scott, "William Spratling and the New Orleans Renaissance," *Louisiana History* 45, no. 3 (summer 2004): 294.

"Prominent in the art life of the 'old quarter'": G. William Nott, "A Tour Through the Studios of the Vieux Carre Artists," *Item-Tribune Magazine,* 4 January 1925, 15.

"A small group of friends": Frederick Oeschsner [*sic*], "N.O. Man Wins Wide Notice," *Morning Tribune,* 16 October 1927, 2.

"As everyone did": Oliver La Farge, *Raw Material* (Houghton Mifflin, 1945), 127.

Gatherings at his place: Natalie Vivian Scott, "Don Guillermo of Taxco," *New Orleanian,* 15 November 1930, 30.

237 **"A party of the unique kind":** Natalie Scott, "Peggy Passe Partout," *States,* 28 September 1924.

Tulane courses: Recollections of Bernard Lemann, in *Talk About Architec-*

ture: A Century of Architectural Education at Tulane, ed. Bernard Lemann, Malcolm Heard Jr., and John P. Klingman, 74 (Tulane University School of Architecture, 1993).

237 **"Slight and dark as a Mexican":** Elizabeth Anderson and Gerald R. Kelly, *Miss Elizabeth: A Memoir* (Little, Brown, 1969), 83.

"An artist to his fingertips": Interviews with W. C. Odiorne, Hollywood, California, 15–16 February 1963, CCC 11.1.

"Always arranging people's lives": Anderson and Kelly, *Miss Elizabeth,* 276.

Raw eggplant for breakfast: Interview with Joyce McClure, New Orleans, 20 March [1960?], CCC 9.14.

"Regretted that Spratling didn't show up": Unsourced clipping, 7 November 1924, in MSS 247, Arts and Crafts Club collection, THNOC.

Introduced him to Le Petit Theatre: John W. Scott, *Natalie Scott: A Magnificent Life* (Pelican, 2008), 246.

Caroline Durieux took him to museums: Anderson and Kelly, *Miss Elizabeth,* 84.

238 **Sketching classes in the French Quarter:** Recollections of James Marston Fitch, in Lemann et al., eds., *Talk About Architecture,* 79.

Natalie Scott found work for him: Scott, *Natalie Scott,* 246.

"Disappearing overseas": Lyle Saxon, "What's Doing," *Times-Picayune,* 25 October 1925, 2.

239 **"Talk of the town":** Unsourced clipping, 7 November 1924, in William Spratling folder, THNOC.

"Master of his craft": Meigs Frost, "Splendid Exhibitions at Orleans Arts and Craft" [*sic*], *States,* 18 November 1924.

"Glaring nude": Jack Gihon, "Exhibit of Arts Club Combines Craftsmanship and Delicacy," *Times-Picayune,* 17 November 1924.

Painted on Majorca: Scott, "William Spratling and the New Orleans Renaissance," 302.

Showed *Ulysses* to his students: Lemann et al., eds., *Talk About Architecture,* 74.

"Likes high art": "Popular Bachelors of New Orleans," *New Orleans Life* 2, no. 7 (March 1927), 17.

Lecturing at Delgado: "Spratling Speaks," *Morning Tribune,* 11 October 1926, 8.

Tulane yearbook: *Jambalaya,* 1925.

Socks of two colors: Lemann et al., eds., *Talk About Architecture,* 84.

Women linked to Spratling romantically: Scott, "William Spratling and the New Orleans Renaissance," 319, 317.

Influenced by Frans Blom: Spratling, *File on Spratling,* 19.

240 **Showed Mexican work at Arts and Crafts Club:** Oeschsner [*sic*], "Man Wins

Wide Notice"; Vera Morel, "Sculptured Soap at Art Club Exhibition," *Morning Tribune*, 29 October 1928, in Ellsworth Woodward folder, THNOC.

240 **Mexican friends at Arts and Crafts Club:** Scott, "William Spratling and the New Orleans Renaissance," 312.

Durieux in Taxco: Scott, "William Spratling and the New Orleans Renaissance," 312n.

WILLIAM FAULKNER

Sketch based on Joseph Blotner, *Faulkner: A Biography,* vol. 1 (Random House, 1974), and W. Kenneth Holditch, "Rising Star," *Gambit Weekly,* 22 September 1997, unless otherwise indicated.

241 **"Strange young man":** William Spratling, *File on Spratling: An Autobiography* (Little, Brown, 1967), 22.

"Sort of person you wouldn't have looked at twice": Stella Pitts, "The Quarter in the Twenties," *Dixie* (*Times-Picayune* magazine), 26 November 1972, 44.

"Odd fish": James K. Feibleman, *The Way of a Man: An Autobiography* (Horizon Press, 1969), 37.

242 **Tweed jacket, raincoat, haircut, nicotine stains:** Interviews with Lucille Antony, New Orleans, 14 September 1962, CCC 1.13; Julius Friend and Lillian Friend Marcus, New Orleans, August 1951, CCC 6.26; Joyce McClure, New Orleans, 20 March [1960?], CCC 9.14; Harold Levy, New Orleans, winter 1963, CCC 8.40.

Women made him awkward: Feibleman, *Way of a Man,* 276.

Pitot quote: "A Contemporary Composer Talks about Her Works," interview with Pitot by Kenneth Holditch, 18 May 1978, in the Jambalaya Program Records, 1975–1980, City Archives, New Orleans Public Library.

Flo Field quote: Interview, 7 January 1962, in Flora Field collection, Newcomb Archives, Newcomb College Center for Research on Women.

Goldstein quote: Jim Amoss, "William Faulkner and Other Famous Creoles," *Lagniappe* (*States-Item* magazine), 6–12 March 1976, 6.

"Loved to put things over on people": Elizabeth Anderson and Gerald R. Kelly, *Miss Elizabeth: A Memoir* (Little, Brown, 1969), 100–101.

"Always a leg-puller": Spratling, *File on Spratling,* 27.

"Imagination takes precedence": Quoted in Kate Crawford, "A Literary Tour of New Orleans," *Ciao! Travel with Attitude,* February 2003, www.travelwithattitude.com/Literary New Orleans.htm.

243 **Scaling the balconies:** Jay Parini, *One Matchless Time: A Life of William Faulkner* (HarperCollins, 2004), 75.

***Double Dealer* introduced him:** "Notes on Contributors," *Double Dealer,* January–February 1925.

243 **Crippled aviator in story:** Sherwood Anderson, "A Meeting South," in *Southern Odyssey: Selected Writings by Sherwood Anderson,* ed. Welford Dunaway Taylor and Charles E. Modlin (Univ. of Georgia Press, 1997), 16.

"Little Confederate": Hamilton Basso, "William Faulkner, Man and Writer," *Saturday Review,* 28 July 1962, 12.

"Rude as hell": Amoss, "William Faulkner and Other Famous Creoles," 6.

"Miss Elizabeth": Irving Howe, *Sherwood Anderson* (Methuen, 1951), 145.

"Nice, pleasant Southern boy": Panthea Reid, "The Scene of Writing and the Shape of Language for Faulkner When 'Matisse and Picasso Yet Painted,'" in *Faulkner and the Artist,* ed. Donald M. Kartiganer and Ann J. Abadie (Univ. Press of Mississippi, 1996), 83.

"Drank constantly": Spratling, *File on Spratling,* 29.

Binge that included some fights: Feibleman, *Way of a Man,* 276.

244 **"Somewhat strange, totally independent":** Pitts, "The Quarter in the Twenties," 44.

RAF surgeon: Interviews with W. C. Odiorne, Hollywood, California, 15–16 February 1963, CCC 11.1.

Shakespeare and Company: Bart H. Welling, "Faulkner's Library Revisited," *Mississippi Quarterly* 52, no. 3 (summer 1999): 365.

Less patience than Spratling; "More funny folks": John W. Scott, "William Spratling and the New Orleans Renaissance," *Louisiana History* 45, no. 3 (summer 2004): 300–301.

Sat on the floor and drank: W. Kenneth Holditch, "William Faulkner and Other Famous Creoles," in *Faulkner and His Contemporaries,* ed. Joseph R. Urgo (Univ. Press of Mississippi, 2004).

245 **Supper at Galatoire's:** Holditch, "William Faulkner and Other Famous Creoles."

"I don't come back much": Joel Williamson, *William Faulkner and Southern History* (Oxford Univ. Press, 1993), 216.

ELIZABETH ANDERSON

Sketch based on Elizabeth Anderson and Gerald R. Kelly, *Miss Elizabeth: A Memoir* (Little, Brown, 1969), and William A. Sutton, "Elizabeth Prall Anderson (1884–1976)," *Winesburg Eagle* 1, no. 2 (April 1976): 5–7, unless otherwise indicated.

246 **Lillian Marcus; apartments in New Orleans:** Walter B. Rideout, *Sherwood Anderson: A Writer in America,* vol. 1 (Univ. of Wisconsin Press, 2006), 539, 545.

Floors sanded: Joseph Blotner, *Faulkner: A Biography,* vol. 1 (Random House, 1974), 389.

247 **Put up $300:** Interview with Marc and Lucille Antony, New Orleans, winter 1963, CCC 1.13.

"Quiet priestess of the temple": William Spratling, *File on Spratling: An Autobiography* (Little, Brown, 1967), 17.

248 **Taken over management of his funds:** W. Kenneth Holditch, "William Faulkner and Other Famous Creoles," in *Faulkner and His Contemporaries*, ed. Joseph R. Urgo, 31 (Univ. Press of Mississippi, 2004).

Golden Bough: Interview with Elizabeth Anderson, Taxco, Mexico, 1959, CCC 1.11.

Shipped out as mess boy: Rideout, *Sherwood Anderson*, 545.

Tried to make him sit at his desk: Interview with Marc Antony, New Orleans, 1 and 3 February 1965, JBP 2479/004.

Urged him to go on lecture tours: A note from Blotner says Marc Antony told him this. The note is on an interview with Elizabeth Anderson, Taxco, Mexico, 29 January 1965, inserted on page 2 of an interview with William Spratling, Taxco, Mexico, 28–30 January 1965, JBP 2479/004.

"Make his unpolished genius acceptable": Irving Howe, *Sherwood Anderson* (Methuen, 1951), 145.

249 **Translated poems:** Sor Juana Inez de la Cruz, *Ten Sonnets from Sor Juana Inez de la Cruz, 1651–1695: Mexico's Tenth Muse,* trans. Elizabeth Anderson (Guerrero, 1943).

Score-settling memoir: Anderson and Kelly, *Miss Elizabeth.*

ILLUSTRATION CREDITS

NEARLY ALL ILLUSTRATIONS not credited below are out-of-copyright or are otherwise in the public domain—e.g., those from newspapers or ephemeral publications of the 1920s. I have used a few that may be protected by copyright without permission when I was unable to locate the possible rights-holders. Anyone who knows that a copyright has been violated should get in touch with me.

PAGE CREDIT

2 Courtesy of the Brodsky Collection, Center for Faulkner Studies, Southeast Missouri State University.

15 (*top*) Courtesy of the William Faulkner Archives, Rowan Oak, Oxford, Mississippi
(*bottom*) THNOC, accession number 1970.22.1.6.

16 Vertical Files, "Arts. Artists. Spratling, William P.," LaRC.

19 Courtesy of the Brodsky Collection, Center for Faulkner Studies, Southeast Missouri State University.

23 Jacket cover by Lou Glanzman copyright © 1953 by Dell, a division of Random House, Inc., from *Mosquitoes* by William Faulkner. Used by permission of Dell Publishing, a division of Random House, Inc.

32 (*bottom*) Courtesy of the Middle American Research Institute, Tulane University.

35 Courtesy of Le Petit Theatre du Vieux Carré.

37 THNOC, accession number 2009.0103.1. Gift of Le Petit Theatre du Vieux Carré.

38 THNOC, T110727.766.1, Le Petit Theatre Program, 1927, "A La Creole."

46 THNOC, accession number 1958.85.145. Gift of Mr. Boyd Cruise.

48 (*bottom*) THNOC, MSS 247, F. 68. Gift of Mr. and Mrs. John McCrady and Mr. and Mrs. Harry B. Kelleher.

PAGE   CREDIT

50 THNOC, MSS 247, F. 438. Gift of Mr. and Mrs. John McCrady and Mr. and Mrs. Harry B. Kelleher.

52 Courtesy of CHRC.

54 From Genevieve Munson Trimble, "Le Petit Salon 1924–1974: A History," in Vertical Files, "Organizations. Le Petit Salon," LaRC. Used courtesy of Le Petit Salon.

57 From Arts and Crafts Club brochure, in Vertical Files, "Arts. Societies. Arts and Crafts Club," LaRC.

58 Courtesy of Lorraine Fletez-Brant.

61 Courtesy of CHRC.

62 THNOC, accession number 1959.156.12.

63 (right) André, oil painting, Caroline W. Durieux, 1933. Courtesy of the Collections of the Louisiana State Museum.

64 Conrad Albrizio (Am. 1894–1973), Jordan, 1935–1937, oil on panel. Collection of the Louisiana Art and Science Museum, Baton Rouge. Used by permission.

70 University Archives, Special Collections, Howard-Tilton Memorial Library, Tulane University.

73 Detail from "[Unloading bananas, New Orleans, Louisiana]," 1900–1910. Photograph, Washington, D.C., Library of Congress, Prints and Photographs Division, Detroit Publishing Company, hdl.loc.gov/loc.pnp/det.4a17030 (accessed October 24, 2011).

80 Photograph by Eugene Delcroix. Collection of the author.

82 John W. Scott collection, LaRC.

83 (right) Vertical Files, "Organizations. Junior League of New Orleans. Junior League Review," LaRC.

87 (right) Detail from Frances Benjamin Johnston, photographer, "1301 Royal St., New Orleans, Orleans County, Louisiana," 1937–1938. Photograph, Washington, D.C., Library of Congress, Prints and Photographs Division, Carnegie Survey of the Architecture of the South, hdl.loc.gov/loc.pnp/csas.01329 (accessed 24 October 2011).

89 Vertical Files, "Arts. Galleries. Green Shutter," LaRC.

100 Lyle Saxon collection, M4, box 14, folder 2, LaRC.

101 THNOC, accession number 1977.312. Gift of Mr. and Mrs. John P. Labouisse.

105 Flora Field collection, Vorhoff Library and Newcomb Archives, Newcomb College Center for Research on Women, Newcomb College Institute of Tulane University.

108 (right) THNOC, accession number 1978.122.7.

113 (right) Courtesy of the University of North Carolina General Alumni Association.

116 (*right*) Courtesy of the Middle American Research Institute, Tulane University.

118 Courtesy of Dex One Corporation. © 1933 RHD Co.

119 (*right*) THNOC, accession number 1995.103.1. Gift of Mrs. Laura Simon Nelson.

121 Courtesy of the Edith Garland Dupré Library, University of Louisiana at Lafayette.

126 (*left*) John W. Scott collection, LaRC.
(*center*) "Pops" Whitesell collection, LaRC.
(*right*) "Pops" Whitesell collection, LaRC.

127 Vertical Files, "Arts. Artists. Spratling, William P.," LaRC.

131 Courtesy of the Middle American Research Institute, Tulane University.

134 (*right*) Samuel Louis Gilmore Jr. collection, M695, box 1, folder 14, LaRC.

142 (*right*) Courtesy of Milton G. Scheuermann Jr.

145 (*right*) Courtesy of Lorraine Fletez-Brant.

147 Courtesy of Lorraine Fletez-Brant.

148 (*right*) "Pops" Whitesell collection, LaRC.

151 (*right*) THNOC, accession number 1979.179.1.

152 THNOC, accession number 1993.71.75. Gift of Mrs. Edmund B. Richardson.

153 Courtesy of State Library of Louisiana.

155 (*right*) "Pops" Whitesell collection, LaRC.

158 (*right*) Roark Bradford collection, M20, box 1, folder 3, LaRC.

159 Lyle Saxon collection, M4, box 1, folder 6, LaRC.

162 (*right*) © New Orleans *Times-Picayune*. Used by permission.

165 (*right*) Courtesy of James L. Kelly.

172 (*right*) "Pops" Whitesell collection, LaRC.

180 (*right*) Lillian Friend collection, Vorhoff Library and Newcomb Archives, Newcomb College Center for Research on Women, Newcomb College Institute of Tulane University.

185 (*right*) Evelyn Soulé Kennedy collection, Earl K. Long Library, University of New Orleans.

186 Courtesy of the family of Dr. and Mrs. Ignatius Martin Dematteo. Image provided by the Neal Auction Company, New Orleans.

190 THNOC, accession number 2004.0237. Gift of Mrs. Anice Doak Temple.

192 (*right*) Elina Gardère Cherbonnier collection, Earl K. Long Library, University of New Orleans.

201 (*right*) "Pops" Whitesell collection, LaRC.

202 From Henri Schindler, *Mardi Gras Treasures: Costume Designs of the Golden Age* (Pelican, 2002). Courtesy of Henri Schindler.

203 "Pops" Whitesell collection, LaRC.

ACKNOWLEDGMENTS

I AM GRATEFUL TO Gaines Foster and the Louisiana State University Department of History for the lecture invitation that began this whole business, and for their hospitality in Baton Rouge. I also thank the staff of the LSU Press, who have been a delight to work with. Particular thanks to Rand Dotson, who was involved in this almost from the beginning; Lee Sioles, who ably and uncomplainingly oversaw the complicated job of production; and Laura Gleason, who did the splendid design and layout. I'm especially grateful that the Press indulged me (usually) in the matter of illustrations. My view that a blurry, grainy, pixelated image is better than none at all is not always shared by publishers. I am also beholden to Derik Shelor, whose copyediting caught far too many solecisms, inconsistencies, and downright errors of fact. He also asked some embarrassingly penetrating questions that led me to rewrite not just the odd sentence but several whole paragraphs.

The last of the Famous Creoles died in 1998, so I missed the chance to meet any of them, but fortunately Joseph Blotner, Carvel Collins, and Kenneth Holditch each interviewed many of the principals, often at length, and thoughtfully archived transcripts which I read with delight. (I also had a very agreeable and informative lunch with Professor Holditch.) I thank them for their assiduous research. I'm likewise indebted to the biographers of individual Famous Creoles, especially four whose help went beyond writing useful books: Chance Harvey, Taylor Littleton, John W. Scott, and Anthony Stanonis.

Without Lisa Eveleigh's hard work and organization I would still be trying to get permission to use some of the illustrations in this book. Lisa and I had the good luck to deal with a great many obliging people (many of them archivists and librarians, who are God's gift to the world of scholarship). Sean Benjamin at Tulane's Louisiana Research Collection, Ann Case at the Tulane University Archives, and Eric Seiferth at the Historic New Orleans Collection deserve special mention, but others include Judith Bonner, Charlene Bonnette, Sybil Boudreaux, Marcello Canuto, Lorraine Fletez-Brant, Robert Hamblin, Rebecca Hamilton, Daniel Hammer, Christine Hernandez, Fran Huber, Jennifer Ickes, Mary-Allen Johnson, Pat Kahle, Kathe Lawton, Tony Lewis, Leon Miller, Meg Partridge, Henri Schindler, Elizabeth Sherwood, Lisa Speer, Eira Tansey, Margaret Tenney, Susan Tucker, I. Bruce Turner, Elizabeth Weinstein, Lisa Werling, Mary Lynn Wernet, and Cindy Woessner. By the way, I particularly appreciate those individuals, organizations, and archives who let me use their images (and in some cases reproduced them for me) without charging extortionate fees—that is, most of them.

For hospitality in New Orleans and other miscellaneous favors, I'm grateful to Jane and Corny Apffel, Curtis Wilkie, Lolis Elie, Brett Anderson, and David Cuthbert, as well as Harry Watson and Josh Lynn at Chapel Hill's Center for the Study of the American South (they know why). John Mark Ockerbloom, editor of the Online Books Page, has done enormously useful work on copyright that saved me a great deal of trouble, and the foreign language skills of Philip Lewis and E. Christian Kopff helped to make up for my lack of any. I wrote much of this book while a visiting fellow at Clare Hall, Cambridge, and David Houston, Richard King, and Tony Badger read and commented on an early proposal, and Jim Cobb did the same for the almost-finished manuscript. I'm much obliged to all of them.

Finally, I thank Dale for her help—and for having the idea in the first place.

INDEX

Page numbers in italic refer to illustrations.